Voices of a New Generation:

A Feminist Anthology

Sara Weir and
Constance Faulkner, Editors

Western Washington University

Boston   New York   San Francisco
Mexico City   Montreal   Toronto   London   Madrid   Munich   Paris
Hong Kong   Singapore   Tokyo   Cape Town   Sydney

Senior Editor: Jeff Lasser
Editorial Assistants: Andrea Christie, Sara Owen
Marketing Manager: Krista Groshong
Senior Editorial-Production Administrator: Deborah Brown
Composition and Prepress Buyer: Linda Cox
Manufacturing Buyer: JoAnne Sweeney
Cover Coordinator: Linda Knowles
Editorial-Production Service: Susan McNally
Electronic Composition and Layout: Galley Graphics

For related titles and support materials, visit our online catalog at www.ablongman.com

Between the time Website information is gathered and then published, it is not unusual for some sites to have closed. Also, the transcription of URLs can result in unintended typographical errors. The publisher would appreciate notification where these errors occur so that they may be corrected in subsequent editions.

Library of Congress Cataloging-in-Publication Data
    Voices of a new generation : a feminist anthology / edited by Sara Weir, Constance Faulkner.
        p. cm.
    ISBN 0-205-34414-3
    1. Feminism.   I. Weir, Sara.   II. Faulkner, Constance.

HQ1111.V65 2003
305.42dc21

                                                                2003054136

Printed in the United States of America

10 9 8 7 6 5 4 3 2   07 06 05

for our students

Voices of a New Generation:

A Feminist Anthology

 # c o n t e n t s

p a r t   t h r e e
Contradictions: Theory and Activism 93

preface

Two insights motivate the creation of this anthology. One is our longstanding belief in the value of feminist theory and practice broadly conceived. We came to gender issues late in our graduate studies. After years of navigating, mostly successfully, largely male professional worlds, our lives were changed by feminist analyses. It was through feminism that our broader critical voices emerged.

Second, we have learned lessons only time could have taught. Dissertations, tenure, and years of teaching women's studies and other courses reminded us that feminist praxis, like all critical approaches, is constantly changing. Feminism remains important to our students, but their views reflect the post-modern, multi-cultural, and global influences of a new generation. For this project, we sought out voices like theirs to join an ever-changing conversation about issues ranging from the theoretical implications of feminism to its effect on everyday life.

Many of the authors in this volume want more from feminism—more inclusion, more guidance in facing deeply imbedded power relationships that continue to shape women's experiences. These demands make us uneasy, creating a level of intellectual discomfort necessary for our own growth and change. As a result, we have learned from these authors just as we have from our students. Beyond their common commitment to a broad vision of feminist consciousness, the authors bring different educational and life experiences to their writing. We thank them for their honesty in expressing this commitment and for their contributions to the body of literature on feminism.

In addition to the contributors many others must be acknowledged and thanked. Sue Scally was involved in the project from the beginning, offering creative ideas and helping to write the book proposal. As graduate students in the political science department at Western Washington University, Margaret Chapman and Shelly Frazier approached Sara Weir, asking to study feminist theory at about the time that work on this book was beginning. An independent study led to their involvement in the project. They provided ideas, editorial suggestions, and ultimately articles for the anthology. David McIvor provided editorial advice and organizational discipline to the text. He is a wonderful copy editor and thoughtful critic, whose support gave the project continuity. Other editorial assistance was provided by Pamela Pearsall and Kathryn Faulkner.

We would also like to thank Western Washington University and especially the Bureau of Faculty research and its director, Geri Walker, for providing financial support for the project. The editors at Allyn and Bacon, Jeff Lasser and Andrea Christie, have remained enthusiastic and supportive, even when we needed more time to complete the project. Susanna Brougham, copy editor for Allyn and Bacon, did an outstanding job in identifying problems with the manuscript.

To our families, friends, and colleagues, we express our deepest appreciation. Peter and Jim supported us at home, and the staff of the political science department, Joan Blackwell and Deborah Engebretson, made it possible for Sara to make time for the project while serving as department chair.

This anthology is dedicated to the strong, independent women we have had the good fortune to know, especially our students from whom we continue to learn more than can ever be expressed.

introduction

Sara Weir
Constance Faulkner

The post–World War II era, and especially the social activism of the 1960s and 1970s, brought feminist theories into college classrooms across the United States. These came both in the form of women's studies programs and as isolated courses in other disciplines. Although there has never been agreement on a single definition of feminism or feminist theory, the idea of feminism as critical of the status quo was widely shared by feminists and their critics. The consciousness raising and questioning of knowledge and ways of knowing that were fostered by such courses led to important changes for many academic disciplines.

Academic feminism *has* made a difference. It has challenged ideas ranging from theories of moral cognitive development in psychology to use of scientific methods that assumed one could generalize from male subjects about the health of women. In the study of economics and sociology, academic feminism exposed as false the assumptions that women were unsuccessful in the economic sphere because they made "bad" choices. And in literature, feminists have challenged the exclusion of women from the literary canon and forced recognition of the fact that women have earned the right to be there.

Women's studies itself emerged from a political movement[1] and its implied political character remains at issue today. As has been the case with other disciplines whose very names imply a political stance, many faculty in women studies programs began a move toward less controversial, less action-oriented approaches. Some of these changes were signaled by new, less specific names of disciplines, such as gender studies and American cultural studies. Often, as was the case with environmental studies and some ethnic and other minority studies programs, the choice was between a less controversial approach and survival in a particular institution—both for the program and for the faculty.

Defining Feminism

According to Alison Jaggar, a professor of philosophy and women's studies at the University of Colorado,

"Feminism" was originally a French word. It referred to what in the 19th-century United States was called "the woman movement": a diverse collection of groups all aimed, in one way or another, at "advancing" the position of women. When the word "feminism" was introduced into the United States in the early 20th century, however, it was used to refer only to one particular group of women's rights advocates, namely that group which asserted the uniqueness of women, the mystical experience of motherhood and women's special purity. . . . Now, "feminism" is commonly used to refer to all those who seek, no matter on what grounds, to end women's subordination.[2]

There are many categories of feminism, but the limitations of the most prominent forms of feminist theory are well documented. Although feminisms, such as liberal feminism, Marxist feminism, or postmodernist theory, could be considered inclusive of *all* women, they are often used to privilege the experiences of a narrow class or group of women. According to Patricia Hill Collins, "African-American, Latino, Native American, and Asian-American women have criticized Western feminisms for being racist and over concerned with White, middle-class women's issues."[3] The issues specific to sexual-minority women have also been marginalized in feminist theory. This lack of explicit inclusion has led to the development of other critical theories by, among others, Hill, bell hooks,[4] Gloria Andzaldúa,[5] Kimberlé Crenshaw,[6] and Mari Matsuda,[7] but much work remains to be done.

Because there are so many definitions and less defined ideas about just what feminism and feminist theory are, we offer our own definition, from which we (but not necessarily all the authors) work. Our definition is drawn from our own experience and from the articles that appear in this volume. For our purposes, then, feminism is the belief that the female perspective and experience are both legitimate and illuminating of *human* experience and that to marginalize this part of the human experience is to construct a false picture. Feminism directly challenges the power relationships resulting from dominant viewpoints, theories, categories, and understandings of the world, and thus it directs a revolutionary, emancipatory practice. This practice demands that existing economic, political, and social structures be changed. As a corollary to this, a feminist is one who believes that women's experience, historically and cross-culturally, illuminates all human experience; believes and acts on the idea that women's experience has been violated, undervalued, negated, and often trivialized and laughed at; and whose philosophy of life includes the idea of emancipation for all people whose lives have been so defined.

Feminist theories are theories of change; thus, definitions of feminism include the impetus to "act," to correct the injustices. This imperative is present, either implicitly or explicitly, in the essays in this volume. Although each of the authors has seriously engaged feminism and/or feminist theory at some point in his or her life, not all identify themselves either as feminists or activists. As a consequence the differences among their views are greater than that which holds them together. Still, we believe that "what holds them together" is significant. By raising issues relevant to a feminist consciousness, each adds to our understanding of the reality of women's lives, including their joys and their struggles. Sometimes the articles seemingly contradict one another, which is further evidence of the variety of "feminisms" and the resulting necessity to cultivate a tolerance for ambiguity and to challenge dichotomous thinking.

Aims of the Anthology

We, the two editors of this book, are activists and intellectuals. Students electing to take our classes (meaning those not *required* to do so) say they were attracted by the implied political content that would help inform their understanding of the world and actions designed to change it. This does not mean these students are revolutionaries—although some would certainly identify themselves as such—but rather the vast majority seek a way out of the confusion created by mixed messages they have received about important social issues facing their generation: inequality, poverty, U.S. involvement in other countries, the role of wealth in the United States, and so on. When asked what is missing from their texts, most students replied that voices similar to their own were never heard. They wanted to hear from others deeply concerned about the same issues, others of their own generation, scholars other than those widely anthologized, and voices generated from a greater diversity of backgrounds. When we sought texts to answer these concerns, we found none. It is our hope that this volume both validates and challenges students and offers others new ways of understanding how younger women see themselves in the world in the twenty-first century.

Others who have written for this book would also define themselves as activists, although the nature of their activism varies widely. Some are teachers, some work with social interest groups (including feminist groups), some have "taken to the streets" on many occasions, some are social movement organizers, one writes of her experiences as the mother of a mixed-race child, and one writes about growing up with a feminist father. Because of our interest in how younger women—those too young to have participated in the activism of the 1960s—view feminism today, the contributors were drawn primarily from that population. They include primarily White women, women of color, straight women, and lesbians. There are, however, one man and several women over fifty, the eldest in her midsixties. They fill in gaps in the subjects covered and give different perspectives.

Although some contributors address issues of global significance, the focus of the book is mainly on the ideas and challenges of North American women. Our intention is not to privilege the experiences of these women. Instead, it is to focus on what we are most familiar with, not making claims of expertise beyond the scope of our knowledge and experience.

NOTES

1. See Shari Popen's article in Part IV.
2. Allison Jaggar, *Feminist Politics and Human Nature* (Totowa, NJ: Roman & Allanheld, 1983), 5.
3. Patricia Hill Collins, *Black Feminist Thought: Knowledge, Consciousness, and the Politics of Empowerment,* 2nd ed. (New York: Routledge, 2000).
4. bell hooks, *Feminist Theory, from Margin to Center* (Cambridge, MA: South End Press, 1984). Many others of hooks' writings add to our understanding of feminist theory from the perspective of the women *most* oppressed by sexism: non-white and poor white women.
5. Gloria E. Anzaldúa, *Borderlands/La Frontera: The New Mestiza* (Spinsters/Aunt Lute Book Co., 1987).
6. Kimberlé Crenshaw's contributions have come not only through what she has written but also through her work in editing. Particularly valuable is *Critical Race Theory: The Key Writings That Formed the Movement* (New York: The New Press, 1995), which she edited with Neil Gotanda, Gary Peller, and Kendall Thomas. Crenshaw's article "Mapping the Margins: Intersectionality, Identity Politics, and Violence Against Women of Color" is included in that volume.
7. Mari Matsuda, "Color Blindness, History, and the Law" in *The House That Race Built*, Wahneema Lubiano, ed. (New York: Pantheon, 1997); and *Where Is Your Body? And Other Essays on Race, Gender, and the Law* (Boston: Beacon Press, 1996). Like Crenshaw, Matsuda is a leader in the critical race movement. Both are trained in the law.

Voices of a New Generation:

A Feminist Anthology

part ONE

The Uses and Limitations of Feminist Theory and Feminism

Teaching courses in women's studies, especially when the discussions and debates focus on feminism and feminist theory, is an exciting undertaking. The impact on many students, intellectually and personally, is profound. Some questions remain the same, but with new technology and new generations of students, alternative ways of understanding feminism and feminist theories emerge. As teachers and lifelong supporters of women, we have wondered how younger women—many born after 1970—view feminism today. What are the benefits and shortcomings of feminism and feminist theories for these women, educated in the last years of the twentieth century, during what is sometimes called the "third wave" of feminism? The essays in this section focus on a number of issues faced by younger women. Some are new, but most are older problems that have not gone away. The authors speak in clear and critical voices about challenges facing women today.

All of the authors in this section have learned about feminism through their own life experiences and through women's studies courses, at the undergraduate and in some cases the graduate level of study. While they have strengthened their critical voices in these courses, their life experiences, the challenges they face in everyday life, and their increasing awareness of domestic and international social problems draw attention to the limitations of feminism and feminist theory in overcoming these challenges and directing action that could provide solutions.

In the opening essay, "*Mujerista* Economics: The Creation of a New Economic Paradigm," Brenda Aníbarro draws attention to ways in which academic feminism marginalizes the struggles of women of the "global south." She calls for *mujerista* economics, explaining, "*Mujerista* economics takes the essence of what it means to be a *mujerista,* working collectively with our communities for justice." She urges North American feminists to "listen to the voices of women of the global south and women of color in the United States."

Carolyn Finney, drawing on her feminist understanding that the way we *know* things is limited by the dominant culture, asks why environmentalism ignores the relationship between black people and nature. "Where are the black folks?" She asks how, using the tools of feminist theory, to "uncover, reclaim, and represent the truths of the African American environment 'experience'"?

Monica McCallum's essay on raising a multiracial child speaks to the help she got from feminist writings on parenting and on racism. Feminists "talked about race, they talked about mothering and both discussions validated me." However, it was in reading about women of color who identify themselves as feminists that she came to understand the limitations of feminism in answering the questions of a white women mothering a multiracial son.

All three of these articles—by Aníbarro, Finney, and McCallum—seek to make feminism more inclusive and therefore more reflective of the experiences of *all* women.

The final three essays take up issues commonly discussed in women's studies courses: reproductive choice, violence against women, and body image. Each essay illustrates how complicated and challenging these problems remain for young women today.

In writing about her experience working in a battered women's shelter, Sarah McCarry broadens what most have thought of as "feminist" by demonstrating that all women who struggle and have struggled against violence in any of its many forms share an unrecognized bond. Becky Statzel, too, is writing about a form of violence: the contradiction between reproductive rights and population control, "where the individual loses her freedom of choice under the onus of controlling population," a contradiction seen by few feminists.

And finally, Shelly Frazier writes about the damage done to young females because of *bodyoma,* the "craze for thinness." As she says, "I know that dealing with my own bodyoma severely limited my ability to think in feminist terms. I, like most women with a body image disorder, was selfish in my pursuit of the perfect body." Like so many women, she sacrificed her health for concerns for "how I looked and what others thought of me. It was only with motherhood and feminism that I managed to rearrange my priorities."

Brenda Aníbarro

Mujerista Economics: The Creation of a New Economic Paradigm

A mujerista *is someone who makes a preferential option for Latina women, for their struggle for liberation.* Mujeristas *struggle to liberate themselves not as individuals but as members of a Latino community.*

—Dr. Ada Maria Isazi-Diaz, *My Name Is Mujerista,* 1993

Young women of color have found themselves to be heirs to a tradition of liberation informed by the experiences of women of color, low-income women, and women of the global South. This tradition has taken feminism to task for failing to address the importance of differential power dynamics *between* women and the need for feminism to allow space for a multiplicity of voices to be heard. As we enter the twenty-first century it is time that we, the heirs to this tradition—the daughters of difference—name those spaces where we can build unity in our struggle. *Mujerista* economics is an attempt to synthesize the voices that have clamored to be heard, that have dared to ask, "Where is *my* struggle in your movement?" *Mujerista* economics takes the essence of what it means to be a *mujerista,* working collectively with our communities for justice, and pushes us to see how this identity can be the starting point of a paradigm that brings together our work for economic justice. By bringing to-gether *mujerisma* and economics we place the restructuring of the economy not only as a priority, but also as a project that is informed by our struggle as women of color in our communities. As feminists, as *mujeristas,* we need to make the restructuring of the economy a priority in our theories and our actions. Women of color, low-income women, and women of the global South need to take the lead in creating an economic paradigm in which the experience of oppression and the struggle for liberation lead to a reevaluation of priorities within our communities and at the global level.

Women of the global South have been asserting the need to deconstruct and rebuild the workings of the global economy throughout history. During the past forty years these voices have struggled to be heard by the larger feminist movement. In her book *Let Me Speak!,* Domitila De Chungara describes her life as a Bolivian tin worker and the fight for worker control in the

Bolivian economy.[1] When Domitila raised this issue in 1975 at the International Women's Conference in Mexico, her comments were ignored and refuted by prominent feminists. A number of years ago I interviewed my mother, a Bolivian who emigrated to the United States at the age of seventeen, on her views of the feminist movement. In the interview she explained why she identified with *mujerisma* over feminism. "It does not mean that I give up fighting for my rights as a woman, but I will fight for my rights as a woman within my community while holding the hand of my *companero* who is also fighting economic oppression."[2]

To answer the call put forth by women like Domitila De Chungara, American feminism must be informed by the sites of struggle faced by women of color and low-income women, and it must develop a theoretical framework that works for economic justice. As women of color we have the unique possibility of drawing from lived experiences in our communities as a basis for constructing an economic framework that recognizes the value of human life and our environment. This essay proposes a new paradigm in which we come together as women and as communities to answer these calls.

The need for a new economic paradigm is best understood by first examining the economic theories lying behind policies that have created institutionalized systems of economic disparity. Studying these models also reveals how feminism has engaged each theoretical framework (or how it hasn't). Though myriad economic theories seek to account for how we define, distribute, and create resources, the two that are currently receiving the most attention, and thus affecting the creation of economic policy, include the discourse of development and the political philosophy of neoliberalism.

Development Theory and Practice

Development is a buzzword tossed around by everyone from economists to activists to signify a process that seeks to engage the global South with the economic and social possibilities of the global North.[3] Development as a political and social project was publicly ushered in by President Truman's 1949 inaugural address when he stated, "We must embark on a bold new program for making the benefits of our scientific advances and industrial progress available for the improvement and growth of underdeveloped areas."[4]

While such a statement may seem harmless enough, critics have argued that the implications of the term *development* and its metaphorical connection to evolution and progress have placed people of the global South in a crucible—to be defined, problematized, and "fixed" by the North. Gustavo Esteva has written of the effects of the term, stating, "It [development] converted history into a programme: a necessary and inevitable destiny. . . . The metaphor of development gave global hegemony to a purely Western genealogy of history, robbing peoples of different cultures of the opportunity to define the forms of their social life."[5] The domain of development theory is vast and has thus encompassed divergent approaches in the formation of projects and policies. The creation of the multilateral economic institutions at the Bretton Woods meetings of 1944 were largely influenced by the developmentalist assumption that the North should have a hand in creating macroeconomic rules and regulations that would allow the "underdeveloped" countries to "catch up" and follow the lead of the economic superpowers. In this vein, the International Monetary Fund was established as a lending institution and the

World Bank as a financier of reconstruction and development projects. Initially intended as part of the United Nations, these institutions were instead given room to operate under their own jurisdiction and a weighted voting system—a political structure that allots power to national governments that provide the institution with the most funds.[6]

Developmentalism, as a domain of thought and action, has also effected the creation of participatory projects, in what has been termed "people-centered development." These projects include micro-credit banks and small-trade networks. Despite the more grassroots approach of these projects, the assumptions remain that economic possibilities and expertise reside in the technology and resources of the North. Powerful institutions such as the World Bank claim to practice people-centered development yet undertake no critical reflection of the power relationships perpetuated by their institutions. Further, under the rubric of people-centered development, the World Bank has pursued policies to decentralize or completely disband human services provided by the state.

In the 1990s many social theorists took up the task of examining development as a discourse. Arturo Escobar's work, *Encountering Development: The Making and Unmaking of the Third World,* argues that development is "an efficient apparatus that systematically relates forms of knowledge and techniques of power."[7] Escobar, and others who have pursued similar aims, have created a space in which the "power of the West to define" can be challenged. Escobar applies Chandra Mohanty's critique of mainstream feminism's construction of Third World women to that of development, writing, "there exists [in development literature] a veritable underdeveloped subjectivity endowed with features such as

powerlessness, passivity, poverty, and ignorance, usually dark and lacking in historical agency, as if waiting for the [white] Western hand to help subjects along and not infrequently hungry, illiterate, needy, and oppressed by its own stubbornness, lack of initiative, and traditions."[8]

The space created by deconstructing development so that "the task of imagining alternatives can be commenced" is invaluable and must continue as we build alternatives to Northern-centric, top-down models of development. In addition, many feminists engaged with development theory—both from within institutions and from the outside—offer critiques and visions of what could emerge in response to the dominant paradigm.

Feminists Respond to Development: WID and GAD

The precarious position that development created for women of the global South led to the creation of two different schools of thought. Throughout the 1970s, the term *women in development (WID)* defined an approach where women were "added and stirred" to the project of economic growth. The primary goal of WID was to increase women's accessibility to economic and political institutions. In response to this line of thinking, institutions such as USAID established WID sections within their organizations to devise ways for their projects to engage women. While some significant inroads were made, the WID approach to development did nothing to challenge the basic premise of development or ideas of economic growth and progress. Later, the *gender and development (GAD)* approach went further by questioning issues of power, arguing that women could not be understood without examining their location in social relationships. The GAD approach also critiqued the top-down policy directives of multilateral institutions. Unfortunately, this analysis has been neglected by mainstream development theorists and practitioners, who argue that there is no way to integrate the critique and insights of GAD into practice and policy.

From Developmentalism to Neoliberalism

The project of development initially favored Keynesian, welfare-state type policies. Moreover, the Bretton Woods institutions at first had a limited capacity to extend their political and economic policies into recipient countries: "When these institutions were created at Bretton Woods in 1944 . . . they had no control over individual governments' economic decisions, nor did their mandate include a license to intervene in national policy."[9]

Despite their Keynesian beginnings, the Bretton Woods institutions were soon influenced by neoliberalism, a political philosophy conceived by Friedrich von Hayek and expanded by Milton Friedman, which calls for unregulated flow of capital, privatization of state resources, and limited controls on investment. This philosophy was a minority position during the 1950s and 1960s but gained ascendancy when President Reagan and Prime Minister Thatcher applied its tenets to their national policies. The spread of neoliberalism within the halls of international economic institutions and policy circles eventually influenced the creation of the World Trade Organization (WTO). Though many countries of the global South had earlier suggested the idea of an international trade body, with the goal of creating a more level playing field, previous attempts to begin one had not succeeded due to the unwillingness of the eco-

nomic superpowers.[10] Instead the General Agreement on Tariffs and Trade (GATT) was created and became a forum for opening markets and decreasing regulations on investors. The United States and other powerful countries began to see the benefits of creating an international trade body that could enforce trade laws favorable to investors. The World Trade Organization would serve such a purpose.

Both neoliberalism and development theory have not provided most of the world's people with a means to attain a secure and sustainable livelihood. On the contrary, these theories have led to economic policy that distributes wealth in such a way that the technology, access to resources, and profits stay in the hands of a small percentage of the population. So the question must be asked: where do we go from here?

Coloring Outside the Lines: Creating a New Paradigm

Mujerista economics is the synthesis of our struggles as women, people of color, and low-income communities—groups who have never been invited to the table to determine how, and for whom, economic policy is created. It is the lump in our throats that we have felt as the daughters of difference . . . the recognition that we have a truth to speak. It is building upon the lessons learned during kitchen table dialogues. It is our poetic monologues put into practice. At this time *mujerista* economics is built upon three central ideas. The first is that how we define value must be reexplored, reexamined, and reconstructed. The second is that due to the present effects of development and neoliberal economic practice, we must be vigilant in challenging unjust economic policies and their effects. The third is that our paradigm must be rooted in a politics of place—the process of building a more just economic framework must stem from our local movements, with an understanding of the specific needs, desires, and resources of a given community while simultaneously working together at a global level.

The question of how we, as a society, determine value has been central to the development of economic theories long before David Ricardo and Adam Smith put their thoughts to paper. It is crucial that we return to, and in many ways reclaim, this question if we are to come to any conclusions regarding how we approach exchange and allocation of resources. This area needs to be explored within our communities, where we can simultaneously honor traditional value systems and create new relationships with other people and with our natural environment in the most sustainable and equitable manner possible.

While *mujerista* economics is concerned with the building of equitable and just exchange relationships, it must also develop new means to challenge the dominant and unjust economic order of the day. This means focusing on institutions and governments that create and implement economic policy that negatively affects the majority of the world's women. A great example of this is the practice of ethnography termed "studying up," proposed by anthropologist Laura Nader.[11] Nader has argued that anthropology has historically focused its inquiry on the peasant community or village; it must now examine those arenas that have had the privilege to remain behind closed doors.[12] Developing ethnographies of the boardroom, of international trade bodies, and so on, might provide us with a better means to understanding these institutions and their role in society. The practice of studying up can be powerfully integrated into *mujerista* economics as we research, expose, and challenge the ideologies, policies, and practices

that siphon wealth and resources from the public purse and into the coffers of the private sector.

This last element of the paradigm requires rooting our questions and answers in communities and local movements, thereby avoiding grandiose, overgeneralizing theories. This further begs us to revisit questions of what defines a community. Is it defined geographically, ethnically, or according to certain issues or identities? Rooting our approach in this way makes sense from a practical perspective when assessing a community's needs, desires, and resources. This is not to say that one policy or prescription will serve as an economic panacea, curing all the economic imbalances of our community. Rather, *mujerista* economics is a space for us to develop questions, refine our approach, and share our struggles.

While making sure that we ground our work in our community, it is also critical that we remain global in outlook. Many processes that drive the international development policies which detrimentally affect women in the global South are the same ones that lead to urban gentrification and privatization of social services in the United States and Europe. Creating and utilizing existing networks of social movements can bring our communities together to share ideas and resources regarding the struggle for economic justice.[13]

Conclusion

Mujerista economics is a point of convergence for people of color, low-income communities, and our allies to come together and build a new economic paradigm from our experiences in the struggle for liberation. It is a space to unite women who have been challenging feminism to take into account the multiplicity of struggles faced by the most oppressed in our world, so we can work toward a new feminism, a *mujerisma* that includes all our voices. The specificity of the paradigm will be built through our experiences working in our communities to challenge the economic status quo and work toward economic justice. Much within the paradigm has yet to be fully elaborated and articulated. This essay provides the seeds for the development of this new framework. It offers no quick solution or simplistic blueprint for change. Rather, *mujerista* economics begs a set of questions that might lead each of our communities toward building more equitable and just economic relationships.

NOTES

1. Domitila De Chungara, as told to Victoria Ortiz, *Let Me Speak!: Testimony of Domitila, a Woman of the Bolivian Mines* (New York: Monthly Review Press, 1978).
2. Interview with Susana Saravia-Ugarte, May 1997.
3. Naila Kabeer has discussed the term *development* as follows: "In its narrow meaning, it refers to the planned process by which resources, techniques, and expertise are brought together to bring about improved rates of growth in an area variously defined as the Third World, the developing world, the periphery, the South and so on." Naila Kabeer, *Reversed Realities: Gender Hierarchies in Development Thought* (London: Verso, 1994), 69.
4. Wolfgang Sachs, ed., *The Development Dictionary: A Guide to Knowledge as Power* (London: Zed Books, 1999), 6.
5. Ibid., 9.
6. At the present time the United States has veto power within both the IMF and the World Bank.
7. Arturo Escobar, *Encountering Development: The Making and Unmaking of the Third World* (Princeton: Princeton University Press, 1995), 10.
8. Ibid., 8.
9. Susan George, *Global Finance: New Thinking on Regulating Speculative Capital Markets,* ed. Walden Bello, Nicola Bullard, and Kamal Malhotra (London: Zed Books, 2000), 27.
10. In 1947 a group of countries from the global South convened in Havana, Cuba, to form the International Trade Organization. The intent of this organization was to manage international trade and allow countries of the South to pursue protectionist policies. Instead, the United States and other surplus countries pushed for the creation of the General Agreement on Tariffs and Trade (GATT), which called for reductions in tariffs and protectionist measures.
11. Laura Nader, "Up the Anthropologist—Perspectives Gained from Studying Up." In *Reinventing Anthropology,* ed. Dell Hymes (New York: Pantheon Books, 1972), 284–311.
12. The work of some economic anthropologists and economic geographers is beginning to move in this direction. Mapping wealth and creating ethnographies of power have the potential to bring scholars and community members together to work for economic justice.
13. Many networks have been actively working for a number of years to bring social movements and communities together. More recently, there has been an upsurge in this type of cross-border engagement. See Beverly Bell, *Social Movements and Economic Integration in the Americas* (Albuquerque, NM: Center for Economic Justice, 2002).

Carolyn Finney

Can't See the Black Folks for the Trees

"Chile, they've got some of us everywhere."—Words of Colleen McElroy's grandmother,

—Colleen McElroy, *A Long Way from St. Louie,* 1997

I'm coming out. No, I'm not talking about a revelation of my sexual identity. I'm talking about my love affair with the Outdoors. I'm talking trees, dirt, mountains, and blue sky. Hiking for days without a shower. Sitting on a rock, high above the world, nursing my blisters—marveling at the earth as it lies before me. Miles to go before I sleep? Bring it on! Or lying on a beach, enjoying the smell of the sea while watching the sunset. Or sitting on the stoop of my apartment building, letting the warm spring air caress my skin. And I am Black. Say what? That's right— stop the presses—I is OUT. I am a Black woman who loves the outdoors. Camping is NOT a four-letter word. Environment is not some abstract idea that only White folks can understand. I am a Black woman who loves the outdoors and I AM NOT GOING ANYWHERE. Except maybe on another hike.

How did this happen? How does a black girl from the U. S. of A., with its history of cotton fields, lynchings, and WHITES ONLY signs, come to have a love relationship with Nature, the Great Outdoors, the Wilderness?

Here's the thing, second question first: I call myself, among other things, a Black feminist geographer. The geography part means I want to understand why people do what they do where they do it. As a feminist, I challenge the way we come to know things in academia and in the world at large: What is truth? Whose truth are we talking about? Who gets to represent this truth? And as a Black woman, or African American, I want to know what race has to do with . . . well, everything. Ask me to tell you in academic parlance my research interests and I would say I'm interested in understanding nature/society relationships particularly as they concern groups whose ideas, values, histories, and beliefs are not part of the dominant narratives (masquerading as The Truth) that define and inform our world. But let me give it to you straight: I want to know, when we in the West talk about environment, Nature, the Great Outdoors, where are the Black folks? Where are the farmers, the fishermen, the Black girls rolling around getting leaves in their hair? And this is no frivolous question. The environmental movement is BIG. Adventure/outdoor travel has hit an all time high— look at advertising, look at pop culture (*Survivor,* that Australian dude with the alligators). Travel and nature writing are spurred on by the popularity of adventure travel and concern for the environment.[1] And you cannot watch the news without some story of environmental disaster filling your television screen. We are constantly reminded that we need to Save the Trees, Save the Whales, and, basically, Save Our Asses, by taking better care of our environment. We all depend on the environment in one form or another, whether it's the air we breathe, the fish we fry, the tree we lean on after a long day. But when is the last time you've seen an advertisement on environmental issues that includes a Black person (or, for that matter, any person of color)? I nearly fell over in a store when, as I flipped through a copy of *Mother Jones,* I saw an advertisement for saving the salmon with Robert Kray (a Black musician) and his guitar, standing on some rocks in a stream, touting the need to protect the salmon.[2] Now THAT's radical. You may laugh at me. But I'm a Black woman who is tired of being stared at when I gaze in awe at the Grand Canyon. Or being asked downright stupid questions when booking airplane tickets to go trekking in Nepal (is that your home country?). Along with *Ms., Oprah,* and *Utne,* I love to read *Outside, National Geographic,* and *Adventure Geographic.* And I rarely see my skin color represented anywhere in magazines that focus on the environment, the outdoors, or adventure. A few years ago, Eddy L. Harris, an African American writer, wrote an article in *Outside Magazine* entitled "Solo Faces."[3] I was thrilled at his willingness to discuss his experience of being a Black man in the outdoors but disappointed that in years of reading these magazines, it was the first article by an African American that I had ever seen. I *expect* to see my skin color reflected back at me when there's talk about poverty, inner cities, prison issues, crime, and education. But I want to go where few Black folks have gone before. No—that's not right. I want to show people that Black folks HAVE gone before, are there now, and will continue to be around. This land is your land, this land is MY land. And if we're not there, it's not simply because we don't like the outdoors/environment. Let's talk about spatial mobility, economic disparity, fear, and exclusion.[4] Or maybe White folks just haven't noticed us. Or perhaps it's as Zora Neale Hurston once said: "The answer lies in what we may call THE AMERICAN MUSEUM OF UNNATURAL HISTORY. This is an intangible built on folk belief. It is assumed that all non-Anglo-Saxons are uncomplicated stereotypes. Everybody knows all about them. They are the lay figures mounted in the museum where all may take them in at a glance. They are made of bent wires without insides at all." She then goes on to say:

> But for the national welfare, it is urgent to realize that the minorities do think, and think about something other than the race problem. That they are very human and, internally, according to natural endowment, are just like everybody else. . . . Argue all you will about injustice, but as long as the majority cannot conceive of a Negro or a Jew feeling and reacting inside just as they do, the majority will keep right on believing that

people who do not feel like them cannot possible feel as they do. . . . It is well known that there must be a body of waived matter, let us say, things accepted and taken for granted by all in a community before there can be that commonality of feeling. . . . Until this is thoroughly established in respect to Negroes in America, as well as other minorities, it will remain impossible for the majority to conceive of a Negro experiencing a deep and abiding love and not just the passion of sex. That a great mass of Negroes can be stirred by the pageants of Spring and Fall; the extravaganza of summer, and the majesty of winter.[5]

So, I reiterate—where are the voices, histories, ideas, and beliefs of Black folks and the great outdoors? As a feminist, how can I uncover, reclaim, and represent the truths of the African American–environment "experience"? And why is this necessary?

I believe that many of the histories, ideas, and beliefs that Black folks have regarding the environment can be found in the personal—in the stories of their lives and those of their families. Like a thread, each story can be woven together to bring into focus a rich and complex tapestry of a Black environmental experience that considers the individual life story, the collective memory, and the historical context in which all our lives are grounded.

Let me talk a bit about my "natural" history. I was fortunate to have spent much of my childhood among green grass and trees—my father was the caretaker for a large estate outside of New York City, and we lived in the gardener's cottage within a rock's throw of The Big House, where the owners would stay for weekends and

holidays. While the land was not our own, we kids were allowed to run wild on the property, as though it were. The long driveway became Piranha river, and clusters of rocks became the hiding place of the stolen, sacred animals we were sent to retrieve. The pond was the secret world of large turtles and sunfish, and a game of hide-and-seek could go on for hours. And I loved rolling around in the leaves and getting bits and pieces stuck in my 'fro.

I felt comfortable in the outdoors, and Nature just let me be.[6] I was not just a young Black girl, taking advantage of the space around me, unconsciously trying to find my place. I was a natural part of things, a piece of the landscape, like the big rock I pretended was a horse, like the weeping willow that looked like it was dripping tears into the pond.[7] It was natural for me to run through the grass, stare at clouds, and row a boat across the water. It was natural for me to walk through the woods, assiduously avoiding anything that looked like poison ivy. Sure, I had some fears of the Outdoors. The woods at night seemed particularly frightening, and spiders were (and still are) a major phobia. I saw the movie *Krakatoa, East of Java* starring Frank Sinatra, and I became convinced that a volcanic explosion was imminent in my neighborhood. But regardless of my fears (rational or not), I still believed it was natural for me to be there.

However, this was not so in the wider neighborhood in which I lived. A wealthy area, where big houses were the norm, my family was the only Black family for at least a three-mile radius. We looked about as natural in this neighborhood (this was the 1960s and the 1970s) as Rush Limbaugh might look in an all-Black church singing the gospel. But this was *my* landscape. I had grown used to my surroundings, walking home from school underneath the shade of the trees that lined the street I lived on, recognizing squirrels that my mother complained about (they ate the birdseed she left out for the birds). Yet, within the wider neighborhood, I was the BLACK girl who lived with the BLACK family, who worked for the So-and-So's. And being a BLACK girl meant different things to different people. For the cops who regularly patrolled my neighborhood, it meant asking me where I was going and if I worked in the neighborhood (I was ten years old). For some of the neighbors to whom I delivered newspapers and Girl Scout cookies, it meant dealing with someone who was fairly nonthreatening and very inconsequential. For the German Shepherd who chased me regularly, it meant something tasty to chew on. For the Black girls I went to school with, who lived outside the three-mile radius, it meant reminding me of my place, limited as it might be, by any means at their disposal.

I knew nothing about a nature/culture dichotomy, Blacks' association with the primitive, or the social construction of me. Yet two things were clearly happening. I was developing an appreciation for nature/outdoors AND discovering that my being in certain spaces/places was not expected, welcome, or "natural."

I had a number of environmental "teachers," *Audubon Nature Encyclopedia, Wild Kingdom* (Sunday nights after *Disney*), and my parents. While books and television opened my eyes to Nature beyond my community, my parents influenced my more immediate, day-to-day interactions.

My dad was intricately involved with the natural environment. He mowed the grass, planted the flowers, grew vegetables in the garden. He cleaned up the bird shit that the geese left around the lake, complained about the groundhogs digging up the flowerbeds, and chased away teenage White guys who'd sneak onto the property, hoping to take a dip in the owner's pool without being noticed. He had a particular lack of affinity with the geese. He would load up his gun and regularly shoot them, for they made his job infinitely harder. Yet he was frustrated at the geese's lack of comprehension of why he was killing them and lost sleep worrying about his role in the depletion of their population. My mother said he'd wake up in a cold sweat, looking panicked, after dreaming about the geese coming after him. My father was even quoted in the local newspaper about the excess proliferation of geese and how different residents were dealing with it.

My mother is a naturalist. Not in the academic sense (she never went beyond high school), but in the lived-it, observed-it sense. She can tell you about the various trees, which ones have died and why, the squirrels with their individual characteristics, the seasonal migration of the birds, and why the appearance of deer on the property is a sign of the times. She knows about the bushes that grow there and has a special fondness for a cherry blossom tree given to her by my dad on their anniversary. And her run-in with an oversized snapping turtle is legendary in our family.

Work issues overlapped with my parents' concerns for the environment, the natural space they inhabited, while race and class issues (their lack of ownership, being the only Black people in the neighborhood) played a subtler role in their day-to-day experiences.

"I have the blood of three races in my veins . . . white, black, and Indian, and nobody asked me *anything* before."[8]

So, what is Black folks' perspective? There is no monolithic Black Folks' Environmental Perspective (feminists are still smarting from a similar one-track approach to understanding women). But my guess is that many Black folks could relate to some broad issues and concerns—areas within the common context of struggle where stories are told, alliances are born, and new ideas take root.[9] Our collective memory of our interactions with the environment is a starting point for reconsidering the processes and events that have informed our relationship to it. But when was the last time Black folks were asked their collective opinion of the environment? Whom do we ask? Who does the asking?[10] Who gets to represent our views? And it's not only supporting "new voices" in a dialogue or debate—it's also equally valuing these voices and opinions, not slipping into tokenism to appease political correctness and those addicted to it.

In academia—in the classroom, when teaching feminist theory, gender, and environment, BIG IDEAS about the environment—how bold are we to include Black voices, "traditional" and nontraditional, not as an addendum to business as usual but as an embodiment of lived experience that disrupts dominant narratives and the underlying assumptions that cloud our vision(s)? Can we assert that subjectivity is integral in the production of knowledge, challenge the ability of anyone to produce knowledge that's all-encompassing and always true,[11] deconstruct ideas that sustain relations of domination in order to make room for more creative thought,[12] firmly embrace the idea that identity is not static, that we all comprise multiple identities that should be brought to bear on any issue? We are remiss if we dismiss, ignore, leave out any voice, any possibility that might

reveal a way to effectively deal with tough issues. It's time to harshly interrogate those voices that have historically constructed an image of you or me, rooted in limitations.

It's just that little colored children listening to that proper white woman would never hear their own cadence in her words. They'd come to believe that they would have to abandon their own language and stories to become a part of her educated world. They would have to forfeit Waller for Mozart and Remus for Puck. They would enter a world where only white people spoke. And no matter how articulate Dickens and Voltaire were, those children wouldn't have their own examples in the house of learning—the library."[13]

One of my professors admonishes us to pursue the Big Questions in our research. These questions, within geography, should address major environmental issues such as climate change, global warming, food security, deforestation, and poverty.[14] And I struggle with how I can show that I'm asking the Big Questions, that I'm doing what's important. During my musings, it occurred to me that asking the Big Questions means getting the Big Answers. And these questions and answers depend on certain underlying assumptions, namely, the Big Ideas that our society is built upon. And the development and proliferation of those Big Ideas have left out the voices of major segments of the population. So, here I am, lone Black girl/woman, picking leaves out of my dreads, asking myself the Big Question—what can *I* bring to the debate surrounding these questions?

First, I want to ask some of my *own* questions. Do White folks think we can't understand environmental concerns, particularly around conservation issues? Do they think we're not interested? Are Black folks interested? Is it just that we don't prioritize environmental concerns because we're overwhelmed with economic and education issues (to start with)? Or, as Price Cobbs, coauthor of *Black Rage,* says, have we "shrunk our ledge" and led ourselves to believe that we are limited in what we can understand, what it means to be authentically Black, and what we feel our voice should be lent to? Cobbs asks, "Do you collide with the ledge? Do you write about something non-black, like French cinema, and broaden the ledge?"[15] What are the truths about the environment and how Black folks relate to it? What are *our* Big Ideas? How do they figure in the environmental debate and human/environment relationships? How can we participate in creating, as Gloria Anzaldua calls it, our *conocimientos*—"alternate ways of knowing that synthesize reflection with action to create subversive knowledge systems that challenge the status quo"?[16] But I get ahead of myself. How can we discuss when we're not even at the table? But why should we wait to be invited? What are *our* terms?

I want to underscore something: This is not just about the White oppressors and how they've made it impossible for Black folks to speak. This is also about how Black folks have "shrunk their ledge"—dismissing some issues as unimportant, as something White people do, while elevating others, thereby limiting our ability as individuals to fully realize who we are. It's about agency—that even though we still may be left out, silenced, dismissed, and devalued, we still have the ability to think, to be creative, to resist, to have Big Ideas.[17]

For example, let's take nature writing as one venue to which African Americans can lend their voice. Counter to the perspective that African American nature writing is frivolous,[18] it has in fact had an enormous impact on society's thinking on Nature and the Big Ideas of those White men who have come before. Black voices have impacted environmental policy, conservation ideals, the design of our national parks, who makes decisions about the environment, who has access. Michael Eric Dyson, self-proclaimed Hip Hop Public Intellectual, underscores the importance of writing as a way for Black folks to invent and reinvent who they are. He says,

> Writing is enormously important to try to figure out what the past is about, what the present is about in relationship to the past . . . and a way of reinventing the very character and texture of experience in light of one's own writing. When one is writing, one is literally writing into and writing from. . . . Especially for African-American people who are preoccupied with literacy, who are preoccupied with the articulation of a self through narrative, writing becomes a most important avenue of both revealing and inventing the future of the race.[19]

Nature writing is one way to transform the historical Black/nature association as one of negativity—Blacks as natural objects; Blacks, like nature, having no voice; Blacks equated with animals; Blacks like land, seen as a commodity. We need to claim and reclaim all avenues that can showcase our views about the environment. We can challenge ourselves to think beyond our own self-imposed box as well as the ones designed for us by others.

Black folks understand that debates in academia have big consequences for their material interests. According to Dyson, "We already see the connections between the academy and the 'real world,' because the real world looks to the academy to justify its prejudices, to dress them up in scientific discourse that allows them to gain legitimacy and power."[20] Well, I am questioning that legitimacy and power. As put forth by Chandra Mohanty, discourses are central sites of political contestation. And they should be grounded in and informed by the material politics of everyday life. Bringing their lives to the table is just the beginning. As a feminist, I must continually contest and disrupt what it means to employ feminist thinking in my work and my everyday life. I/We must question the role of feminist theory and pedagogy in the "real world" in order for feminism to evolve as a relevant and meaningful tool, vehicle, and framework for making the personal political and for engendering positive social change.

In a conversation with my dad, we asked the question: If there were a nuclear war or plague and only a few people were chosen to survive, whom would you choose? A scientist? A political leader? A teacher? My dad said, someone who knew the land, who understood the environment, because we need food for survival—we *need* the environment. This from a man with a twelfth-grade education who took care of someone else's land for forty-five years. Don't tell me Black folks aren't concerned about the environment.

NOTES

1. I feel the need to mention some African American writers that have written about travel and the environment: Alice Walker, Colleen McElroy, and Eddy L. Harris.
2. *Mother Jones* (May/June 2000).
3. Eddy Harris, "Solo Faces," *Outside Magazine*, December 1997.

4. I must acknowledge the environmental justice movement, in which academics and activists of color have been waging a battle for years to place the environmental concerns of people of color and the poor on the table. See the work of Robert Bullard and Laura Pulido.
5. Zora Neale Hurston, "What White Publishers Won't Print," reprinted in Alice Walker, ed., *I Love Myself When I am Laughing . . . and Then Again When I Am Looking Mean and Impressive: a Zora Neale Hurston Reader* (New York: The Feminist Press, 1979), p. 170.
6. Nature has been defined in numerous ways: as something separate from humans, as something we've constructed, as something opposite to culture, as something that we're inherently a part of. In respect of my memories, Nature, as seen through the eyes of a child, was all life, other than human, outside the four walls of my home.
7. I use the word *natural* on purpose—part of the process of creating and giving voice to a narrative is also reclaiming certain words for ourselves. *Natural* has often been used to mean primitive, the opposite of cultured, and consequently, when Blacks have been described as natural, the implication has been negative. I define natural as being down-to-earth, real, connected to something larger than myself and conscious (proud?) of that fact.
8. Alice Walker, "Looking for Zora," in Walker, *op. cit.,* p. 301.
9. See Chandra Mohanty's work on Third World opposition struggles.
10. See, for example, David Sibley, *Geographies of Exclusion: Society and Difference in the West* (London: Routledge, 1995).
11. See Donna Haraway's work for an in-depth discussion of subjectivity.
12. Helan E. Page eloquently explores making the personal political within in the academy in her chapter "Teaching Comparative Social Order and Caribbean Social Change." In *Spirit, Space, and Survival: African-American Women in (White) Academe,* ed. Joy James

and Ruth Farmer (New York: Routledge, 1993).

13. Walter Moseley, *White Butterfly* (London: Pan Books, 1992), 56.

14. This is not meant to be an exhaustive list.

15. Erin Aubry Kaplan, *Utne Reader* (July/August, 2001), 92.

16. Analouise Keating, *Gloria E. Anzaldua: Interviews* (New York: Routledge, 2000), 5.

17. See bell hooks's work on resistance in the margins.

18. David Lionel Smith, "African-Americans: Writing and Nature," in J. Elder, ed., *American Nature Writers* (Farmington Hills: Gale Group, 1996).

19. Sidney L. Dorbin, "Race and the Public Intellectual: A Conversation with Michael Eric Dyson," in G. A. Olson and L. Worsham, eds., *Race, Rhetoric, and the Postcolonial* (New York: State University of New York Press, 1999), 85.

20. Ibid.

Sarah McCarry

Laundry: Writing on Feminism

At two in the morning I am done washing windows. It's snowing, the third time in this odd and unreasonable winter, a sure omen of strange times ahead. The phone hasn't rung in an hour; the last call was a woman fed up with her manipulative abuser and patronizing family. She's schizophrenic, happy on her meds, and cranky about being told she doesn't know what's best for her. *I mean, goddammit, I'm fucking crazy! I'm not a fucking idiot!* We are both laughing when she hangs up. The other night I cut off all my hair, a weight I no longer wanted to carry. Now when I catch sight of my reflection in clean-scrubbed glass my head looks too large, crowned with an unwieldy chrysanthemum. I am thinking of Linda J. in her jail cell, her face against the bars, her children taken from her. She hasn't been told where they are yet. Her black eye is slow to fade. What they have done with the body of her husband I don't know; neither does she. He molested their daughter, beat her into emptiness, hunted her across state lines. There's a memorial scheduled: *Beloved father, husband, son.* Beloved father. Linda J. kept her stories close until the police came. By then it was too late.

I sleep in a house full of women who have survived. Survived as women survive—swimming upstream. Women who have survived because they thought ahead to hide the car keys, saved thirty-five cents and five minutes for a single phone call (*I have to leave please help me before he kills me*). Women who ran with the clothes on their backs and their children in their arms. Women who waited until he left for an hour, went to work, passed out drunk. On the overnight shift I sleep on a pile of blankets on the shelter office floor, phone next to my head, one ear primed for the sound of footsteps or loneliness, a woman asking for night meds, a child up too late, someone's abuser at the door. I generally don't sleep well at work. Tonight I'll sleep safer at the thought of snow. I stood outside for a while and watched the thick flakes fall in a neighborhood that will wake to a world turned white. It's been a long week.

Names and other identifying details have been changed. But all of these stories are true.

In Lowell, Massachusetts, in 1834, a woman was fired from her job. The newly developed textile industry demanded young, unmarried women—literally, spinsters—to work industrial spinning machinery. In protest, a shopful of women left their looms. One climbed atop the town pump, from which she delivered what was described in a newspaper report as "a flaming Mary Wollstonecraft speech on the rights of women and the iniquities of the 'moneyed aristocracy' which produced a powerful effect on her auditors and they determined to have it their own way, [even] if they [had to die] for it."

What I do is women's work. What I do has always been women's work. The movement of women, the long slow surge. Our tide rising with the pull of centuries. My friends block roads, hold marches, picket, protest, resist. My friends organize, steal, subvert, dissent, squat, occupy. I answer phones and do laundry. I listen to stories. Sometimes—folding sheets late at night, running yet another load of blankets, unlocking the meds cabinet for Maria's sick child, dispensing housing referrals and food stamp information, asking Denise how her day was—sometimes I wonder what I am really doing. Shuffling women in the front door and out again, strategizing, safety planning, talking about what a healthy relationship might look like, over and over. This is the work I do, this endless and sometimes exhausting sisterhood. There is no glamour in being a listener of stories, no glory in hearing the accounts of violence both horrific and mundane. Sometimes I lock myself in the office and cry. There is no end to the movement of women. There is no end to the men who lurk, stalk, assault, molest, terrify, batter, hunt, harass, belittle, pursue, and destroy. There is no end to the litany of names the women I work with have been given by lovers, husbands, caseworkers, or the government: lazy, stupid, hopeless, helpless, crazy, deserving, bitch, cunt, slut, whore. There is no end to the strength of women. There is no end to women's ability to resist.

In March 1776 Abigail Adams wrote to her husband, "If particular care and attention are not paid to the ladies [in your revolution], we are determined to foment a rebellion, and will not hold ourselves bound to obey the laws in which we have no voice of representation." One hundred and forty-four years later, after decades of struggle, white women won the right to vote.

When I first meet Linda J., the right half of her face is swollen purple. She has driven here from another state after shooting her husband, although I do not know this at the time. Before his death Linda J.'s husband held a gun to their daughter's head and explained if he felt like it she would die. Linda J.'s daughter does not sleep well at night. Some time after I meet her Linda J. will share the front page of the paper with a Texas woman convicted of murdering her five children. The paper will report that Linda J. hit herself in the head with a paperweight in order to claim abuse. The paper will also report that the Texas woman, although she had attempted suicide multiple times, been hospitalized for depression, and methodically drowned her children in order to save them from the grip of Satan, was not in fact insane at the time of their deaths but guilty of "the ultimate betrayal of a mother to her children." On the third page of the same paper two small, one-paragraph items will appear; the first, the story of a Vancouver man charged with killing his six children and setting fire to their home with their bodies inside, and the second a brief account of an Oregon man suspected of shooting his four children and his wife before turning the gun on himself. The motives of both incidents will be listed as unknown and pictures of the men will not appear beside the stories.

I work with women consumed with the struggle to rewrite histories penned in blood and broken bones. I have read enough feminist theory to disbelieve gender binaries. But here is a binary for you: masculine—a gun, a knife, a fist, a cock, a baseball bat, a fireplace poker, a frying pan, boiling water, lit cigarettes; feminine—thirty-five cents and five minutes for a single phone call *I have to leave please help me before he kills me,* the clothes on her back and her children in her arms, wait until he leaves for an hour, goes to work, passes out drunk. I have a hard time thinking outside that one sometimes. People ask me, *How can you possibly stand to do the work that you do?* I say this: The women I work with are warriors. The women I work with are the bravest women I have ever met. The women I work with make me feel like a warrior too.

In the midst of the Great Depression, Black mothers in Cleveland became angry about a local power company shutting off electricity for families who could not pay their bills. In protest they hung wet laundry over every utility line in their neighborhood. Their power was restored. When the Cleveland Emergency Relief Association denied them benefits, they left crying babies on the desks of caseworkers, refusing to retrieve the infants until free milk had been provided for each child. Some years later, the civil rights movement in the United States began as a network of African American women organizing through churches in the South. Rooted in three centuries of African American women's struggle in this country, the organic and far-reaching network of women's groups, ladies' clubs, and church groups had been in place long before the day in 1955 when Rosa Parks of Montgomery, Alabama, refused to give up her seat at the front of the bus.

Why doesn't she just leave? I am frequently asked. If he's so violent, if it's so terrible, if the children are in danger, if he takes her money, her family, her friends, her self-worth, her life, if he promises to change, if he tells her he loves her after he hits her, if he tells her she's crazy, if she loves him, why doesn't she just leave? What kind of woman is she? What kind of mother is she? What did she do to make him so angry? Why did she ask for it?

This is my history, a history written in bodies, in blood, birth, and strong arms. This is the history of women. I name myself feminist and when I say *feminist,* I mean Watsonville, California, where sixteen hundred Latina women went on strike for eighteen months beginning in the summer of 1985, supporting families on their strikers' benefits of fifty-five dollars a week, going on hunger strikes when the pickets failed, and finally ending their resistance in a Catholic pilgrimage on their knees to a local church where they prayed for justice. When I say *feminist,* I mean women in New York and across the United States whose sisters, children, lovers, friends died on 9.11.01, women who say out loud and strong, *I do not want a war in my name, in the names of those I love.* When I say *feminist,* I mean women all over the world, women in Palestine, in the Philippines, in Zimbabwe, India, Indonesia, China, Afghanistan. When I say *feminist,* I mean the Pacific islands, where starting in the 1950s women began to experience radiation effects from U.S. test bombings in the Marshall Islands. They called the children they birthed "jellyfish babies," children born without ears, eyes, legs, arms. By the 1970s they were involved in a constant movement of small protests, demonstrations against dumping, blockades of roads used to transport nuclear materials. By the mid-1980s the movement was visible globally. In June 1984, the National Party government of New Zealand fell over the issue of whether to permit nuclear-armed vessels into New Zealand waters. The opposition Labor Party came into power on the basis of its nuclear-free platform. This is the history of the women I work with, the women fleeing terror into freedom, women who tell the oldest stories in the world. This is a history older than words.

Linda J. will ultimately go to jail. Though this story has not yet spun itself out, I can tell the ending from here. Most likely Linda J. will never see her daughter again. Linda J. never had the chance to tell her daughter that she could sleep safe at night because her father was dead. I am folding sheets, washing windows, watching the snow fall. I am reminding Laura to mop the kitchen floor, wondering how Angela is doing in her new house, waiting for the phone to ring. *I need to leave. I am done. I am tired of living my life in fear.*

These are the stories of women all over the world, wealthy women, poor women, women of color, white women, queer women. Warriors all. This is the history of my body, the history of my blood. This is the story I will tell.

SOURCES CITED

Castillo, Ana. *Massacre of the Dreamers: Essays on Xicanisma.* New York: Penguin, 1994.

Morgan, Robin. *The Demon Lover: The Roots of Terrorism.* New York: Simon and Schuster, 2001.

Ruiz, Vicki L., and Ellen Carol DuBois, Eds. *Unequal Sisters: A Multicultural Reader in U.S. Women's History.* New York: Routledge, 2000.

Zinn, Howard. *A People's History of the United States.* New York: HarperCollins, 1995.

article 4

Becky Statzel

Genocide, Liberation, Self-Determination, and the Politics of Abortion: A Critique of Mainstream Feminism

On the twentieth anniversary of *Roe v. Wade,* I celebrated by trekking up to an abandoned wall in my hometown with my two best friends to paint a giant crossed-out coat hanger. I was seventeen and had always lived with the freedom to choose to have an abortion. It was a chilly night; the spray paint numbed the tips of our fingers, cars buzzed by below with the occasional honk of support. Afterwards, standing away from our work, paint drying on our freezing hands, I was in awe of the potency of the symbol, and the weight of the struggle for reproductive rights.

As an idealistic teenager raised by a feminist mother, I recognized the significance of reproductive freedom as a central component of the emancipation of woman, although like most women of my generation I found it difficult to imagine the fear of living under anti-choice legislation. Although my primary activism involved environmental issues, I actively supported the movement for reproductive rights.

I was born into a working-class logging and mining community in the Idaho Panhandle, to White working-class-to-middle-class parents. For the first couple of years of my life my parents and I moved around northern Idaho, following my father's logging jobs. We then moved to a medium-size city in Washington State. Following my parents' divorce, my mother began a steady climb up the economic ladder, bringing my brother and me into the solid middle class. Although poor or near poor until I was almost a teenager, we always had enough food to eat, and once my mother graduated from college and got steady accounting jobs, we received all the privileges of the middle-class life, including living in White, middle-class neighborhoods and attending good public schools.

In high school I cut my activist teeth running our school's environmental club. Organizing activities from trail restoration to setting up a recycling program, I saw myself a part of a growing international movement and felt empowered by the notion of participating in the movement to save the earth. As part of the environmentalism I embraced, I identified overpopulation as a significant environmental problem and supported groups such as Zero Population Growth (ZPG) for their efforts to spare the earth of the pressure of a burgeoning human population.

I, sadly, was not alone in holding beliefs connecting human population size to environmental protection. Messages about the overpopulation "problem" are pandemic in the media, in the progressive community, and even in feminist and pro-choice circles. A recent issue of *Ms.* magazine had a short commentary on a sperm-bank advertising campaign in Brazil, with the comment "We thought there was an *over*population problem." On a popular radio program recently, a DJ listed random "interesting" facts and commented, "If the population of China were to walk by you in a single-file line, it would never stop due to population growth. Now that's *scary!*" Currently a massive advertising campaign sponsored by Planet, a coalition including Planned Parenthood, hosts a variety of ads depicting women and couples from around the planet encouraging us to "dream, discover, demand, and defy"—to stand up for the right to birth control and abortion. The coalition also sponsors ads showing a bleak clear-cut forest and a woeful-looking monkey, with the caption, "In many developing nations, lack of family planning doesn't just degrade human life." It insinuates that such environmental catastrophes could be avoided if Third World women had access to birth control.

Like many feminists, I did not see the contradiction between reproductive rights and population control—where the individual loses her freedom of choice so that population can be controlled. After first hearing the proposition that population control is fanned by racism and misogyny, I had a difficult time setting aside my previous assumptions about the connections among increasing population size, resource extraction, and impending environmental doom.

While in college I encountered the environmental justice movement, a grassroots, justice-focused movement led by people of color and challenging global environmental racism. Becoming familiar with this movement shook the very foundations of my previous paradigm, forcing me to reflect on the White, mainstream environmental movement in which my first activism flourished. I began to see my activism for what it was: monocultural, lacking justice, and representing a disconnect between people and the environment.

A long journey began with that challenge to my belief in the need for population control, leading me to rethink my entire orientation to the world. I had to delve into the murky world of social constructions—the layers of assumptions that create the lenses through which we see the world. For me to understand this critique of population control, I needed to see my place in the world and to grapple with how my race, class, nationality, gender, and sexual orientation create this position. To become a more effective and honest activist, I needed to understand the history of not only the movements I belonged to, but the history of myself and my people. For, as long as history is ignored, we are bound to repeat it.

Among academics, I notice a trend in which White/privileged writers mention at the beginning of a piece that they are interested in a topic because they are working on antiracism concerns as allies of people of color. Although this positioning is important, much of the time the theorist/writer stops here at acknowledging this position and motivation, as though this absolves them from any other responsibility as allies. However, it is not that simple. Hegemonic beliefs are tenacious; even when we White people attempt to challenge our white privilege, we often unintentionally ensure its perpetuation.

In this effort I am very self-conscious about my research, attempting to challenge any sort of self-entitlement about where and what I can research. Instead I will focus on analyzing the discourse around reproductive rights with my position as focal point.

Population Control 101

The concept of population control is based on the relationship between numbers of people and a decreasing quality of life. Although each human inherently must use resources to survive, creating some amount of stress on the environment, there are innumerable ways for people to interact with their environments and use resources. Disparate levels of resource use have been well documented: "First world people are responsible for 75% of global pollution. If the poorest 75% of the world's population were successfully controlled out of existence there would only be a reduction of pollution by 10%."[1]

The relationship between economic status and population is often misunderstood. Oftentimes, overcrowded slums are depicted as evidence of the population problem. However, if we look at two of the most densely populated countries in the world, Holland and Japan, it is clear that per capita density has little to do with economics. Both countries offer some of the highest standards of living and lowest rates of poverty in the world. Conversely, sub-Saharan Africa, often touted as an area hard hit by the population crisis and having one of the lowest standards of living on the globe, actually has a tremendously lower per capita population than Holland or Japan. The problem then isn't so much about land or resources, but about the distribution of each. Africa is drained of its resources (crops, minerals, and precious gems) without gaining economic benefits from them because international corporations own and exploit and garner the profits. Resource-rich Africa thus falls at the bottom of the global economy.

This strains the logic of the population paradigm, which directly connects environmental degradation to overabundance of people. People are social, not purely biological creatures. Their patterns of resource use, mediated through economic and cultural means, determine environmental impacts and quality of life. So why the focus on numbers? Truly effective curbing of resource depletion and pollution would require changes in the economic system, changes in patterns of resource use, or targeted population reduction, meaning reduction of First World peoples—hardly a tenable option. Ironically, the *entire* focus of the population control movement is on Third World peoples. Since the conclusion arrived at by population control advocates is not the most effective or logical conclusion, it must be asked, What assumptions cause them to conclude that population control is the final desired outcome?[2]

For people who believe in the need for population control, the above argument may challenge so many of their basic assumptions that they may not really hear the critique. The main clarification I need to make is that this is not an anti-choice argument. Criticizing population control is *not* criticizing the need for every woman to have safe and easy access to a variety of forms of family planning and birth control. Every woman deserves to be able to decide when and how many children she'll have or won't have and be able to protect herself from STDs. However, the idea of population control *is* fundamentally anti-choice, for it does not give individual women the right to choose their own family planning. It instead reduces women to aggregate breeders whose fertility must be regulated. Is this not the opposite of "freedom to choose"? There is certainly a need for poor women to have more access to contraceptives; however, supporting access to family planning is quite different from supporting population control.

The difference between a reproductive rights framework and a population control framework is stark. Support of reproductive rights includes the right to birth control that does not threaten the health of the woman. However, population control groups advocate experimental or proven carcinogenic forms of birth control. Depo-Provera and Norplant, the most commonly prescribed, are both hormonal forms of birth control that may increase a woman's risk for cancer. A true reproductive rights campaign would advocate for sustainable, easy-to-use forms of birth control that do not adversely affect the health of the woman.

Eugenics, Birth Control, and "Overpopulation"

The history of population control and the historical period in which it gained momentum are telling. In the United States, racism, eugenics, and population control formed a terrible trio, scarring many communities of color through state-sponsored eugenicist offices. Until the 1960s many states operated such offices with the attempt of stopping groups dubbed "degenerates" (typically poor women, women of color, and disabled women) from procreating. These offices have since closed down, but their legacy persists. Although these offices specifically supported eugenics (literally meaning "good genes") and not population control, their explicit purpose was to protect the "public" (read the privileged) from the degenerates (those different from the white mainstream by race, class, or ability). These offices were part of a centuries-old

debate on the role of a society's responsibility toward the poor.

The theoretical ringleader of the population control movement, the clergyman-turned-economist Thomas Malthus, wrote in the late eighteenth and early nineteenth centuries about a connection between poverty, land, and population size in England. Mathus's thesis blamed social ills on a natural inclination for human populations to increase, creating competition over decreasing resources in an environment where, with natural selection, only the fit survive. Does this sound like social Darwinism? Darwin gave credit to Malthus's "Essay on the Principle of Population" (1798) as providing a foundation to his theory of natural selection and evolution. Malthus wrote that without "preventative checks" human populations would double every twenty-five years, requiring intervention.[3] The responsibility of intervention was bestowed on the rich, to regulate the size of poor families. Karl Marx, who came of age at the time of Malthus's death, also wrote about the treachery of poverty but proposed quite different solutions. Marx also agreed that too many people were living in poverty, but his solution was to challenge poverty itself and build a more equitable economic system. The Malthus/Marx debate at its base level was, and remains, eliminate the poor or eliminate poverty.

Populationism, influenced by Malthus, grew strong roots in the large eugenicist movements of the early 1900s. The notion of controlling population even influenced the development paradigm and was an inherent goal of global economic development.[4] This is the backdrop against which birth control, including the pill, was first created and distributed in the United States. Margaret Sanger, grandmother of the birth control movement in the United States and founder of Planned Parenthood, published a magazine called the *Birth Control Review.* As early as the 1920s the *Review* published eugenicist articles. By the 1940s a birth control movement had come of age in the United States and was tightly entangled with the eugenicist movement. Although Sanger's own views on eugenics are deeply contested today, many coalitions existed between birth control advocates and eugenicists.[5]

The Birth Control Federation of America, the precursor to Planned Parenthood, developed a "Negro Project" in 1939 that made the following statement: "The mass of Negroes, particularly in the South still breed carelessly and disastrously, with the result that the increase among Negroes, even more than among whites, is far from that portion of the population least fit, and least able to bear children."[6]

This organization largely created the pressure to develop the birth control pill, which leads to the question, Was the birth control pill created to propel a eugenicist agenda? Probably not— but failing to acknowledge eugenicist support for birth control gives an incomplete history.

In the 1950s a new focus emerged on the problem of "overpopulation." In 1952, John D. Rockefeller III held a conference with Planned Parenthood, conservationists, demographers, and development experts out of which came the Population Council. Rockefeller's motivations for the council are evident in this statement: "The relationship of population to material and cultural resources of the world represents one of the most crucial and urgent problems of the day."[7] The Population Council is still possibly the leading population control group.

Population Control and Colonialism

At the core of populationism is a unilateral subject/object relationship. The subject is the thinker who "understands" the problem and creates the solution; the object is the population masses who are only acted upon. Thus, First World citizens (white industrialized peoples) hold the responsibility of solving the problems of the poor Third World people (illiterate people of color). In this relationship, solvers have power, and those with the problem lack power. If we acknowledge the global economic system that allows a minority of the world (read the privileged in industrialized society) to live in relative luxury due to the exploitation of the labor, land, and resources of the majority of the world (read poor, Third World peoples), we see that the power imbalance in the population paradigm is far from natural. This power imbalance also follows the same lines as European colonial expansion—wealth poured from the Third World countries to the First. Thus, capitalism transports resources from the poor to the rich and from poor nations to rich ones in the same direction as colonialism directed wealth to Europe and Europeans for hundreds of years.

Privileged Americans, particularly White Americans, typically understand our political and economic status in the world as either natural or arrived at through hard work and perseverance (sometimes called the pioneer ethic). Thus we render invisible the exploitation that must exist to float our lifestyles by normalizing our position in the world. It is easy to embrace the population paradigm because it is based on so many of our cultural ideals. In short, populationism fails to challenge capitalism and the unequal global economic and political divisions that capitalism perpetuates. Instead of reevaluating our own consumption, our role in the global economy, and our colonial history (which created the stratification of rich and poor), we conveniently blame the current global environmental dystopia on there simply being too many people "out there." This disowning of responsibility puts the blame on poor women of color, the people who have the least amount of power on a global scale; thus they are the most easily controlled. Populationists can convince themselves that they are not speaking for their own interests, but for the good of the environment, mother earth, and our collective interests. Their colonialism is based on good intentions, which sadly follows a long-standing trend.

Birth Control and Racism

Population control literature features an interesting constant—the people pictured are brown or black and almost always are women. Portraying women of color in an attempt to sell the idea of overpopulation comes with a complex, historically grounded set of messages. Colonialists for centuries have used images that depict people of color as though they are not fully human, but rather objects who are in need of "our" collective white or Western help. The effects of this racist and colonial thinking have scarred many women of color.

During the 1970s the Indian Health Service *sterilized 25 percent of American Indian women in the United States without their consent.*[8] While the mainstream reproductive rights movement was desperately fighting to ensure women's access to abortion, Native American women were sterilized at significantly high rates against their will. The story of the Native women who worked against this is not fully acknowledged in the history of reproductive rights. But is not the fight for the right of a woman to choose *to* have children just as much a fight for reproductive rights as the fight for the right of a woman to choose *not to* have children? Placing this sterilization campaign in the context of the larger five-hundred-year genocide program against Native Americans sponsored by European interests, including the U.S. government, shows the magnitude of this issue.[9]

In *Abortion Without Apology,* Ninia Baehr attempts a radical history of the birth control movement. The focus of the work is to provide a history of the abortion rights movement to enlighten abortion activism in the 1990s. Although Baehr's history is more inclusive than most writings about abortion, the work fails to present a racially inclusive history. She begins in 1959, describing the work of the "Army of Three," who worked in California to abolish anti-abortion laws. Baehr quotes Lana Clarke Phelan, one of the "Army of Three," describing her experience with an illegal abortion. Her story is blatantly told from a White perspective and directed to a White audience, a limitation that Baehr does not address. Phelan explains how she received an illegal abortion in a Cuban settlement in Tampa, Florida. After the abortion she experienced complications and had to go back to the Cuban midwife for help: "It was so dark. I went around the side of this woman's little shack. . . . After she cleaned me up, she came around the gurney and put her arms around me. This great big woman, big Black woman, with big motherly arms, and, you know, a wonderful warmth about her."[10]

Phelan's description of the abortionist so closely fits the stereotype of the mammy, an image of Black women constructed by Whites to promote Black female subordination and servitude, that Baehr's failure to acknowledge this stereotype is significant. The entire passage is a description of Phelan's venturing into the community of the "other," leaving the White norm behind to receive an abortion. Although the book's topic is purported to be a history of abortion, it is obviously a focus of White activism.

The story of the Cuban woman who performs the abortion is left untold, along with the circumstances of her and her community's sexual health and reproduction issues.

Where Do We Go from Here?

There is clear evidence that since its inception, the birth control movement has not met the needs of women of color and often helped perpetuate racial oppression. However, women of color, just as White women, need safe, effective, and easy access to birth control. The needs are different, however, in that, as Chandra Mohanty has stated, "For poor women of color, the notion of 'a women's right to choose' to bear children has always been mediated by a coercive, racist state."[11] Therefore, in order to achieve reproductive rights for *all* women, the movement must focus on ending racism, classism, heterosexism, and ableism, to ensure equal access to resources.

I believe we need a new way to interpret history based on the notion of intersectional oppression, one not based on binaries. On the one hand we need to challenge the activists who, intentionally or not, perpetuate racism and colonialism; we still must learn from their victories and mistakes, build on their successes, and tell their history without vilifying them.

Although the mainstream birth control movement is guilty at times of supporting white supremacy, to depict a binary relationship between a monolithic birth control movement as oppressor and a monolithic group of women of color as victimized, with me the writer and you the reader helping to solve the situation, only perpetuates the same stymied relationships. It is important to recognize that many communities and activists of color have actively fought for reproductive freedom—both for legal birth control and against racist infringement on their right to have children. African American groups, for example, have participated in reproductive rights politics for centuries. Between 1919 and 1945, the Black press published numerous articles advocating for the legality of birth control, although some of the motivations differed for Black women and White women. Jessie M. Rodrique writes that from 1916 through the early 1930s, Black women's fiction frequently depicted Black women refusing to bring children into a racist world and decried the criminalization of birth control.[12] Loretta Ross writes that during slavery African Americans "used birth control as a form of resistance to slavery. . . . When Black women resorted to abortion, the stories told were not so much about the desire to be free of the pregnancy, but rather about the miserable social conditions which dissuaded them from bringing new lives into the world."[13] Yet this acceptance of birth control did not include a coerced acceptance of sterilization abuses. Rodrique writes, "Blacks took a significant stance against sterilization, especially in the thirties. Scholars have not sufficiently recognized this point: that blacks could endorse a program of birth control but reject the extreme views of eugenicists."[14]

There is great fear within the mainstream birth control movement that telling an honest history of the movement, airing its dirty laundry, would vilify the White woman activists who helped push for abortion reform. I believe this fear is based on binary thinking, whereby individuals are seen either as good or bad, accepted or rejected, hero or villain. We need to break out of this limiting thinking. However, we can't ignore that most White reproductive rights activists have historically worked for themselves and other White women alone, have often perpetuated racism, and have not challenged their own privilege in the way necessary to build successful coalitions with women of color. As reproductive rights organizers worked for the liberation of White women, they may well have perpetuated or ignored the oppression of women of color.

To fully achieve reproductive freedom for all women, the reproductive rights movement must embrace a critique that extends beyond birth control. If women are choosing freely not to have children based on not wanting to bring them into a racist world, not having the means to support them, or fearing the pollution in their neighborhood will impede the development of a child, what sort of "choice" do they really have? The following statistics show the unequal access to safe prenatal care and child rearing in the United States, which result in unequal family planning options:

- Twenty-five percent of Black pregnancies end in miscarriage.
- Babies born to women of color have twice the neonatal mortality rate of White babies.
- Black babies die at a rate of six thousand more per year than White babies in the same geographic region, due mainly to low birth weight.
- Twenty-five to thirty percent of inner-city Black women receive little or no prenatal care.
- By 1982, 15 percent of white women were sterilized, compared with 24 percent of Black women, 35 percent of Puerto Rican women, and 42 percent of Native American women.[15]

It was easy for me as a White American to identify with the goal of population control, for I understand colonialism and my place in the world on a subconscious level. Even though I was raised to support human rights, my very understanding of the world was formed by the culture I grew up in, which is deeply influenced by the centuries-old history of colonialism, the foundation of the white American experience. Until I began to understand the effects of my position on my understanding and my own internalized sense of supremacy, I could not engage in effective activism nor work in effective multiracial coalitions.

I also found it easy to identify the continued legal access to abortion as the primary focus of the reproductive rights movement. I could not have fathomed that my experience might include a denial of the right to have children. Just as I needed to go through tremendous changes to come to grips with my whiteness and grow into a more effective activist, so too does the feminist movement. Particularly because of current threats to reproductive rights in the United States, it is crucial to learn from the past mistakes of the pro-choice movement to ensure more successful future outcomes.

The familiar coat-hanger symbol is powerful yet emblematic of only part of the movement for reproductive rights. Challenging the institutional racism that backed the mass sterilization of women of color in the United States, particularly Native American women, is just as much a reproductive rights issue as supporting continued legal access to abortion. Posing support of population control as though it belongs in the reproductive rights movement is only continuing the history of exclusion and collusion with racism from which the movement must break free.

To move forward inclusively, we must be boldly honest and build a new focus with input from a truly diverse group of women. I believe we need a new symbol for reproductive rights—one that unites us, as women, in a truly common movement without centering on the experience of one group at the expense of all others. As the younger generation, this is our task.

NOTES

1. Andy Smith, "Malthusian Orthodoxy and the Myth of ZPG." In *Defending Mother Earth: Native American Perspectives on Environmental Justice,* ed. Jace Weaver (Maryknoll, NY: Orbis Books, 1996) 125.

2. In my experience with challenging population control, there is a common place in the argument that makes people get stuck. I feel it is noteworthy enough to address this here. Many people have so entangled the idea of population control with the pro-choice movement that they feel that attacking population control is somehow attacking a woman's right to choose. However, critiquing population control is not denying the need to support and recognize every woman's right to safe, easy access to all forms of family planning and birth control. I am saying that the idea of population control is fundamentally anti-choice. The focus is not on giving individual women the right to choose their own family planning, but instead reduces women to aggregate breeders whose fertility must be controlled. Can you imagine neighborhood Population Control clinics being visited by U.S. women for birth control and abortion? Would you feel comfortable going to a clinic with such a name?

3. Betsy Hartmann, *Reproductive Rights and Wrongs: The Global Politics of Population Control and Contraceptive Choice* (New York: Harper & Row, 1987) 13.

4. Arturo Escobar, *Encountering Development: The Making and Unmaking of the Thirld World*

(Princeton, NJ: Princeton University Press, 1995) 35.

5. Hartmann, *Reproductive Rights and Wrongs,* 97.

6. Susan E. Davis, *Women Under Attack: Victories, Blacklash, and the Fight for Reproductive Freedom* (Cambridge, MA: South End Press), pamphlet no. 7.

7. John D. Rockefeller III, quoted in Hartmann, *Reproductive Rights and Wrongs,* 101.

8. Andy Smith, "Malthusian Orthodoxy and the Myth of ZPG," 124.

9. Davis, *Women Under Attack,* 22.

10. Quoted in Ninia Baehr, *Abortion Without Apology: A Radical History for the 1990s.* (Boston: South End Press, 1990) pamphlet no. 8, p. 13.

11. Chandra Mohanty, "Introduction: Cartographies of Struggle." In *Third World Women and the Politics of Feminism,* ed. Chandra Mohanty, Lourdes Torres, and Ann Russo (Bloomington: Indiana University Press, 1991), 12.

12. Jessie M. Rodrique, "The Black Community and the Birth-Control Movement." In *Unequal Sisters: A Multicultural Reader in U.S. Woman's History,* ed. Ellen Carol DuBois and Vicki L. Ruiz (New York: Routledge, 1994).

13. Loretta Ross, "African American Women and Abortion After Roe," in Rickie Solinger, et. al., *Abortion Wars: A Half Century of Struggle, 1950–2000* (paperback edition, Berkeley: University of California Press, 1998), 144.

14. Rodrique, "The Black Community and the Birth-Control Movement," 337.

15. Quoted in Paula Giddings, "The Last Taboo." In *Words of Fire: An Anthology of African-American Feminist Thought,* ed. Beverly Guy-Sheftall (New York: The New Press, 1995) 245–246.

Monica McCallum

Seeing in Color

Every day as I drop my son off at day care, I read the short message inscribed on the poster overhanging the door. The poster is simple, just the message "Love Sees No Color," accompanied by a black and white photo of two children's arms stretching down in a "V" to two entwined hands. One dark-skinned arm, one light-skinned arm.

In some ways, I appreciate the simplistic format of the poster. At first glance, it challenges centuries of racism, without being brash. Looking at the picture, I see a positive reflection of my own light-skinned hand entwined with my son's dark one.

But I also dread having to face that photo and those words every day. When I read the poster, I read a between-the-lines message encouraging "colorblindness." This nags at me. It glares at me. It sees my nasty secret.

You see, I am sharply aware of the racial differences between my Latino son and me. As a White single mother of a multiracial child, I feel it is my responsibility to openly and honestly discuss race and racism. We comment often on the shades of our skin and the ways they change throughout the seasons. We talk about hair color and eye color and cultural and racial biases.

Our conversations become easier as I realize more and more that our family is becoming more

the "norm." In February 2000, *Parenting* magazine reported that "the percentage of interracial families has more than tripled in the last 30 years."[1] Indeed, I have seen this trend among my own friends and peers, many of whom have interracial relationships and/or children. Unfortunately, simply having these relationships does not make them any easier to maneuver. In addition, parenting resources and social commentaries have not reflected this trend adequately, leaving those of us who have interracial families with little guidance and support.

Nonetheless, as a mother, I still sought resources to help me better define the intertwined dance of my son's life and my own. Sadly, most mainstream parenting magazines, books, and Internet resources neglect issues of race, racism, multiculturalism, and interracial families. The few resources that do mention race primarily address transracial adoption or Dr. King's "I Have a Dream" speech—but they slightly pervert his original message to promote mere "tolerance" of diverse cultures and "colorblindness," as opposed to not judging the quality of one's character by the color of one's skin.

The day-care poster extends this watered-down message of colorblindness to children. "Love Sees No Color" is one of many messages displayed in public schools and day-care centers meant to teach racial tolerance to youngsters around the country. The philosophical premise of these messages is to promote a society in which people are not judged by a good/bad label based on ethnocentrism. However, on a realistic level, colorblindness exudes a sense of whiteness as the norm, and many of the messages are aimed specifically at White people.

Looking at the more subtle repercussions of the way race is taught to children, I assume I will be spending most of my son's school years un-teaching the assumptions propagated through the school system. Colorblindness is just one example of a general teaching that is inappropri-ate for interracial families. The very notion of colorblindness is based on having the option to see or not see color, and thus it is a privilege that can only be used by the dominant (White) cul-ture. It stems from an assumption that whiteness is the central perspective and that all other per-spectives must in some way conform to white-ness. Once conformed, people of varying races can be seen as "individuals."

However, in an interracial family, we do not have the option of ignoring color. My searches for writings about race and single parenting led me to more progressive writings about parent-hood. A logical evolution in my search came when a friend handed me a copy of *Listen Up: Voices from the Next Feminist Generation.* Poring over this anthology for the first time, I began to feel a sense of solidarity with these other young women. Though their names were not familiar (I didn't even know most of the people they referred to), many of their concerns were person-ally engaging: body image, abortion issues, race, and even mothering. Even though all of these issues were never merged in a single es-say, the connection was clear to me: feminists

talked about race, they talked about mothering, and both of these discussions validated me and encouraged me to expand my own point of view.

As I explored more feminist literature, I discovered the writings of bell hooks, Gloria Anzaldua, Patricia Hill Collins, and other women of color. I found the writings of women of color particularly helpful because they intro-duced me to histories that I had not traditionally learned about, and they addressed issues regard-ing the limitations of feminism. bell hooks makes clear the line between the multilayered resistance struggle of "revolutionary feminism," which aims to openly address and eradicate all oppres-sion, and the mainstream mass media feminism that caters to White women who strive to access ruling-class wealth and power.[2]

I began to see a parallel between hooks's examination of the limitations of feminism and the limitations I saw in the parenting industry. As a mother trying to sort through issues of race, gender, class, and sexuality—all within my little family—I found the glossy, smiling parenting magazines, which dedicated space to simplistic discipline tactics and product advertising, vacu-ous and threatening to much of what I stood for as a parent and woman interested in building healthy communities. I found solace in combin-ing ideals of revolutionary feminism and pro-gressive parenting to create a vision of a community dedicated to eradicating oppression and increasing communication along lines of race, class, sexuality, ability, and age.

Theory and real life are different, however. This became painfully clear to me the day my three-year-old son told me he wanted to cut all his skin so it would grow back white. When I asked him why he thought his skin would grow back white, he pointed to a patch of scarred skin that indeed had grown back a lighter tone than his coffee-with-cream hue. When I asked him why he wanted white skin, he replied that it was because he wanted to be like Jesse and do the things that Jesse did. (Jesse was the protagonist of his favorite movie at the time.)

I was utterly taken aback by my son's desire to change his skin. I felt unprepared for this because I had read in parenting books that children didn't have an awareness of racial "difference" until they were about kindergarten age, yet here it was, a full two years early. Even with the early onset of racial awareness, though, hadn't I done a good enough job of exposing him to a variety of people, cultures, races, and beliefs? Hadn't I affirmed him and loved him enough? In my mind, I had been creating a symbiotic balance by merging theories of whiteness, womanhood, mothering, and race; but in real life, my son wanted to cut his skin off. Where did I go wrong?

I thought I was ultra-progressive, yet here was my son needing comfort and answers in a way that I felt utterly inadequate to give. It was the first time in my son's short life that I really missed the presence of the father he never knew and the man I left when I was only eight weeks pregnant. I began questioning my ability to be a suitable single mother for a child of color. I was feeling my privilege as a negative burden that manifested itself as a sense of complete and utter failing in my duties as a mother. I felt that the solution for our conundrum lay in my finding a way to examine my own whiteness, White privilege, and the ways I reflected those beliefs in my son's upbringing (watching movies with all-White casts, for example).

I was faced with the daunting task of helping my son find healthy ways of developing his burgeoning racial identity, while simultane-ously reconciling myself with the relationship, based predominantly on exoticism, that helped to produce him. I found myself wondering about how to teach my son elements of his Peruvian, Chinese, and Norwegian heritages. I wondered about the broader social implications of being part of an increasingly international global community. Perhaps most significantly, I began to question how I could work through my own issues of racism without ultimately exploiting or exoticizing my own child.

Along with a friend, I decided to take my son on a three-week trip to Mexico as a way of helping him strengthen his racial comfort with himself. As we got ready for the trip, I talked with my son a lot about all of the things people with different skin colors do: swim, have friends, play (he was three, remember?). We talked in a simple way about the cultural background connected with his skin and with mine. I reminded him that he also carries my history with him, even though his skin may not reflect that.

Once in Mexico, we stayed mostly in hotels where Mexican families stayed. We rode buses, spoke in Spanish, and pointed out brown-skinned people doing everything from walking down the street to driving boats. My son freely began to express his adoration of horses, playing at the beach, and his noticeably darkening skin. He felt proud when his skin tanned nicely as mine reddened and burned.

And now, nearly three years later, I can say with satisfaction that my son is proud of his color. As his understanding grows, so do the concepts we discuss. We talk about everything from the science of melanin to the reasons why people might stereotype us and the definitions of labels and identities such as *Latino* and *indigenous*.

I sometimes still mourn the things I can't provide for him. But in these cases, I try as much as possible to be honest and open. I let him know that I can't provide him with a real Peruvian cultural experience. As he gets older, I'll continue to speak openly about racism, White privilege, and our experiences.

I wonder how the differences between him and other Latino children are going to affect him. Now that my son is school age, it is beginning to become clear to me just how much his life is going to differ from the lives of other Latino children. Just as bell hooks speaks about the limits of liberal White feminism, I wonder if I can raise my son within the liberal White paradigm that is comfortable for me and still expect him to become a proud man of color.

I hope that subverting this parenting paradigm with a sense of social justice is enough to help him develop a healthy, happy sense of self. Within all this, I know that I must see myself, see race, and know what being White means to me. Through this knowledge, even its harsher and guilt-ridden sides, I see my son—in all of his color. I feel a sense of subversive pride, knowing I have done my part to break down some of the barriers of "whiteness," "colorblindness," and simplistic "tolerance" for cultures beyond the hegemonic norm established for the convenience of the majority culture in the United States.

And still, at the center of all of this is my son—my bright, inquisitive, and engaging son. When he asks questions about race, I do my best to answer him honestly. I tell him that his experiences are going to be different than mine because people will see him differently. I also tell him that I call him "Latino" and "multiracial" and "Peruvian," but he does not need to call himself these things. He is free to define himself as he sees fit. He is free to live his life with all of his colors. He has a right to be honored and respected. And he has a right to be loved unconditionally for it—which he is.

NOTES

1. http://www.parenting.com/parenting/article/article_general/0,8266,1952,00.html
2. bell hooks, *Killing Rage, Ending Racism* (New York: Henry Holt, 1995) 98–100.

Shelly Frazier

Bodyoma

The craze for thinness is everywhere. It has infiltrated the lives of almost all women and has managed to leave some of its deepest scars on young adolescent girls. Moreover, the craze is not just for thinness; it calls for "thinness to the extreme." What were once considered normal and healthy sizes for young girls and adult women are now ostracized and deemed as "chubby" or "fat." The ideal size for women and adolescent girls is plastered on magazine covers, newspaper ads, bulletin boards, and television commercials and is further mobilized by the food and exercise industries.

Corporations make millions of dollars by pushing the image of frail-thin women onto consumers. The food industries have created entire lines of products geared to dieting. Diet foods have become so popular that they are mainstays in many homes. Even people that are not dieting buy many "low-fat" or "fat-free" foods that, while low in fat, do not offer any nutritional value. Potato chips, cookies, ice cream, candy bars, and many more types of snack foods are now offered as low-fat or fat-free, so that even if you are dieting, you can still eat junk food. Brands such as Snackwells and Healthy Choice have made millions of dollars by reducing fat in food and marketing it as a healthier alternative. Of course, this food is usually loaded with calories and preservatives, making the decrease in fat content irrelevant. The exercise industry, which includes health spas and gyms as well as the makers of exercise equipment, capitalizes on an image of thinness to draw people toward their products. Their hundreds of infomercials advertise "new and improved" devices that guarantee the loss of inches in weeks, or new training programs and techniques that guarantee weight loss that will make us look like the people in the ads. The examples of food and exercise companies making profit from penetrating the lives and health of consumers with images of the perfect body and perfect lifestyle are endless.

Almost all of this advertising uses our culture's ideal woman or young girl to advertise their products, regardless of whether the products are directed at women or men. We all know what *she* looks like. *She* is tall and thin to the point that we can see bones protruding through her skin. *She* is completely emaciated with eyes set back deep into her face, and her cheekbones look as if they have been carved. If it were not for her breast implants, *she* would look like a prepubescent girl or boy. Now this image is not only required for the fashion model on the catwalk; it is also prescribed as the norm for women and girls in all walks of life.

The advertising world has pushed her image into every consumer market. You can find her in almost all media industries, including film, music, and television—even into markets that would seem off limits, such as teen-oriented magazines and television shows. Young girls shown on television are now completely emaciated with their rib bones protruding beneath their halter tops. Even female athletes are shown in magazines and advertisements as thin and frail as opposed to healthy and strong. I remember reading about the diets of some of the popular actresses who were losing weight in order to have better chances for more parts in movies or television shows. By healthy standards they were not overweight or even chubby, but the entertainment industry calls for thinness "to the extreme." Jennifer Aniston, who at one point in her career weighed a whopping 130 pounds, chose to lose twenty pounds in order to be at a competitive size. And now, like all of the others, she is finally thin enough.

This craze for thinness has pervaded the lives of young girls and women and has resulted in an obsession with body image that I call "bodyoma." What was once categorized by way of eating disorders such as anorexia nervosa or bulimia has now taken on many forms, all of which stem from a compulsive struggle for the perfect body image. Bodyoma often exists in the gray area between anorexia and bulimia. Young girls and women with bodyoma are not necessarily starving themselves to death or binging and purging on a regular basis. They are living lives that are regulated by the incessant counting of calories, consistent attempts at crash diets, mornings filled with anxiety over that crucial moment when they step on the scale, opting for cigarettes and diet sodas for lunch and dinner instead of healthy meals, eating only "fat-free" or diet foods, and the hours spent in front of the mirror, pinching and poking themselves and looking for fat or cellulite that they cannot seem to lose. Compulsions such as these are home for many women and young girls. In fact, I do not have one friend who is not fixated on her body image to the point of some compulsion, whether it is excessive dieting, obsessive exercising, or hours spent depressed over her inability to lose the weight that is preventing her from looking like the women in all the advertisements.

My own battle with bodyoma first began when I moved to California. Born and bred in the Midwest, my self-perception was cushioned by the accepted image of girls raised on meat and potatoes. I was considered "strong and healthy" by my family and peers because I was an athlete. Sizes eight, ten, and twelve were accepted as the norm fifteen years ago in the Midwest. Young women like myself in my high school were conscious of our weight, but the norms allowed us much more room to be comfortable with ourselves. Upon arriving in California, however, I soon realized that by their standards, I was *not* healthy, but fat. The thin look was "in" as opposed to a healthy or athletic one. Young women were size two or four at the most. Size six was somewhat acceptable, but it would still have put me in the chubby category. In California, advertising is everywhere. With all of the shopping malls, magazines, newspapers, and billboard ads, no one can escape the idea of a woman's "perfect" body. I lived close to Los Angeles, so women were not only thin to the extreme, but they were also perfectly sun-tanned and beautiful. These images of what I was supposed to look like crashed down on me and completely annihilated any sense of self-worth or self-confidence. Within six months of being in California, I started exercising and dieting like mad. I decided that I needed to lose thirty pounds in order to be thin enough, which took me over a year and a half to do. I remember spending mornings in front of the mirror in tears because the weight was not coming off fast enough. In my mind, I was too fat to wear a bathing suit on the beaches, too fat to buy clothes that looked like everyone else's, and way too fat to have a boyfriend.

Although I had never counted calories or fat grams before, I quickly taught myself how to do it. Amid the food industry's fat-free and low-calorie foods, I was inundated with what to eat and what to stay away from. In a short amount of time, I was like all of the other women that I met in California: I drank diet sodas, smoked cigarettes, ate only fat-free foods, and exercised every day for hours. I compulsively weighed myself four to five times a day to make sure that I was not putting on the weight that I had worked so desperately to get off. Who I was as a person was no longer centered on the values that I had been taught in the Midwest—such as kindness, intelligence, and sincerity; it was now solely based on how I looked in the mirror.

One of the biggest problems of bodyoma, however, is that this vicious cycle of dieting, exercising, and obsessing never leaves you. Even though I lost some weight and manage to wear a size that I am comfortable with, I still have bodyoma. In fact, until I found out that I was pregnant, I was still weighing myself once a day and counting every calorie and fat gram that I ate. Looking back, I finally realize that I looked fine. I was not overweight or in need of any sort of dieting or rigorous exercise, but when you have bodyoma, it is impossible to see yourself clearly. All that I could see was myself in comparison to the rail-thin women in all of the ads and commercials, which always left me wanting

to be thinner. It was not until the recent birth of my daughter that I was able to get any true perspective regarding my body and my health. Pregnancy allowed me to view myself and my body differently. Because I was committed to taking care of myself in order to have a healthy baby, I forced myself to put the dieting and exercising on hold. I began to eat well, to rest, and to take care of myself. After a while, I actually started to enjoy my body and the fact that I was able to carry and eventually have a baby. But the remnants of my bodyoma are still always in the background. I will always fear being overweight by society's standards. And more important, I doubt that there will ever be a day when I am completely satisfied with my body. I have to make a conscious effort to enjoy my body and my health and not to fixate on an "ideal" body image that I will never have.

Only through my commitment to feminism and motherhood have I been able to identify these aspects of my personality and recognize them as part of a bigger problem facing women and adolescent girls. As the mother of a daughter, I have had to work hard at not succumbing to the pressure and anxiety that accompany my bodyoma. I do not allow myself to read any magazines or newspapers that have advertising directed at marketing any form of body image. I do my best to refrain from watching television shows or movies where normal women look like chic heroin addicts. I make myself eat foods that are good for me, regardless of their fat or calorie content. And I have promised myself to eat meals with my daughter without guilt or anxiety because I am truly committed to not passing my bodyoma on to her.

Through my struggles, I have also recognized that I am not alone. All of my friends struggle with some form of body obsession. Whether they are constant dieters trying each new dieting gimmick, excessive exercisers, consistent fasters, smokers, or diet soda drinkers, they are all struggling to make that "perfect" weight. As feminists, we make concerted efforts to discuss our bodyoma with each other as honestly as we can, so that we can somehow make sense of our behavior. We recognize the weaknesses that we share and are consistently trying to find ways to ward off our feelings of pressure and anxiety. We are also trying to find ways to bring the problems associated with bodyoma to light in the feminist community. This is especially important now that there is mounting evidence that adolescent girls are being plagued with the same pressures. Fortunately for myself, operating somewhere in the gray area between an eating disorder and obsessive behavior did not begin until my early twenties. For many adolescent girls, it is beginning as early as the age of ten. They are dieting more, exercising more, and experiencing more anxiety about their weight, while being more affected by the media than ever before.

Research shows that the numbers of anorexic and bulimic adolescent girls are on the rise, and the numbers of young girls dieting and exercising are also dramatically increasing. In her book *Fasting Girls,* Joan Brumberg reports that 80 percent of girls in the fourth grade in San Francisco are dieting. And at three private girls' schools in the D.C. area, 53 percent of the girls were unhappy with their bodies. Brumberg's research also shows that as girls get older, the number of them dissatisfied with their bodies also increases. She cites a *Glamour* magazine survey of thirty-three thousand women between the ages of eighteen and thirty-five, which

showed that 75 percent believed they were fat, although according to clinical standards only 25 percent were actually overweight.[1] The age of young women with symptoms of a body image disorder is becoming younger and younger. And their behavior is becoming more and more drastic. As Brumberg's research shows, young girls between the ages of ten and sixteen (who should be establishing a basic confidence about themselves) are being inundated with information that promotes self-loathing instead of self-liking.

Research by Levinson, Powell, and Steelman shows that body image is the chief concern among females. Adolescent girls are reported as being much more dissatisfied with their weight than are males, and this dissatisfaction is correlated with an overall anxiety about body image—mainly because young women face harsher social consequences when they are not within the socially accepted boundaries of what is a desirable physical appearance. When comparing adolescent body perceptions as being underweight, normal weight, or overweight with the perceptions of their parents and their physicians, the effects of social forces become apparent. Young white women were almost twice as likely to report themselves as being overweight than their physicians or their parents did. These adolescents are responding to social forces from the advertising world and the media that do not affect parents and physicians. The research does show, however, that unlike physicians, parents are somewhat more attuned to the social forces that determine acceptable body size. Parents judge their adolescents more critically than their physicians do. Although parents do not judge their adolescents as harshly as the adolescents judge themselves, they are more likely to adhere to social, rather than healthy, standards.[2]

The connections between women, their bodyoma, and the media are inextricable. The idealization of extremely thin women in our society has given way to a culture of thin. Research by Brewis shows that body image distortions are perpetuated by our fat-stigmatizing or thinness-promoting media. It is important to note the differences between fat-stigmatizing advertising and thinness-promoting advertising. In our society, being fat is clearly stigmatized. What is beautiful and desirable is rarely, if ever, portrayed by obese people: it is almost always relegated to those who are thin or of medium size. The problem, however, and the point of distinction, is that our media in the United States do not promote average or medium sizes. Instead, almost all advertising is geared toward extremely thin, anorexic-looking women. In this way, the media may not be stigmatizing the average or the medium sizes as they do obese ones, but they certainly do not promote them. These studies show that women in industrialized societies have greater body image distortions, which can be associated to the omnipresence of a thinness-crazed media. Brewis finds that young women not only perceive themselves to be larger than they are, they also are inaccurate in their perception of what body sizes men find most attractive. The young women studied selected much slimmer figures than did the men, thus perpetuating their own dissatisfaction with their bodies. Brewis cites this point as evidence of the fact that the media misinform women not only as to what they should look like, but also as to what men are finding desirable.[3]

This trend is in keeping with our capitalist market. Corporations make money by keeping people unhappy with themselves and the things that they have. The only way to sell their products is to convince us that we need them, which is why the ideal woman has become thinner over time. Companies have to keep us dissatisfied with ourselves so that we will buy their exercise products, gym memberships, clothing, and diet foods.

Young girls, who should be learning to express themselves with confidence, are instead learning self-loathing. They are at the mercy of a world of overstated body images created by selfish and shallow adults. As feminists, how can we expect young women to find a place in our movement—which operates completely outside of their reality? In other words, how do we push messages of equality, strength, and solidarity, when the young women coming up behind us are not even eating? Our culture of thin teaches young girls how to be skinny, look pretty, be sexy, and buy whatever the market is selling. When the majority of what society sells is beauty and sex, how can there be room for feminist concepts such as independence, equality, choice, and, most important, confidence and self-love?

I know that dealing with my own bodyoma severely limited my ability to think in feminist terms. I, like most women with a body image disorder, was selfish in my pursuit for the perfect body. I was rarely thankful for my health because I was so focused on how I looked and what others thought of me. It was only with motherhood and feminism that I managed to rearrange my priorities, to put my disorder in the background, and to focus on my family, my studies, and my commitment to feminism. The question, however, is how do we as feminists reach out to young adolescent women, who clearly need our message, especially when we are competing with our greater society that is so clearly focused on physical appearance, sex, and material consumption?

Feminism needs to find space to deal with problems facing young women. Problems that are not necessarily in the traditional scope of feminist ideology need to be addressed and brought to the forefront. Young women are our future and we cannot ignore the problems that they are facing, especially given the fact that in their dealings with social problems, they are not likely to see the value in feminist thinking. Most feminists already recognize the differences between our generations and we must find ways to bridge the gaps. As it is, many young women see no need for feminism. They do not see the need to support choice, to fight for equal pay, or to push for better political representation in government because they see themselves as having enough in those regards. I have heard many young college women say that these issues are issues of the past. Because of this attitude, we need to address the issues that are plaguing their generation. We need to reach out and teach them confidence, independence, and the need to support both traditional and new feminist issues. We need to get them thinking about poverty and welfare reform, racism, sexism, choice, and the future of women everywhere in the world. But we cannot do this if we ignore the fact that many of them are starving themselves to be thin or buying breast implants to be beautiful. We cannot move them from their self-oriented perspective to a world-oriented perspective unless we give them the tools to find confidence and respect for themselves, despite the influences of our culture.

I propose that we find a way to market images of strong, healthy, independent women who are finding their own way in this society in contrast to the images of sex-crazed, frail, young women doing everything they can to attract boys. We need to sell images of young women who are confident and respectful of themselves: an image that is obtainable by all young women and, more importantly, one that is accepted by everyone. As feminists we have the means to advertise a strong, healthy image of women. We need to start using feminist magazines, music, and books as vehicles for our new image of women. We have to start discussing these issues in our feminist circles as a way to raise consciousness for all generations of feminists—to get mothers thinking about their daughters, sisters thinking about other sisters, and, most important, older feminists thinking about young women coming into adult life.

When I think of my daughter having to grow up in a society monopolized by physical appearance and material consumption, I often feel overwhelmed. I am grateful every day for the freedoms and opportunities that this country does offer, but I am disappointed that the images and role models our society idealizes are skinny women with breast implants wearing sexy clothes. The role models for young women are Britney Spears and those like her, instead of competent, intelligent, and healthy young women. Unfortunately, as a society, we idolize the rich and famous and the images they convey instead of hardworking, intelligent people with whom we should be able to identify. There is a void, which feminists have the power to fill. As bell hooks states in her work, *Feminism Is for Everybody: Passionate Politics,* "No feminist-oriented fashion magazine appeared to offer all females alternative visions of beauty. . . . all females no matter their age are being socialized either consciously or unconsciously to have anxiety about their body, to see flesh as problematic. . . . seldom do articles have a feminist perspective or feminist content."[4]

We need to fill this void and offer an alternative vision of beauty for young women: one that is real and looks like us. I believe that the first step is ours. If we can find ways to celebrate our *own* beauty, health, and independence, and pass that celebration on to young women, instead of continuing this vicious cycle of self-loathing, then at least we have made a start.

N O T E S

1. Joan Jacobs Brumberg, *Fasting Girls: The History of Anorexia Nervosa* (New York: First Vintage Books Edition, 2000).

2. Richard Levinson, Brian Powell, and Lala Carr Steelman, "Social Location, Significant Others, and Body Image Among Adolescents," *Social Psychology Quarterly* 49 (Dec. 1986), 330–337.

3. Alexandra A. Brewis, "The Accuracy of Attractive-Body-Size Judgment," *Current Anthropology* 40 (Aug.–Oct. 1999), 548–553.

4. bell hooks, *Feminism Is for Everybody: Passionate Politics* (Cambridge, MA: South End Press, 2000).

The Uses and Limitations of Feminist Theory and Feminism

 d i s c u s s i o n   q u e s t i o n s

- The articles in this section range from scholarly studies to personal narratives in their approach. Do you respond differently to each? Which carries the most authority with you? Why?

- How did you first encounter the term *feminism?* Was your view of it positive or negative? How has it changed?

- What is feminism missing? How would you broaden the content of feminist theory? What would be gained by these changes in scope or content?

- Do you have to be a feminist to be a supporter of women?

 f u r t h e r   r e a d i n g s

Bell, Beverly. *Social Movements and Economic Integration in the Americas.* (Modified from report by same name commissioned by the Rockefeller Foundation.) Albuquerque, NM: Center for Economic Justice, 2002.

Chossudovsky, Michel. *The Globalization of Poverty: Impacts of IMF and World Bank Reforms.* Penang, Malaysia: Third World Network, 1997.

Cuenca, Alejandro Martinez. *Sandinista Economics in Practice: An Insider's Critical Reflections.* Cambridge, MA: South End Press, 1992.

DuBois, Ellen Carol, and Vicki L. Ruiz, eds. *Unequal Sisters: A Multicultural Reader in U.S. Women's History.* New York: Routledge, 1990.

Escobar, Arturo. *Encountering Development: The Making and Unmaking of the Third World.* Princeton, NJ: Princeton University Press, 1995.

Finlen, Barbara, *Listen Up: Voices from the Next Feminist Generation.* Seattle, WA: Seal Press, 2001.

Fried, Marlene Gerber, ed. *From Abortion to Reproductive Freedom: Transforming a Movement.* Cambridge, MA: South End Press, 1990.

Gordon, Linda. *Woman's Body, Woman's Right: A Social History of Birth Control in America.* New York: Grossman, 1976.

Guy-Sheftall, Beverly, ed. *Words of Fire: An Anthology of African-American Feminist Thought.* New York: The New Press, 1995.

hooks, bell. *Black Looks: Race and Representation.* Cambridge, MA: South End Press, 1992.

———. *Killing Rage, Ending Racism.* New York: Henry Holt, 1995.

———. *Feminism Is for Everybody: Passionate Politics.* Cambridge, MA: South End Press, 2000.

Isazi-Diaz, Dr. Ada Maria. *My Name Is Mujerista.* http://users.drew.edu/aisasidi. See also, *En La Lucha—Elaborating a Mujerista Theology.* Minneapolis: Fortress Press, 1993.

James, Joy, and Ruth Farmer, eds. *Spirit, Space, and Survival: African-American Women in (White) Academe.* New York: Routledge, 1993.

Kelly, Rita Mae, Jane H. Bayes, Mary E. Hawkesworth, and Brigitte Young, eds. *Gender Globalizations and Democratization.* Lanham, MD: Rowman & Littlefield, 2001.

Petchesky, Rosalind Pollack. *Abortion and Woman's Choice: The State, Sexuality, and Reproductive Freedom.* New York: Northeastern University Press, 1984.

Silliman, Jael, and Ynestra King, eds. *Dangerous Intersections: Feminist Perspectives on Population, Environment, and Development.* Cambridge, MA: South End Press, 1999.

part TWO

Defining Ourselves, Being Defined by Others

The articles in this section focus on the complex, often competing ways in which women define themselves and the ways they are defined by society. In the first article, Camellia Phillips draws attention to the relationship between violence against Black women and their continuing criminalization. Central to this relationship, she argues, are negative cultural and social representations of Black women. She calls for the construction of "antiviolence and progressive social justice movements that can address the multilayered causes of violence against women of color." The second article, by Denise Cooper, focuses on Hip Hop as an art form created by Black people and its significance as a cultural force. She places contemporary debates about the cultural character of Rap and Hip Hop in the broader historical context of "class connotations and internalized racism" within Black society. Like Phillips, Cooper focuses the continuing struggle Black women face to redefine themselves as neither "bitches" nor "queens," as an explanation of why relatively few Black women "fit into the world of Hip Hop or Rap."

In the third essay Wendy Somerson begins her exploration of gender roles and "the definitions of gender itself" with a story about the year in her childhood when she (and her best friend) decided to be boys. Somerson links this childhood gender choice with her continuing effort to negotiate gender as a "feminine-identified dyke." She concludes by calling for the acknowledgment of gender extremes and "more freedom to alter the definitions of gender itself."

Like Wendy Somerson, Constance Faulkner draws upon childhood experiences to explore her identity as a socialist feminist. Focusing on aspects her early life in a Mormon family, she asks hard questions about gender, White middle-class privilege, and the role of the church in shaping her feminist consciousness. Although she is not sure why she left the church, she acknowledges the many "positive lessons about women's roles, that she has internalized." She is still learning that leaving the church does not have to mean giving up her heritage.

In the fifth article Philomena McCullough contrasts her Native American grandmother's childhood with her own experiences, seeking her identity as a tribal member today. McCullough's description of her hunting a deer opens the door to a powerful discussion of the role women and food play in subsistence cultures. The author calls for a feminism that embraces the daily efforts of poor women to feed their families and the cultural value the provision food plays for many native people.

Drawing upon the lesbian film *If These Walls Could Talk II: 1972,* Anne-Marie Basso and Kim Morrison critique "the strategic formation of distorted representations of women of color" in lesbian film. The authors argue that the film reinforces "a biased history" in much the same way as heterosexist film. "The universal experience strategy is not lost in the queer subculture, it is only transferred, inverted regarding sexuality and repeated regarding skin color and class."

The final article, by Cara Ann Thoreson, uses her relationship with her father to raise questions about men and feminism. The story begins with an acknowledgment that "feminist men" have influenced the person and activist she has become. Highlighting the tensions and contradictions she experienced growing up with a feminist father, Thorsen makes a strong case for the inclusion of men in feminist activities and for allowing men to have their own versions of feminism, "just as women have made allowances for each other in the feminist movement for decades."

Camellia Phillips

Criminalizing Black Women: (Re)Representing History, Sexuality, and Violence

The history of violence against Black women is inseparable from the history of their hypersexualized representation and the institutionalization of racism and sexism in the United States. The devaluation of the bodies, sexuality, and morality of Black women is embedded within historical and contemporary representations, images, and stereotypes. These representations were not only born of, while supporting and justifying, the institution of slavery, but also have played a vital and violent role within law, social policy, and public discourse into the present. At the center of the contemporary criminalization of Black women lie the abuse and exploitation of their sexuality and reproductive rights throughout the history of the United States. Simultaneously, the silencing of Black women's voices has accompanied their targeting as locations and transmitters of inherent poverty, sexual immorality, and subsequent criminality. Valuing and centering the experiences of Black women, from slave narratives to contemporary interviews, not only challenge the representations that silence and discredit them but also challenge the social, political, and eco-nomic systems that continue to enforce and perpetuate individual and institutional violence against Black women. The criminalization of Black women has affected in both practice and ideology the decriminalization of intimate violence committed against them.

Throughout the history of the United States, sexual violence against and reproductive abuse of Black women's bodies have been both a matter of daily assault and a terrorist method of control. The realities of slave women's lives clearly illustrate this institutionalized attack through intimate violence. In her 1997 book Dorothy Roberts traces the history of the reproductive abuses leveled by the state and by individuals against Black women from the inception of slavery to the late twentieth century. She grounds her analysis of this history in the physical and ideological exploitation of Black women through the intersections of representation, public policy and law, and the threat of violence unchecked. She explains that

> every indignity that comes from the denial of reproductive autonomy can be found in

slave women's lives—the harms of treating women's wombs as procreative vessels, of policies that pit a mother's welfare against that of her unborn child, and of government attempts to manipulate women's childbearing decisions through threats and bribes. *Studying the control of slave women's reproduction, then, not only discloses the origins of Black people's subjugation in America; it also bears witness to the horrible potential threatened by official denial of reproductive liberty.*[1]

Valuing the testimony of slaves and ex-slaves as reliable historical documents portraying the real yet often officially denied history of Black women can strengthen contemporary arguments and activism against racism and sexism and their intersections with other forms of oppression. Linda Brent, or Harriet Brent Jacobs, recounts her sexual exploitation as a female slave in her book *Incidents in the Life of a Slave Girl,* one of the best-known slave narratives. The importance of Brent's insights has been noted by many scholars, including Traci West in her 1999 book investigating the contexts and realities of violence against Black women. West notes that Brent's "narrative itself is an inspiring act of resistance both in substance and form,"[2] then goes on to quote the following passage from Brent's testimony in which Brent admits how her owner, Dr. Flint, "told me I was his property; that I must be subject to his will in all things. My soul revolted against the mean tyranny. But where could I turn for protection? No matter whether the slave girl be as black as ebony or as fair as her mistress. In either case, there is no shadow of law to protect her from insult, from violence, or even from death; all these are inflicted by fiends who bear the shape of men."[3]

Brent describes the connections between institutional and individual violence in her own life and the lives of all slave women when she states that "there is *no shadow of law to protect her* [the slave girl] from insult, from violence, or even from death; all these are inflicted by fiends who bear *the shape of men*" (italics mine). The sexual and physical violence which slave owners inflicted upon their "property" was enforced by the law, compounding the violation. At the same time, this violence and sexual exploitation were sanctioned by popular belief while being officially encouraged through the lack of laws protecting or even addressing Black women.

As Brent describes, she was forcefully named by her master and the law as property and thus was at the mercy of her owners, with no recourse or protection. Her body, her labor, her reproduction (her potential or existing children) were the possessions of her master; her sexuality was at his ideological and physical disposal. As Dorothy Roberts explains, "female slaves legally could be stripped, beaten, mutilated, bred, and compelled to toil alongside men. Forcing a slave to have sex against her will simply followed the pattern. This lack of protection was *reinforced by the prevailing belief among whites that Black women could not be raped because they were naturally lascivious. . . . for most of American history the crime of rape of a Black woman did not exist.*"[4] Reinforcing the lack of legal protections, the construction of slave women as "naturally lascivious" and therefore unrapable enabled White men and White society overall to justify such abuses on moral and legal grounds. Black women themselves, rather than the intimate violence against them, were rejected by the dominant discourse as immoral.

Stereotypes and social systems have worked together to create a self-supporting dialogue of justification, facilitating the dismissal and dehumanization of Black women as both unvirtuous women *and* incompetent mothers. Roberts concludes that the "construct of the licentious temptress served to justify white men's sexual abuse of Black women. The stereotype of Black women as sexually promiscuous also defined them as bad mothers."[5] As a result, Black mothers have been represented as genetically and morally inferior—as carriers of "incurable immorality."[6] While motherhood itself did not signal a change in slave women's status as immoral and sexually exploitable property, it did add to the complexity of Black women's enslavement as they were forced to bear children for their masters, including those conceived in rape or sexual coercion.

Integral to the devaluation of Black motherhood was the coupling of economics and violence in the lives of slave women. Awareness of the impact of economic roles in their own lives was a constant for slave women, who were clearly classified as property. As Linda Brent recounted, her owner was very explicit in defining her and her children's status within the U.S. economy and legal system. Many authors cite the economic bind of slave women in their conflicting roles as both producers[7] of goods through their labors and reproducers of slaves and the labor force through their own bodies (and the labor of childbirth). Caught in this bind of survival within an oppressive system versus reproducing through their own bodies the main components of the system which enslaved them, slave women inhabited a complex reality which bound them tighter every day. As noted by Linda Brent, the inescapability of internal conflict and external abuse forcefully imposed itself after girlhood gave way to womanhood and the property value of a female slave increased with her reproductive potential. As a slave, a woman's options for resolving these conflicts and escaping abuse were virtually nonexistent.

Linda Brent, in her personal account of the forced sexual roles of slave women, realizes the tendency of her mostly White audience to locate the evils and "sins" of slavery within slave women. She appeals to her White female readers when she asks that "ye happy women, whose purity has been sheltered from childhood, who have been free to choose the objects of your affection, whose homes are protected by law, do not judge the poor desolate slave girl too severely!"[8] Brent understands that her readers will not relate to her as a fellow woman, so she argues the realities of her exploitation as a "poor desolate slave girl." She recognizes that, if taken out of context, her act of having an out-of-wedlock relationship with a White man other than her owner and bearing children by him would reinforce the popular belief in the immorality of Black women.

After emancipation, slavery itself was also incorporated into the images used to degrade and devalue Black women, in effect blaming Black women for their own enslavement. Traci West explains that in "academic treatments that began in the postbellum period and continued into the early twentieth century, *it was understood that black women's sexual 'depravity' stemmed from the legacy of slavery,* when they developed a 'permissive' response to white male overtures" (italics mine).[9] The approach of scholars and policy makers was, for the most part, to blame women for the situations under which they were forced to live and survive. Black women have consistently been portrayed as either consciously or unconsciously responsible for their own financial or moral impoverishment (if they are poor or without formal education or on welfare) and therefore accountable for any sexual violence committed against them.

Images of degenerate Black mothers (welfare queens and crack babies) reinforce the implied claim that Black women are carriers of "incurable immorality." By locating the sexual immorality *within* Black women themselves, those who violate them sexually are not in fact subject to questions of the morality of that violation. In a chapter describing "A Sampler of Cultural Assaults," Traci West explains that one of the pervasive rationalizations of violence against Black women is that "Black Women's Faults Invite Violence."[10] Looking deeper, she examines how "contentions about black women as flawed and blameworthy are embodied in *persistent stereotypes* of them as lazy, emasculating heads of households, and promiscuous. . . . Stereotypes about laziness are pinned on poor black mothers in particular, and can help *sanction male violence against them*" (italics mine).[11] Within the image of the welfare queen in particular, where stereotypes of "laziness" and "promiscuity" converge, poor Black mothers are defined as lazy (being on welfare, they are either unwilling or too stupid to work) and sexually promiscuous (they are veritable breeding grounds for hordes of degenerate children who will in turn become burdens to [White] society). Another image of Black women as mothers of crack babies also combines poverty and laziness (drug-addicted mothers who are unable to hold "real jobs" but instead wallow in their poverty and drug addiction at the expense of their children and the [White] taxpayers who are forced to pay for their damaged children) and sexual immorality (women who cannot even recognize the direness and immorality of their own circumstances but instead continue to "breed" indiscriminately). Both of these images have been used to enact legislation that criminalizes Black motherhood, such as welfare "reform" that limits additional child benefits and targets poor single mothers and incarceration of pregnant crack users.[12]

Even when not explicitly articulated, the assumed criminality of Black women, especially poor single Black mothers, informs the content and creates the context of governmental policy. For example, welfare "reform" discussions in the late 1990s defined Black mothers as social "problems" in need of management and control. The 1995 Personal Responsibility Act, proposed by congressional Republicans as a part of their Contract with America, used the image of Black welfare queens and criminal Black single mothers to justify cutbacks in social service programs. The act claimed that "the likelihood that a young black man will engage in criminal activities doubles if he is raised without a father and triples if he lives in a neighborhood with a high concentration of single parent families." Traci West exposes this thinly veiled racism and sexism by explicating the legislation: "According to Congress, when black single moms are present in high concentrations in a neighborhood, the cumulative effect of their innate attributes somehow causes crime to soar."[13] According to governmental policy, Black women represent the primary cause of crime and government overspending, while racism and poverty as causes are ignored. When Black women are portrayed as exploiting the hard-earned money of [White] taxpayers, the crimes committed against them can easily be dismissed, ignored, or simply never allowed to be verbalized.

In another twist, the sexual immorality of female slaves has been applied to the Black community as a whole in the myth of the Black rapist. Angela Davis responds to this myth in her essay

"Rape, Racism, and the Myth of the Black Rapist," where she expands the analysis of this stereotype of Black men through its connection to stereotypes of Black women and how these paired representations reinforce sexual violence against Black women. She writes that

the portrayal of Black men as rapists reinforces racism's open invitation to white men to avail themselves sexually of Black women's bodies. The fictional image of the Black man as rapist has always strengthened its inseparable companion: the image of the Black woman as chronically promiscuous. For once the notion is accepted that Black men harbor irresistible and animal-like sexual urges, the entire race is invested with bestiality. If Black men have their eyes on white women as sexual objects, then Black women must certainly welcome the sexual attentions of white men. Viewed as "loose women" and whores, Black women's cries of rape would necessarily lack legitimacy.[14]

The representation of Black women as "chronically promiscuous" is silently imbedded within even those stereotypes not directly leveled against them. Black women, like other women of color, occupy a unique space within the White supremacist and patriarchal hierarchy of the United States: they are oppressed and devalued both through their race and their gender and, as a result, their real or perceived class status. It is only natural that, within the system of racist and sexist discourse and policy, Black women are subject to stereotypes based on race and gender as well as a combination of the two. Attacks aimed at the Black community, in this case Black men, contain within them implicit attacks on Black women.

The experiences and social positionings of Black women can only be understood and theorized within their historical context. Just as rape of Black women was not even acknowledged as a violation until recently, the realities of violence against and exploitation of Black women has remained invisible within legal and public discourse. Working from the concept of "critical race theory,"[15] Kimberlé Crenshaw examines the way that the hypersexualization of Blacks has been used to discredit Black women as victims of sexual violence.

Much of the problem [in anti-rape activism and law] results from the way that certain gender expectations for women intersect with certain sexualized notions of race—notions that are deeply entrenched in American culture. Sexualized images of African-Americans go all the way back to Europeans' first engagement with Africans. Blacks have long been portrayed as more sexual, more earthy, more gratification-oriented; *these sexualized images of race intersect with norms of women's sexuality,* norms that are used to distinguish good women from bad, madonnas from whores. Thus, *black women are essentially prepackaged as bad women in cultural narratives* about good women who can be raped and bad women who cannot. (italics mine)[16]

The images that reinforce the "rapability" of black women as "bad women who cannot [be raped]" are so "deeply entrenched in American culture" that in many ways they have become both invisible and distinctly integrated into the laws and policies of the government, courts, and even anti-rape and anti-sexual-violence campaigns.

Stereotypes like the welfare queen and the mothers of crack babies have led to the criminalization, even incarceration, of the women who can be forcibly fit into these stereotypes. As reported in a recent issue of *ColorLines Magazine* guest-edited by Angela Davis, "In 1970 there were 5,600 women in federal and state prisons. By 1996, there were 75,000. 60% of that population are black and Latina."[17] The outrageous distortions of criminality represented in the numbers of women of color imprisoned by the United States court system directly as a result of laws and policies informed by racist and White supremacist discourse and stereotypes about women and men of color cannot be overlooked. In a 1997 essay and speech entitled "Race and Criminalization: Black Americans and the Punishment Industry," Angela Davis recognizes that statistics such as those in *ColorLines Magazine* have been largely dismissed as irrelevant or simply evidence of the criminality of women of color. Explaining the process of criminalization, she writes that "historically, the imprisonment of women has served to criminalize women in a way that is more complicated than is the case with men. This female criminalization process has had more to do with the marking of certain groups of women as undomesticated and hypersexual, as women who refuse to embrace the nuclear family as paradigm. The current liberal-conservative discourse around welfare criminalizes black single mothers, who are represented as deficient, man-less, drug-using breeders of children, and as reproducers of an attendant culture of poverty."[18]

As in the past, the lives and experiences of Black women in the United States are represented and evaluated not by the women themselves but by those who hold economic, social, and political power over them. The popularity and public acceptance of blatantly racist and sexist arguments that blame Black women for the poverty, crime, and moral depravity of Black communities testifies to the continuing devaluation of Black women. Current descriptions of black women as "breeders" highlight the connections between slavery and current rhetoric.

Because both race and gender enforce the invisibility of Black women and other women of color, campaigns and policies that attack one or the other will in fact further alienate and marginalize them. For example, anti-rape or anti-domestic-violence campaigns that focus on reaching "women" without specifically addressing how race/racism affects the needs and situations of women of color lack the contexts to address these needs fully and run the risk of excluding or denying services to women of color because of unexamined structural racism.[19] Charting the racism within domestic violence support services, Traci West cites her interview with Anna Carlson, a worker in a shelter for battered women, reporting that "some shelter workers were more inclined to consider the possibility that black women who telephoned the shelter were not actually in crisis due to male violence."[20] Carlson reveals that White workers devalued calls for help from Black women because they were viewed as "merely homeless women," drug addicts or "urban crack addicts," or "matriarchs" too strong to be truly abused.[21]

Even within courtrooms, legal regulations, and law enforcement, women of color continue to be represented as sexually immoral and therefore less violable. Kimberlé Crenshaw describes how "rape law serves not only to penalize actual examples of nontraditional behavior but also to diminish and devalue women who belong to groups in which nontraditional behavior is perceived as common. For the black rape victim, the disposition of her case may often turn less on her behavior than on her identity."[22] The results of common perceptions of Black women can be seen in concrete statistics—such as the percentages of incarcerated Black women. As Crenshaw explains, "Black women continue to be judged by who they are, not by what they do."

When not only Black women's bodies and sexuality but also their experiences and testimony are devalued, the act of valuing the narratives and testimonies of Black women from slavery to the present takes on imminent importance as one way of documenting not only the atrocities and violations committed against them, but also the silencing and public denial of the criminality of these abuses. Validating the experiences of Black women and constructing theories of and approaches to antiviolence campaigns that take these experiences into account require that the full spectrum of social and political forces that work against Black women be explored and named. Histories of forced violation as documented by women themselves not only reveal the reality of Black women's lives but also work to directly counter the stereotypes and distortions still active today.

Violence against Black women is a societal problem that demands broad-based activist efforts and diverse strategies. Kimberlé Crenshaw explains that, in order to fully address violence against women of color, antiviolence services and movements need to "confront the other multilayered and routinized forms of domination that often converge in [women of color's] lives," such as poverty, lack of child care, "lack of job skills[,] . . . racially discriminatory employment and housing practices," and abusive and invasive state actions.[23] Similarly, Traci West proposes that communities, activists, and others engage in "justice-making action," which both

requires an understanding and acknowledgment of the relationships between societal, cultural, and intimate violence and "calls for a continuous struggle with the manifold cultural assaults that reproduce the conditions of male violence."[24] Stereotypes of Black women as hypersexual or criminal are key elements of the "cultural assaults" that reinforce and condone male violence; as long as these representations remain unchallenged and unquestioned by the majority of society, violence against Black women will continue as a socially sanctioned practice.

NOTES

1. Dorothy Roberts, *Killing the Black Body: Race, Reproduction, and the Meaning of Liberty* (New York: Pantheon Books, 1997), 23.
2. Traci West, *Wounds of the Spirit: Black Women, Violence, and Resistance Ethics* (New York: New York University Press, 1999), 21.
3. Ibid., 26.
4. Dorothy Roberts, *Killing the Black Body,* 31.
5. Ibid., 11.
6. Ibid., 8.
7. Angela Davis, *The Angela Y. Davis Reader* (Oxford: Blackwell Publishers, 1998), 211–212; Dorothy Roberts, *Killing the Black Body,* 24–26, 33–34, 39–41, 46–47; note especially p. 25.
8. Ibid., 54.
9. Traci West, *Wounds of the Spirit,* 137.
10. Ibid., 133.
11. Ibid.
12. Ibid., 133–136; Dorothy Roberts, *Killing the Black Body,* 150–201.
13. Traci West, *Wounds of the Spirit,* 135–136.
14. Angela Davis, "Rape, Racism, and the Myth of the Black Rapist," in James, *The Angela Davis Reader,* 182.
15. Kimberlé Crenshaw, "Mapping the Margins: Intersectionality, Identity Politics, and Violence Against Women of Color." In *Critical Race Theory: The Key Writings That Formed the Movement,* ed. Kimberlé Crenshaw, Neil Gro-

tanda, Gary Peller, and Kendal Thomas (New York: The New Press, 1995), 357–383.

16. Ibid., 369.

17. Angela Davis, *The Angela Y. Davis Reader,* 70.

18. Ibid., 71.

19. Kimberlé Crenshaw, "Mapping the Margins," 357–377.

20. Traci West, *Wounds of the Spirit,* 143.

21. Ibid., 145.

22. Kimberlé Chrenshaw, "Mapping the Margins," 373.

23. Ibid., 358.

24. Traci West, "Wounds of the Spirit," 197.

Denise Cooper

Hip Hop Feminism:
From Bitches to Queens and
the Varied Experiences in Between

Nearly two years after the fall of the World Trade Center, one has to wonder if the global community is at the beginning of World War III. As we enter a new century, will we experience new values that counter the disillusionment of the twentieth century, just as modernists sought to bring change into the twentieth century and forget Victorian values? Will these values be accompanied by a new burst in creative energy, different from anything we have known today, but somehow reflecting our past? Are we even in an "age," and if so, is Hip Hop the soundtrack for that age, just as rock-and-roll was the soundtrack for the 1960s and 1970s and jazz was the soundtrack for the 1920s and 1930s? If so, what does it mean to be Hip Hop? More important, what does it mean to be a Hip Hop feminist?

Hip Hop is more than music; it is the artistic reflection of an era characterized by urbanization and technology. As jazz did for its time, the rhythm of Hip Hop seeps into the artistic mind. Like jazz, Hip Hop is an art form created by people of color. Nearly sixty years after the Jazz Age, New York became the birthplace for an-other musical tradition that has become the soundtrack for our everyday and artistic lives. Born in the Bronx on street corners, subway stations, and house parties, Hip Hop has become a global art form.

From the beginning, it was more than music; it was a science consisting of four elements: breaking, rapping, scratching, and graffiti writing. Young men and women used it as a platform to express their views about urban culture. Somewhere along the line, the music industry discovered the profitability of the culture and decided to market the most flamboyant element of the art form, rapping. Today sales of rap music exceed $1.4 billion a year. With this profitability come a few drawbacks. Like the blues, jazz, and rock-and-roll, rap music is a Black American art form co-opted by mainstream America and used as a tool for selling anything from shoes to fast food.

Like a new stereo at Christmas, rap music is wrapped in a presentable racist, and sexist package, then sold to make record companies billions. And make money it does, mirroring stereotypical images of Black people as poor, violent drug abusers with highly aggressive men and oversexed women.

Today the creativity in rap music has been quelled by market precision. Music that sells is the music that glorifies violence, money, drugs, and sex. This in itself is not a crime, but today rap music artists seem to concentrate more on making money than on making art.

Some would say that Hip Hop and feminism don't mix. Feminists should listen to woman-centered artists like Ani DiFranco, Tracy Chapman, or Michelle N'dege Ochello, not misogynistic rappers like Jay-Z, Nelly, or Ludacris. But for Black women and other women who have been shaped by this music, Hip Hop is something that begins in the bones and emanates outward. If Hip Hop is the music of a new generation, then Hip Hop must also be the soundtrack for a new wave of feminist Black women.

The love affair with Hip Hop might begin with seeing break dancers in the park on cardboard boxes, spinning on their heads, or it might begin as a teenager listening to Tupac rap about anything from teenage mothers to hustling. Maybe it was the first time you saw Queen Latifah in full head wrap, charging that when it comes to music and life, it is all about "ladies first." Or maybe you were chilling one night real late and Erykah Badu's green eyes caught you unawares as they peeked out from *Video Soul* or D'Angelo's dreaming brown eyes caught you in a trance as his full lips sang about Brown Sugar. Whenever your love affair began, everyone knows it's one of those love–hate relationships that never go away.

For me Hip Hop is everything. It rules the cadence of my walk. The rhythm of my talk. The garments I choose to wear. Hip Hop is the soundtrack for my life. How did it start? Was I an avid consumer of every CD and music video? No, not really. My earliest memory of Hip Hop goes back to growing up in Anchorage, Alaska, living in the Tyee Apartments at the age of five, running around with the carefree "I run this shit" attitude that only a five-year-old can have. I remember staring in young contempt at the teenage boys who stupidly spun around on their heads with only a brown cardboard box to protect their heads from the arctic concrete (secretly, I was a little in awe of them). I remember, at age twelve, riding my bike to my friend's house, only to hear male relatives constantly in front of the TV, watching *Yo! MTV Raps,* the raw sounds of young Black men expressing themselves to slow tempos and nodding temples. I remember listening to the urgent rhythms of Salt-N-Pepa, telling me to push it, push it real hard. I remember Hip Hop.

Now don't get me wrong—our relationship hasn't always been fun and games. I have turned my back on it countless times, but every time there was something that kept pulling me back.

There were times when Hip Hop was just too hard for me and musically didn't do anything for me. I was more apt to listen to Muddy Waters than Chuck D, Nina Simone over Eazy-E. In Anchorage the music was not played in many places—you heard only the most pop-sounding stuff on the radio, and we didn't have cable, so BET and MTV were not an option. So I contented myself by listening to old soul, jazz, and blues classics.

Then the late 1990s came, and Hip Hop made me stand up and pay attention again. Lauryn sang like a songbird while laying down the coldest poetry. Tupac playfully told the whole world to go fuck themselves if they didn't like anything about him. Biggie rapped rhythmically over old R&B favorites while thin, pretty girls hung over his big old guppy-looking self (no disrespect intended to the deceased; he himself said he was "black and ugly as ever"). E–40 had the whole country speaking a new Vallejo Vernacular. I could go on and on and on. Hip Hop became more musical. People weren't afraid to make the sound *soft*.

As I left my teen years behind and entered my young womanhood, things started to fall apart as I fell out of love with the art. I couldn't stand to listen to Tupac call me a bitch on one song then ask me to keep my head up in the next. I couldn't keep saying that I just like the beat when some man kept yelling over that beat to keep shaking my ass, ho. It was too much. Rap had come a long way, but the stuff that was selling was burying my sense of self, so I went underground. Literally.

I stopped listening to MCs who didn't express anything I wanted to hear. I drifted toward lesser-known acts out of New York, Atlanta, Chicago, and California. I became a Hip Hop scholar of sorts. I began to explore music again. I revisited my old musical friends Nina, Jimi, Miles, John, Bessie, and Mahalia.

This amazing transformation began with the music then moved to encompass a larger art form. Hip Hop began to mean different things. Hip Hop became a verb. One could *be* Hip Hop. I started writing poetry, I started free-styling, I started expressing myself. All the while I started to notice the community of people who were doing the same thing. Seattle suddenly became full of rappers, poets, DJs, b-boys, b-girls, graffiti artists, beat boxers. It was all there and it was all one LOVE. Spontaneous expressions of our life experiences, uplifting, inspirational, and transformational. Hip Hop.

Now I can say it. I used to love IT and I still love do. Hip Hop is the defining culture for a whole generation of young people across the world. Hip Hop is a community that bridges distances with the simple act of pressing play on your stereo; I am in love again.

But those nagging feelings are still there. Underneath the umbrella of our newly wedded bliss, I still notice the raindrops of inequalities wetting the ground around our feet. I love Hip Hop because the music seems to speak to me and me alone and at the same time fosters shared experiences and shared knowledge. I hate it because the music disrespects you at the same time. Every free-style cipher looks the same, a group of young boys trading wisdom and clever verbalization over human breath beats. But where are the women who free-style? Where are the women who rap? By the very definition of femininity and masculinity, Hip Hop is a masculine art form. It is aggressive, straightforward, dynamic, showy, and loud. Women who come into the art form are expected to play or leave the game. In this realm of hypermasculinity there are only two places for women: be as masculine as the boys or a super sex kitten. We see this manifested not just in Hip Hop but also in all areas of our lives. We as women are given very narrow roles to play; we can be one of the niggas, a ho, or a queen, but there is no room to move into the spaces in between. Of course these limited definitions of masculinity also leave a narrow box for men and young boys to fit into and manifest themselves in homophobia and other brutal forms of oppression.

Unfortunately for the Black community, these images of Hip Hop masculinity and femininity are flickered before our young children, creating conflicting influences. We as parents, educators, and mentors can't teach our children to value themselves when they are constantly inundated by media images that tell young women that it is okay to use men for money, that tell young men they should keep women like horses in a stable. Magazine pictures teach our little girls that beauty is being buck naked. Our little boys learn that men yell and scream and jump all over the room, flaunting their guns, drugs, and half-naked women.

With these images and audio clips always in the background of our lives, what are the issues that the Hip Hop feminist must address? First of all, as has been said by our literary foremothers like Sojourner Truth, Angela Davis, bell hooks, Ida B. Wells, and Audre Lorde, we must recognize the differences in experience along lines of class, sexuality, race, and education. Different women are dealing differently with issues of gender identity, body image, relationships, and violence.

In different cultures, the terms *masculinity* and *femininity* have different connotations. In the western dichotomous tradition, men are constructed as aggressive, strong, large, dynamic talkers and leaders. Women are constructed as soft, small, nurturing, weak followers and listeners. Of course, if one digs deeper, these constructions play out differently in people's actual experiences. For example, historically, Black women are expected to borrow attributes from both sides. We are encouraged to be the "strong Black woman" but still have the sexy appearance of Halle Berry while standing back and letting our men be men.

For young Black women, many things construct our gender identities. As a generation raised by single mothers, we have been shown at home that women are strong and must take care of the family, while images on the television tell us that women must be attractive armpieces for men. Each image is merely a narrow caricature. Women of color have always been valued for our fullness, but watching women like Oprah struggle to fit into a size eight or watching Janet and J-Lo go from big-hipped fly girls to slim sirens, today the message is clear. Society wants a big butt, but not too big.

The increased sexual objectification of all women in the media affects Black women and other young women of color in two ways. It negates our sexuality yet completely exoticizes it. We can either be asexual like Missy Elliott or hypersexual like Lil' Kim. Hip Hop's most visible quality is the value it places on female sexuality and female appearance. Artists such as Lil' Kim and Foxy Brown are caricatures of Black femininity, appreciated only for their hypersexuality. Some would argue that the bold way these women embrace their sexuality empowers them and other Black women, in a challenge to old sexual stereotypes of Black women; I contend that these women have internalized sexism themselves. They have no clear understanding of what it is to be female. They are limited by a view of females that is superficial in that it fails to move beyond looks and sex. These women lack depth, as they are not allowed to demonstrate other aspects of human personality, such as intelligence or caring.

Hip Hop's objectification of women both informs and reflects the Black community, but other aspects of male domination can be seen in the high rates of domestic violence and rape that still persist in the community. Combine this with the fact that interracial dating and marriage are at their highest rate since the Supreme Court decision on *Lovings v. Virginia,* which obliterated antimiscegenation laws in every state, and one sees the deep divisions between Black men and Black women.

As a life decision, interracial dating is a natural consequence of integration, but the disproportionate rate at which Black men outermarry as compared to Black women raises some questions. Why do Black men not want to marry Black women? Why is it easier for Black men to marry outside of their race? What are the repercussions for Black women as they become increasingly mateless when one considers the number of Black men who are gay, in prison, or married to women of other races? Unfortunately, all these questions point to one conclusion—as Black women and men become further alienated from each other, the Black family begins to suffer. The proof of this is seen in the fact that women head 60 percent of all Black families, and many of them still live below the poverty line. The notion that Black men and women started a "journey" together that they must complete is poetic, but it does not illuminate the difficulty of making that journey. Many obstacles keep Black women and men divided.

Furthermore, the hypermasculinity that Hip Hop manifests is just a verbalization of the masculinity valued by Black men. In a society that attempts to disempower Black men in every other arena, at least Hip Hop allows them to be loud, disruptive, and violent. This possessive investment in masculinity also manifests itself in promiscuous, exploitive behavior as young men judge their self-worth based on whether they can have sex, or "pull," with a lot of females.

The hypermasculinity valued in Hip Hop fosters homophobia and heterosexism. Male homosexual behavior is treated with violence and hostility, while female homosexuality is greeted with contempt and derision or considered a sex-ual fetish. These attitudes, reflected in the larger Hip Hop community, limit conversation about sexuality and gender that might help deconstruct gender and patriarchy.

Lastly, the violence and criminal behavior that Hip Hop embraces affect the many women who lose their men to death, prison, and drugs. Some young sistahs are forced to rely on help from men who make their money in the underground economy, professions that don't typically foster safe, stable environments. Many women experience being mothers to children whose fathers are locked up or dead. Those same women might face being locked up or killed when mere survival demands that they cross the lines of what society and the law deem to be acceptable behavior.

With all that said, it is important to understand and acknowledge the varied experiences of women along lines of age, class, education, race, and sexuality. We are not one homogeneous vat of womanhood, to paraphrase Audre Lorde. More important, older generations of feminists and even some from the newer third wave, must recognize the unique position of young women whose realities are shaped by Hip Hop and the issues of the Hip Hop generation. These issues include, but are not limited to, negative media images of Black men and women, increased criminalization of young people of color, sexual exploitation of women of color, and fragmentation of relationships between the genders and within communities. Everyone involved in the feminist movement must recognize that "your feminism ain't like mine." We have to recognize not only the differences between the professional White woman living in Manhattan and her counterpart, the professional Black sister. We must also recognize the difference between a Black sister in Savannah versus one in Seattle.

We all experience patriarchy in different ways, and our male counterparts access that patriarchy in different ways. Feminism attempts to give voice to those men and women oppressed and restricted by patriarchy, just as Hip Hop attempts to give voice to groups who have traditionally been silenced. With all its flaws Hip Hop is still a valuable tool of the people. It is a grassroots form of communication that can produce discourse that isn't limited to academic texts, anthologies, or talk-show sound bites. That is the heart of Hip Hop feminism.

Wendy Somerson

On the Complications of Negotiating Dyke Femininity

When I was in the third grade, my best friend Lauren and I proclaimed that we were boys. I can't remember the day it happened or the particular reason, but it was based on the specious logic that girls were "dumb" and boys were "cool." We simply called ourselves boys and stopped wearing skirts or dresses, and when we encountered gender divisions in the classroom, we joined the boys. We thought by declaring our gender, we simply made it so. Wouldn't it be ideal if gender were such a simple matter of choice for all of us? It actually didn't go too badly for us as third-graders in the 1970s. Our teacher, Ms. (emphasis on the *Ms.*) Elam, was mostly tolerant of our joining the boys' groups whenever gender divisions occurred in the classroom. But the boys themselves were not so welcoming and taunted us with threats to pull down our pants to prove our "real" gender. That never made sense to me; even back then, I didn't understand why genitalia determined gender.

I remember dealing with the gender contradictions fairly gracefully as a third-grader, without giving them too much thought. When I had to wear my Girl Scout tunic to school, I didn't worry about the group affiliation; I simply wore pants under it and called it a long shirt. Our reassigning of our gender wasn't the only thing or probably even the most important thing going on that year in our lives. Our new gender allowed us to shoot marbles obsessively at recess, play kickball, wear scrappy (preferably muddy) clothes, and disdain "girl" games on the playground. Since we refused to hang out with other "silly" girls, and we weren't really accepted by the boys, we did everything together in a wonderful childhood world of two. In our own little universe, we affirmed each other's gender choices without a lot of discussion and got on with the important business of collecting marbles, playing four square, and jumping off the roof of the tree house (until Lauren broke her wrist). The next year, when we were separated into different classes, we left behind our boy identifications. I don't remember making any conscious decision about it.

Lots of girls spend time in their childhood as "tomboys," and I think this childhood gender choice links to ways that I continue to negotiate gender as a feminine-identified dyke. Masculine or nontraditional ways of being feminine are still part and parcel of my identity, but as a committed feminist, I am now determined to question whether I'm basing my gender choices on denigrating more traditional aspects of femininity. While I may raise more questions than answers in this essay, my intention is to generate more complicated feminist discussions and perceptions of femininity within dyke communities. First, I will look at how femininity has been presented and positioned in a few gender panels and discussions that have taken place in Seattle in the past few years. I will then consider how I negotiate my particular brand of femininity and how feminine-identified dykes engage in complicated gender interactions all the time. My aim is to shine a spotlight on queer femininity, which does not often get discussed on its own but more often as a counterpart to butch, or as the unspoken and unacknowledged Other of "gender transgression" panels and conversations within dyke communities, including my own community in Seattle.

Female Femininity

There has been a recent celebration of female masculinity within dyke communities: a proliferation of drag king shows, butch erotica shows, FTM/butch/transgender panels, and discussions of gender transgression or "transcendence." While I do not want to disparage this trend or disdain female masculinity, I do want to consider what happens to female femininity within this debate and to suggest that we need to be careful not to reproduce and reinforce traditional gender hierarchies within queer communities. Several immediate questions come to mind in light of some of these public performances: Why don't we often explicitly talk about femininity? Do we assume that we already know or understand it? Is there an underlying paradigm in these discussions that as we move farther away from our assigned gender, the more trans-

gressive our gender enactments will become? Many of these panels, including one that I organized for a queer film festival, had no feminine or self-identified femme dykes on them at all, and most of them did not specifically address femininity as an issue of concern or interest for our communities.

A local panel on transcending gender in 2000 brought together two FTMs (female-to-male transgendered people), two dykes who identified as butch, and one dyke who identified as a femme partner FTM. Only one of these five panelists was introduced with a comment on her looks. While the FTM organizer described the other panelists based on their accomplishments, he described the femme panelist as "beautiful." When it came time for her own explanation of her relationship to the issue of transcending gender, she commented that after giving it much thought, she decided that she had "only" one gender and thus was "just a girl." While she did a great job moderating the panel, this apologetic comment lingered in my mind, and it disturbs me still. It suggests that her feminine identity is not as complicated or interesting as FTM or butch identities because she stuck with the gender she was seemingly assigned at birth. The more genders, the more transgressive? Does stockpiling or altering genders confer prestige? Throughout the discussion, several butch women in the audience referred to the femme panelist in order to claim that that their girlfriends looked "just like" her in order (presumably) to indicate that their girlfriends were visibly feminine. Unless she really did have a bunch of identical twins running around, this phenomenon indicates the assumption that we know exactly what "femme" looks like, and it often looks the same. It also suggests that gender transgressors sometimes rely on naturalizing feminine identity in order to measure their own departure from a norm. Although queer femininity may appear less constructed than female masculinity, I insist that it is just as constructed, whether consciously or unconsciously.

In a 1998 butch/FTM borderlands panel that I organized in conjunction with the documentary *The Brandon Teena Story* for the Seattle Lesbian and Gay Film Festival, the panel (of two butches and two FTMs) and the audience struggled to address the socioeconomic issues that the film raised. In the contentious discussion, panelists and audience members alike offended each other with questionable remarks about class, which often stereotyped and scapegoated the working class as "White trash." While class discussions in the United States are consistently fraught, I think that an obsessive focus on female masculinity or gender crossing can stabilize and naturalize other aspects of identity—in this case, class—that may not appear as obvious on a visual level. One of the panelists suggested that Brandon's rape and murder and the 1998 murder of Matthew Shepard in Wyoming could only happen in a small town. While obviously homophobic and transphobic violence occurs everywhere, this comment exemplifies a displacement of these phobias onto rural areas. As the documentary makes clear, Falls City, Nebraska, where Brandon lived for the last few months of his life, became an increasingly dangerous and violent place to live in the 1990s, at least partially because of economic underdevelopment and its corresponding effect on unemployment. One audience member also wondered why Brandon didn't just move to New York City. This shows no acknowledgment that he may not have had access to resources or a desire to move to a big city or that he may have encountered the same kind of violence in a big city.

Another audience participant remarked that she couldn't distinguish among Brandon Teena's girlfriends because they all had "big hair." Marked as "White trash," these women were dismissed because of their classed feminine appearances. Like the femme panelist on the transcending gender panel, these women were lumped together as indistinguishable representatives of femininity. After the discussion, one panelist described Brandon's last girlfriend, Lana, as a "manipulative girl who didn't try to better herself." Meanwhile, both panelists and audience members often described Brandon as a hero for choosing to live his life so bravely. Marked as an individual gender transgressor in this discussion, Brandon was often able to escape the class-biased descriptions that were applied to Nebraska and Nebraskans. Brandon seemingly transcended his location in contrast with the other citizens of these small Nebraska towns, who were marked as homophobic bigots in order for city dwellers to feel better about themselves. While the issues of class, gender, and sexuality in Brandon Teena's situation deserve their own discussion, other identity attributes—in this case, class and femininity—get stabilized, naturalized, and simplified when our focus is purely on visual gender subversion.

Psychic Complexity

At another local gender event, an acquaintance dismissed the possibility of a femme drag show by suggesting, "That seems to be pushing it." Why? Because femininity is not seen as a performance as such? Is femininity seen as performative only when it is done in excess? (Think drag queens.) Roles can work on other levels aside from the visual, and we need to start talking about complexity in gender roles and how other factors, including race, class, ethnicity, and nationality, contribute to and produce various gender roles. There isn't one standard of femininity or masculinity for every race, ethnic group, class, or nation. In addition, someone may present one gender expression in a given context, but that same appearance can indicate something else in a different cultural context. For instance, I might appear more traditionally feminine at a dyke event, but when I work out in the university gym, I don't appear particularly feminine with my unshaved legs and short hair. I'm not sure that the larger culture always recognizes some distinctions we make between butch and femme.

We also have complicated psychic identifications, which cannot be determined on a strictly visual level. At another panel I organized on questioning traditional models of masculinity, one of the FTM panelists made an extremely interesting point about attempting to maintain what he sees as a specifically femme and feminist psychology in his FTM body. That identification isn't something that we can necessarily identify visually; it complicates the notion that we can always understand how someone negotiates gender based solely upon visual appearance. Unfortunately, this continual focus on visually subversive gender roles marginalizes many identities, including femme and feminine ones.

Sexuality is one arena in which complicated psychic identifications occur. For example, in some sexual contexts, I feel the most feminine— sometimes in contrast with butch energy—but that can also shift midscene. With some of my butch lovers, I often started out in what felt like a feminine role of seduction, but as we moved deeper sexually, I imagined myself as a man in my fantasies, while my butch lover became my fantasy woman. At the beginning of my most recent relationship, this mental shifting really

upset my butch lover. She could sense some of my male energy, but she didn't know how to act or what persona to take in relation to my shifts and fantasies. After we negotiated these fantasies for a couple years, we became more comfortable playing with these roles and switching genders. In this case, our psychic realities didn't always correspond with our physical coupling. I don't want to dwell obsessively on my sexual personae, but this is an arena in which queer gender roles often get enacted and exaggerated. Butch–femme roles are useful in providing a difference around which desire can mobilize, but even that desire can be more complicated than visual cues might indicate. At one gender panel discussion, a panelist claimed that gender identities are based on where we obtain power. She claimed that butches feel empowered by a masculine-identified role and disempowered by a feminine role, and femmes feel the opposite. But why can't we gain power from more than one place? Just because I'm feminine, why should that mean that I can imagine myself only in a feminine role in both fantasies and sexual acts?

My Body as Text

In addition to complex psychic identifications, feminine-identified dykes can also have complicated visual appearances, which may include masculine elements. While I am arguing that we need to stop limiting our gender definitions to the realm of the visual, even in this realm, many of us who identify as femme or feminine still have to negotiate femininity with care. I certainly don't feel as if my appearance completely explains or covers my fraught feminine identification, but at various moments in my life, it has highlighted some of these contradictions. An assumption exists that if you identify as a feminine dyke, you "pass" as straight (along with all that implies). We need to disrupt this assumption. Identifying as feminine or femme does not always mean sporting long hair and makeup, and these visual attributes do not necessarily add up to passing in all circumstances. Femininity presents conflicts in any dyke's life because rejecting compulsory heterosexuality in and of itself challenges traditional notions of femininity.

I sometimes identify as feminine; I generally and currently identify as dyke and queer. But my appearance has caused "trouble" for quite some time. When I turned seventeen in the 1980s I identified as a punk rocker and rejected the traditional white middle-class standards of femininity. I shaved the sides of my head, stopped shaving my legs, got my nose pierced, and generally appeared as a "freak," especially because I was living in Columbus, Ohio. While my days as a rocker are long gone, I still have very short hair, never wear skirts or dresses in public, don't shave, and don't feel as though I appear particularly feminine. My clothing and shoes come from both men's and women's departments. I don't think my style is very feminine, but that obviously depends on the definition. Maybe I should be redefining femininity instead of separating myself from the category. I still wonder if my choices are partially based on internalized misogyny. Does that make them less valid? Perhaps they hark back to my childhood belief that skirts were "silly," or perhaps I just don't feel comfortable in them.

When I get my hair cut every six weeks, I get it clippered down to a style one-quarter-inch short of bald. My scalp shows for a week, but I always leave a few slight curls around my face. More than one (butch) girlfriend has pointed to these curls as a difference between us and something that marks me as feminine. And this may

be right; these curls feel feminine, and I like them. But at the same time, I challenge enough traditional elements of femininity that when I taught a freshman college class on the boundaries of identity, my body immediately became a text: students identified my appearance as blurring the lines between traditional masculine and feminine attributes. They pointed to my short hair, lack of makeup, and "masculine" clothes. I am sometimes mistaken for a man (for some bizarre reason this generally occurs at my local Safeway), but because of my features, this occurrence is fairly rare. But I recently realized that I don't know how to talk about this experience. I don't know how to join in the discussions when butches talk about being mistaken for men because the consequences of their gender transgressions often seem more dangerous or violent. I rarely fear actual violence (except when I lived in Columbus, Ohio). I worry that if I bring up my experiences, I will be scoffed at because I identify as feminine but never as butch. I rarely, if ever, hear stories about other femmes or feminine-identified dykes getting mistaken for men.

Suitable Gender

A few years ago, in preparation for an academic conference where I was interviewing for a position as a professor, I embarked upon the adventure of buying a suit. Having credit at Ann Taylor (for returning one of my mom's unfathomable gifts), I began with the goal of buying a suit that would look professional enough for me to interview in without feeling too uncomfortable or too uncomfortably feminine. Having dressed up in my more traditionally feminine attire even to shop for the suit, I arrived at the store, feeling like an imposter on various levels. I felt as if I was performing as more traditionally female than I really was—as someone who actually gets paid enough to live on (not a graduate student who couldn't afford to pay her rent without the benefit of student loans), as a respectable "adult" (that ephemeral category that seems perpetually beyond my grasp). Being a proper adult seems to be linked in my mind with performing the proper gender.

I picked out the simplest, most tailored black suit (jacket and pants) that I could find and successfully avoided getting help from the sales clerks before slinking into the dressing room to try it on. Looking at myself in the mirror under the glaring white lights, I looked like a kid playing dress-up. I didn't know what to think; the waist seemed too high, the shoulders too padded, and my whole look incongruous. When I finally succumbed to creeping out of the stall to look at myself in the three-way mirror and get some help, a saleswoman rushed over and immediately insisted that I had chosen a suit that was two sizes too big. Mortified by my error (which I feared exposed me as an imposter), I agreed to try on another size, but I asked that she bring me just one size smaller than the twelve. She arrived with a size eight, and suggested that I "at least try it on," while I asked her again for a ten, this time with a note of pleading in my voice. Temporarily deferring to her expertise, I squeezed myself into the size eight, but I couldn't stand feeling so constricted or the sight of myself in its form-fitting darts and pinching waist. I felt so exposed. I never wear anything that accentuates my waist or emphasizes my breasts.

Later I wondered, am I simply uncomfortable with my femininity? (I've heard feminine women who don't identify as femme accused of this, while few dykes would accuse a butch of something similar. Isn't that part of a butch's appeal?) Is this a butch feeling? a dyke feeling? a nontraditional woman feeling? a former punk feeling? just my feeling? a discomfort with my body? Why did I have to highlight my body in this way? The saleswoman and I compromised on the size ten, although it still felt a little snug (by this time, I felt transported back to negotiating the endless costume drama of adolescence with my mother). As I stared at myself in the mirror, trying to become accustomed to my appearance in a suit, the saleswoman returned with the dreaded "accessories"—a pearl necklace and knee-highs—which she suggested that I try on with some pumps. Aghast, I mumbled, "Ummmm, no thanks," with a tight smile, and retreated to the dressing room. As I pulled on my jeans, sweater, and clunky shoes, I felt anxious, as if I had failed in my quest to perform my act properly.

> Knee-highs? I'm not even sure what they are, but I can't imagine that they would look good with the matted-down black hair on my legs. Look at my shoes—big, clunky men's shoes—does it really seem likely that I'd wear pumps with my suit? Look at my short hair and multiple earrings, the hole in my nose where my ring was; how could I possibly want to wear pearls? Do women even wear pearl necklaces anymore, except when they are forced into the dreaded role of a pastel bridesmaid in a relative's wedding?

After having escaped the store, shaken but intact, I wondered about how I was making those decisions. How was I choosing to participate in one custom of femininity without another? How was I *constructing* my identity . . . in relation to what gendered norms and images? Was this a valid gendered decision, as worthy of support as it would be if I were describing the experience of buying a men's suit? While I do tell the story to a few of my friends for sympathy and laughs, I never consider it important enough to retell in light of gender panels or discussions. At a party after a gender panel, a couple of butch women were describing their experiences of buying men's suits, and I shared my suit-buying story. While I did feel support and interest, I also felt vaguely uneasy and slightly ashamed. I felt like another kind of imposter; who was I to tell this story when it wasn't as dramatic or transgressive as buying or wearing a man's suit?—now there's a real transgendered experience; there's real oppression for you. But I questioned my own reactions and their link to which gender experiences are validated within queer communities. These are the kinds of stories we need to start hearing and discussing if we want to generate more complicated discussions and perceptions of femininity.

I'm not using this example because it's dramatic, unique, or interesting, but for the very fact that it is actually mundane and fairly commonplace. This is often the realm in which we negotiate femininity. I also realize that layers of privilege exist in this story; I am aspiring to an elite, classed standard of belonging in which femininity can encompass having a career, as long as you appear a certain way. I am not so far outside the standard that I can't shop at Ann Taylor at all. Was the saleswoman really the representative of gender norms, and didn't I have some power over her by virtue of being a customer? I feel that I am distorting the story if I don't include the fact that the other saleswoman—a woman with short hair behind the counter—was clearly sympathetic to my plight. While ringing up my purchase, she gently gave me some tips on how to get the most out of wearing my suit for every possible interview and occasion. I worry about what gets left out when this story is based on my visible identification with some aspects of femininity.

In fact, if I stop here at the realm of visual implications about gender, then I think it is very easy to ignore and thus stabilize other aspects of identity, such as race and class. I believe that a middle-class standard of white femininity (embodied somehow in those pearls!) was being upheld as the standard in this shopping scenario, as it is in many gender discussions, while other racialized and classed representations of femininity exist and complicate this model. These other standards of femininity all but get erased in many discussions. When we assume we know what feminine is, I think we are often assuming a model of traditional White femininity. Whiteness and femininity might be linked together in our collective imagination. To consider what remains invisible in my shopping experience is obviously important because invisibility is at the heart of privilege. My discomfort in shopping for a suit might have been multiplied exponentially if I weren't White and middle-class. If I didn't fit these standards, I would likely be treated differently, especially in terms of what kind of womanhood I might be expected to present and uphold. Would a saleswoman still insist that I wear pearls? Would she help me at all?

Feminist Feminine

I've been told at various times that I "secretly" want to be butch! What does that mean? That I don't have the nerve or the right stuff to do it all the way? Should that be my ultimate goal? Why would it be secret? Masculine expression doesn't have to be about my desire to be butch; it can be part of femme or feminine identity. I've also heard that feminine dykes "never look more feminine than when they are wearing men's clothes." I think these comments function to protect butchness or female masculinity as if it were a scarce commodity by asserting and naturalizing a difference between butches and feminine dykes, so that the lines can never possibly blur. Our definitions need not to be so rigid. We are replicating traditional gender dynamics when we don't allow for more fluidity in expression and classification.

I also worry that this desire to complicate the classifications of butch/feminine will somehow make me seem dull, unsexy, and/or an advocate for strict androgyny. I will become the dreaded spectacle of a "1970s lesbian feminist." I sometimes want to single-handedly reclaim that category! Androgyny, or borrowing from both traditionally masculine and feminine roles, no longer necessarily equates to the stereotype of dykes all wearing the same uniform of flannel shirts and hiking boots. I certainly don't want to suggest that we discard butch/femme roles or that the roles themselves are suspect. I also don't subscribe to the notion that we should all appear butch one day and then feminine the next just to mix things up into a hip, postmodern jumble. But I do want to bring more flux into our tentative gender definitions and fewer rigid assumptions about what defines queer gender roles.

When I got in touch with my childhood friend Lauren on email a couple of years ago after having lost contact with her for at least ten years, I asked if she remembered "the year we were boys." While we exchanged several nostalgic correspondences about our memories as childhood best friends, she never responded to that particular question or made mention of that year. I wonder if it disturbed her (she grew up to be straight) because I had also come out on email. Perhaps she felt implicated in a homoerotic childhood dynamic that she would rather forget. The different paths that Lauren and I took suggest that we should be wary of forcing our childhood memories to correspond in any simple way to our adult identities. As adults, we still pick and choose (with varying degrees of choice, awareness, outside influence, coercion, rewards, and punishments) how we present our gender. This story of my year as a boy doesn't fit in with a seamless feminine or feminine childhood of playing dress-up or with Barbies, but it doesn't exclude that history either. As feminists, it's time to reclaim some of the lessons of lesbian feminism to examine and expand our notions of femininity itself. I believe that we can acknowledge gender extremes within the community at the same time that we acknowledge roles that don't fit into those models. If we insist upon the constructed aspect of all gender roles, then we have more room to negotiate gender and more freedom to alter the definitions of gender itself.

Constance Faulkner

A Feminist Confronts Her Religious Upbringing

Until a very few years ago I could not write publicly about my experience growing up in and later breaking with the Church of Jesus Christ of Latter-Day Saints.[1] For some reason it felt disloyal to my family. Even giving credit to my positive experiences felt hypocritical. I felt like a thief; as if being an outsider, I had no right to claim anything. Was it guilt? I don't think so. Guilt had never been a part of my socialization (or if it was, it certainly didn't take). But I thought about it. A lot. Sounds incredibly naive, doesn't it, for someone with my educational, career, and travel experience, for one who had taught philosophy and social theory, political economy and women's studies? But, it was true.

Oh, I could talk (and write) about personal ancestors, about the strong women, the strong sense of responsibility for others, the importance of family, but not about the institution that supported them. When students asked where my identification with socialism came from, I could not tell them about the United Order or the modern LDS church welfare system.[2]

Two important "events" occurred to change my thinking. The first was a conversation with sociologist Barrie Thorne, sitting across from me at lunch during a feminist theory conference, who gave me the language and the courage to

express myself. And it was so simple: of her own experience she said, "[The Mormon church authorities] may take away my membership, which I rejected anyway, but they cannot take away my heritage!" So obvious and yet, for me, a truly liberating thought. The second "event" was a research leave during which I investigated the role of women in the utopian socialist movement of nineteenth-century England. Robert Owen, founder of the Owenite group, claimed that women were "natural" socialists but that many had been "corrupted" into the cash nexus where money was more important than personal relationships. The language he used to criticize society and propose solutions was so similar to that used to describe both the United Order and the modern LDS welfare system that I realized my heritage, especially of those things I deemed most important to my identity, preceded or occurred simultaneously with the founding of the Mormon church.

I had broken with the church emotionally by the time I was sixteen, and by age eighteen I had quit going to church altogether. Although I've no doubt that part of that break was pure laziness (being an active member required lots more time and energy than I was willing to commit), the impetus seems to have been contradictions that arose in my mind over social issues. My earliest writing about my religious experience confronted what I considered racism in my socialization. This soon became an exercise in self-discovery, leading me to examine the many, many things other than race that I had been taught were not "pleasing in the eyes of the Lord," most specifically homosexuality and gender equality, and how subtle and yet penetrating had been the messages.

Still, that doesn't explain why I began questioning in the first place—and I've been asked for that explanation from many people. Why did I break with the Church? How did I make that leap to becoming a socialist feminist? The simple answer to the first question was that I no longer believed. But that, of course, raises another question, Why not? I've been stymied in seeking the sources of changes in my thinking—not just toward greater sophistication, which one would certainly hope for over such a period, but away from the safety and security of a belief system that gave such comfort and self-assurance. No, it was not because I had become a more sophisticated and critical thinker. Most of those who surrounded me in those early years, and certainly those in my immediate family, are highly intelligent and have become equally "sophisticated" and yet retained their firm belief in the church I rejected. So why me? Writing this current essay forced me not only to confront just what it meant to grow up in a Mormon family but further to admit to the privilege I enjoyed even as a female in a male-dominated religion. More important perhaps is the understanding I've come to that it was probably family and church influence itself that led me to the outside, and particularly to feminism. What I cannot explain is why I was led in that direction rather than to a deeper commitment to religious beliefs,

as had been the case with my siblings and nearly all my friends.

Reading *Honky* by Dalton Conley while struggling with how to write about this question provided an insight that, perhaps ironically, made it easier to think about: "I will never know the true cause and effect in the trajectory of my life. [this about gangs and what happened to other gang members] And maybe it is better that way. I can believe what I want to believe. This is the privilege of the middle and upper classes in America—the right to make up the reasons things turn out the way they do, to construct our own narratives rather than having the media and society do it for us."[3] Thinking about this convinced me that my pursuit of this question— Why me??—was just an expression of my white middle-class privilege. Perhaps I just want to make up reasons for my "deviance" that make me look good. Whatever the reasons, I continue to look.

Looking for clues in my nurturing and socialization that would point to my rebellion against social and church definitions of what was right or wrong or inappropriate too often led to the conclusion mentioned above: I was just plain lazy! Then, for years I convinced myself that my rebellion was caused by the birth order in our family, but that explanation was too easy. Then came the studies in recent years that asserted some things were in fact conditioned by birth order. I still didn't take it seriously and to a large extent still don't, although the descriptions of and conclusions about the experience of middle children certainly resonate with my own.[4] Then, too, the other children in our family were separated from me by at least four years, leaving me alone in the middle while each of them had a sibling within two years of them. Furthermore, I was somewhat disabled. A strep infection when

I was three, before experiments during World War II established the safety and effectiveness of sulfa drugs for children, left my ears permanently damaged. I simply couldn't hear everything that went on in the family. Nor in church!

In our family of five children, the oldest was male, so it is difficult to separate his privileges based on sex from those based on age or the patriarchal religion that dominated our lives. I only know that I grew to understand them as reflecting the first of these, in part because of the way our parents would explain seemingly unequal (and in my opinion, unfair) treatment: "He's a boy." "He holds the priesthood." Particularly difficult for me to accept were the times he was given special privileges or recognition based on his having previous experiences that in turn resulted from privileges he held and I did not. One example occurred when I was invited to go camping with a friend and her family, including her parents, something my brothers were free to do. My parents refused on the grounds that I'd never gone camping before and it wasn't as safe for girls. When I pointed out to them that I'd never get to go camping as long as prior experience was required but never available to me, they just responded with something like "Well, that's the way it is." A catch-22 before the term was created to express it.

Much of what I remember of "conversations" with my parents is of that nature. These "conversations" consisted of my asking unpleasant (to them) questions and receiving unsatisfactory (to me) answers. I would then push for "better" answers, and one parent or the other would respond with "Well, that's just the way it is." Or, when I asked why the "church says Negroes are not as good as we are," they responded, "Because God told us that." I'd press further: "Okay, so they're not as good as we are,

but why should they stay over on the west side of the city instead of living up here by us?"

"Because then our house wouldn't be worth as much money."

"Why?"

"Because they're not as good as we are."

"So if God changed his mind and decided they were as good as we are, could they move in next door?"

"God doesn't change his mind." ["He" did, of course, but that was many years later.]

Why did such questions arise in my mind? So far as I know, none of my friends were interested in such things. As a preteen, the tautological nature of the answers given to what I considered such important questions were a source of great discomfort.

As I grew older, I came to see that much of what had gone on in the family was part of a social pattern, not necessarily created by religion. Particularly important in this realization were my experiences as the only female graduate student in an economics department. The slights I experienced there are not all particularly relevant to this essay, but one is because of what it did for my consciousness: When I got married to another graduate student, the department stripped me of my teaching assistantship with the explanation that they could not afford to support two people in one family. "So why me?" I asked, noting that I was by far the better student. The department chair looked at me with something bordering on incredulity. "Well, because you are the wife, of course." This was in 1959, before the women's movement gave me the language to express my outrage at what was clearly a significant injustice. It meant that I would graduate with a Ph.D. and no teaching experience—a fact that did eliminate thousands of dollars from my first salary, money never to be recovered. And although I immediately saw these long-run implications, I did not yet have the language with which to express just why this was unfair. What I experienced as a student reinforced the idea of my inherent inferiority. Fortunately, I didn't believe it.

One other experience, this one in the early 1960s—postgraduate school, employment related—removed any remaining doubts I had as to the social nature of sexual inequality. I applied to teach in a college history department, but my application was rejected on the grounds that, to quote the department chair who wrote me, "We've all had experiences with female historians and none of us wants to work with one." Outrageous? Yes, of course—and later, patently illegal. But at the time, no response of mine would have attracted any positive attention. I did ask whether anyone in the department had worked with an unpleasant male colleague and whether he decided, on the basis of that experience, never to hire another one. You can imagine the answer: they informed me that I must be crazy. At about this time I began talking with other women about their experiences. Again, this occurred before the consciousness-raising groups accompanying the women's movement had organized later in that decade. But the few of us who were talking began to realize that if we shared so many similar experiences, then probably hundreds, perhaps thousands or millions, of other women did so as well. And what did that tell us about the world in which we lived?!?

I've been asked many times how I made the leap from "good Mormon girl" to feminist and became highly critical of the institutionalized roles into which religion puts women. Ironically, I see now that it was religion itself that started my thinking; the contradictions (what some might call hypocrisies) were just too blatant for me to ignore, even as a teenager. Furthermore, I gained strength from these contradictions because, for whatever reason, I insisted on arguing through them, clarifying and shaping my own belief system. The opportunities available to my brothers, and not to my sister and me, were obvious, and their holding the God-granted priesthood was a huge part of this. There were little things as well. I wanted to join the Girl Scouts of America, as my non-LDS friends did, but was not allowed to do so because the church had an alternative, the YWMIA.[5] For the boys, on the other hand, there was a YMMIA but most of that was connected to church-sponsored Boy Scouts of America troop activities. They went hiking and camping. Their merit badges recognized exciting activities and accomplishments in leather and woodworking, camping, first aid, and so on, while ours were mostly rewards for less physically and intellectually stimulating projects such as cooking and sewing. I lost interest in these as recreational activities early on.

We attended church for several hours on Sundays and then again on one afternoon (or evening as we got older) a week. "Extracurricular" activities such as dances, movies, rehearsals or performances of plays and musicals occupied much of our "free" time. I participated fully and thoroughly enjoyed myself. From the ages of eight or nine, boys and girls took separate classes, engaging in some activities in common but spending most of the time apart. Looking back, I'm convinced that my learning at Primary and Mutual[6] were the most influential.

Primary was held after school once a week. The girls were divided by age and given age-appropriate activities and goals we were supposed to meet. We were, from the start, given a large dose of what would later make us good wives and mothers. In fact, beginning at age nine the groups into which we girls were divided had the overall title of Home Builders. The subgroups were called Larks, Bluebirds, and Seagulls. In the front of each manual (the booklets we used to "guide our journey") the following statement appeared: "The joy of making a house into a real home is the privilege of mothers and daughters. They have ever been in quest of lovely things to make their home more attractive. The ideal home is the one that brings to those who live in it love, happiness and the opportunity to serve others. The cost of the home is not important, nor is its location. The attitude and the habits of the people who live there make it a lovely and a happy place." The manuals went on to say: "Dear Lark [or Bluebird or Seagull], let the girl shown in your Home Builder emblem represent you. As you go out in quest of spirituality, health, service and knowledge, you will understand more fully how you can represent the spirit of home building."

Not unlike the badges earned by Boy Scouts and Girl Scouts, we were awarded "charms" after the completion of a specified number of designated activities. There were four "quests": spirituality, health, service, and knowledge. Each quest included both required and "honor" activities. I am impressed, looking back after nearly sixty years, at the usefulness of much of the information we were to learn. For example, the required health activities included eating "at least one serving of fruit and two vegetables each day for a month" and "telling how to prevent the spread of the common cold." Honor activities included "get ten hours of sleep each night for at least two weeks" and "refrain from eating candy or rich foods between meals for two weeks. Give three reasons why you should do this." Only in the service quest does the sexual division of labor become apparent: "Learn to cook or prepare one article of food for the family," "Help with the dishes once each day; iron the handkerchiefs; clean the wash basin and bath tub after using them." While I was learning these things, my brothers were learning similar tasks outdoors: preparing campfire meals, pitching a tent, washing dishes in the wilderness, and so on.

Primary and Mutual also involved crafts and other creative activities. Mutual was particularly involving because we were older (twelve to eighteen years of age) and could do more things in the evening and on weekends. There were dances, road shows, plays, movies; church was, in fact, an almost total-immersion experience. There was little or no time to stop and think, no opportunity to question. However, two teachers I had were instrumental in making me think. One, "Brother Jacobs," had an explanation of where Heaven is (a fourth dimension) that was not especially satisfactory to me but got me thinking about such questions and raised doubts in my mind about the unsatisfactory answers I was getting. But most important, I learned that even a teacher could raise unanswerable questions. Another teacher, "Sister Stonebraker," did let us ask all kinds of questions but, to her credit, never tried to answer anything with the simple "God said so." Rather, she was willing to say, "I don't know." That example from a teacher, someone who was in authority saying he or she didn't know an answer, was a good lesson for me when I started teaching at the university.[7]

There were, of course, church services on Sunday, as well: Sunday School in the morning; Sacrament Meeting in the evening. These were purely religious, and I remember them primarily because I was so bored and had such a difficult time sitting still.

The priesthood itself played a critical role in all our lives and thus provided another source of my frustration with the church. The priesthood in the Mormon church includes the "right to exercise power in the name of Jesus Christ,"[8] a very powerful right to a believer. The Aaronic priesthood is given to boys at the age of twelve, at which point they assume duties (such as passing the sacrament, similar to communion in other churches) that results in their assuming a presence in the local church (called a "Ward") that no girl ever has. When they are a little older, they have the authority to "administer" (or bless) the sacrament and with each advancing stage assume greater responsibilities within the church. At a very young age I was well aware of the privilege this conferred on boys and imagined a time when I too could have that privilege. I pictured myself "passing the sacrament" or administering to it, performing baptism or confirmation, or holding a baby and giving it a blessing and a name. In some way I knew I could never do this, but this dream was right up there with my dream of becoming the first woman major league baseball player. Sometimes I saw myself as a great pitcher, other times as an incredible first baseman, but always as the greatest hitter that ever came to the plate. Never did I think of this as an instant of what we'd now call feminist conviction—I was too self-centered for that. I never thought of the failure of professional baseball to allow women to play as a form of discrimination or as unfair to all women, just to me. And the same was true of male privilege in the LDS church.

I have no doubt my parents thought they were treating and loving all their children equally. What I firmly believe is that they did not see the externally imposed constraints on that equality as touching their male and female children differently. What was given to the boys, and not the girls, was seen not as special privilege but as "natural," as God-given; it wasn't questioned or even thought about. One of the many things the women's movement did was to give me the language to talk about this difference when earlier in my life it simply made me angry—very angry.

One woman I know, a beautiful, strong woman who bore and successfully raised ten children, told me recently that she has never felt inferior to men—and I'm sure she hasn't. Do I think she is "suffering" from false consciousness? Perhaps, but it is serving her well. However, the power of ideology, and particularly the hegemony of an ideology defining women's roles and responsibilities as inferior to those of men while giving them the character of equality, is as evident in her statement as in many others surrounding religion. Any religion. "Good" church members not only learn to accept what is handed to them; if they are truly devout, they internalize it; it becomes a part of them, their identity. Superiority or inferiority has nothing to do with it. Fulfilling whatever role and responsibility they are handed is a source of satisfaction, an ego builder, a reinforcement of self-respect. As a legacy from the "cult of true womanhood,"[9] Mormon women were, and I assume still are, convinced (and quite rightly) of their importance in the family and in the church. What they lack is society- and church-sanctioned power[10] in realms that are considered instrumental, and power in the most defining element of their lives: the LDS church. That only men can hold the priesthood in the LDS church is not seen as a form of discrimination by any Mormon I've ever known because they (men and women) are convinced that the sphere within which women have (theoretically) at least equal power, the home, is so important. "Motherhood is the greatest potential influence either for good or ill in human life. . . . She who rears successfully a family of healthy, beautiful sons and daughters . . . deserves the highest honor that man can give, and the choicest blessings of God."[11]

What this implies about responsibility for children who act outside the church or the law is obvious: the mother is to be blamed. Furthermore, putting a twenty-first-century light on the matter, the position of the church on contraception, abortion, divorce, and remarriage, coupled with women's inability to hold the priesthood, have led many (including myself) to believe that Mormons have traditionally held women in very low esteem, despite the glorification of motherhood. Although I have seen this statement in print only once, and that as quotation from a Mormon pioneer woman who had just heard a sermon preached by President Brigham Young, my own experience growing up in a Mormon family, and seeing the families of relatives and friends, convinced me that the bottom line is "woman, be she ever so smart, cannot know more than her husband if he magnifies his priesthood. . . . God never in any age of the world endowed woman with knowledge above the man."[12]

With more and more Mormon and other religious women of necessity working outside their homes as well bearing the major responsibility for home and family, with more and more of them attaining higher levels of education, the reality of women's lives, and of women's burdens, has become clearer. So too has the strength of the ideology. Mormon women's inability to "do it all" is seen (by them and others) as inadequacy on their parts. This is not unique to LDS women, or even to religious women in general. The strong social message that my generation, those that went before, and (I'm sorry to say)

some of those who came immediately after were given is that "real" women could do it all—and do it all very well. No wonder so many women—even LDS women who thoroughly internalized the message—suffer from feelings of inadequacy and inferiority, and from depression. Few, especially those without the financial resources to obtain significant domestic assistance, can live up to this incredibly high standard of what it means to be a "real woman."

My mother never held an outside-the-home paid position from the time her first child was born. Certainly she held many positions in women's and children's organizations in the church, and from everything I can remember she was very good at them. She had strong organizational skills (as do many women who have "organized" families), and she knew how to inspire people to work. At home she cared for five children with a twelve-year age span. For years she baked all our bread (six or seven loaves at a time), canned and preserved fruits and vegetables, sewed many of our clothes, did all our laundry (without the aid of an automatic washer or a dryer) and ironing (until we girls were old enough to help without burning ourselves or the clothes), the meal preparation, and the bulk of the house cleaning, although she did insist that my sister and I learn to help at an early age. My brothers helped with the dishes and did the yard work, which consisted primarily of mowing the lawn once a week in the summer—a job I took over when I got to college. We were not wealthy; in fact, even by standards of those days, our father didn't make an "adequate" wage. My parents were perpetually in debt despite the fact that we lived quite simply. But we children did not generally feel deprived, and this was largely due to our parents' ability to maintain the standards of nutrition, cleanliness, activity, and comfort that we saw in other families. We were not a particularly close family, but we did many things together.

Our father was a kind, gentle, generous man who showed his sons through example how to respect and care for a wife. But at the same time, I don't think any of us particularly respected our mother. We didn't look up to her as a source of knowledge, as someone who knew a lot except about housework and child care, things for which no prizes were going to be given. Neither my sister nor I thought as children that we wanted to grow up to be like her. I doubt that my brothers consciously (or even subconsciously) thought they'd like to find a woman like their mother to marry. She was just there, taken for granted, as were most wives and mothers in the 1940s and 1950s as we came of age. And I'm sure my mother knew it, but her consolation (which she consciously seemed not to need) was that God had ordained her position.

Hindsight, as they say, is 20/20. I can now see myself as growing up in a happy, loving, supportive, and secure environment largely made possible by my mother's serious consideration of her role as good Mormon wife and mother. As a strong and able woman, who was actually better at household repair ("men's work") than our father, she was a role model for me and my sister even though we would never have admitted it.

All my adult life I've thought back to my childhood and teen years believing I'd wanted to be a boy; but now that I've vigorously focused attention on that period, found boxes of stuff I'd saved, and reread it all, I realize that all I wanted was to be a girl and do what the boys did. At the same time, I internalized all those lessons about women's roles as well as any Mormon girl, despite my having left the church. As wonderful as

such things are, my greatest joys in life have come not from publishing an article, giving a fantastic lecture, winning a struggle over an academic issue, or even hearing from the many former students who have told of the positive impact I've had on their lives. Rather, I have found my greatest joys in life from home and family. This is hard to admit.

So, do I resent or regret all the time spent on activities of my youth designed to make me a believer and a better housewife and mother? No, not in the least. Even those teachings designed to make me believe that difference (such as race and gender) was, and should be, hierarchal, that whites and males were better than nonwhites and females, played an important and ultimately positive role in my development, both as a scholar–teacher and as a mother. I've no doubt my mental (and sometimes physical) struggles against that training, and the mindset it established, were enormously helpful in establishing who I became. Struggling against something so powerful as religious ideology made me much more aware of what I believed and why. In the process of separating myself from the doctrine, I became a stronger human being. This struggle also allowed me to put "women's roles" into perspective. As a feminist I have always believed that feminism and the women's movement should be about choice and about ways of allowing women to make real, not preconditioned, choices concerning their lives. And ultimately I think that's what I got. But I still never answered the question "Why me?"

N O T E S

1. Throughout this essay I refer to members of the Church of Jesus Christ of Latter-Day Saints as Mormons and the church itself as the Mormon church. In doing so I mean no disre-

spect to the desire of church officials to move away from such usage. It's simply handy. Sometimes, for the sake of variety, I use LDS for either. One other note on the LDS church: from the inside, Mormonism is not seen as "fundamentalist." Orthodox, yes, but not fundamentalist. While they believe the Bible to be "the word of God," they add, in their Articles of Faith, the phrase "so far as it is translated correctly." This has allowed the Mormons to avoid some of what I would view as the excesses of the religious (far) right, while adhering to a more humane interpretation of religious expectations.

2. The United Order (more accurately, United Orders) "refers to the cooperative enterprises established in LDS communities of the Great Basin, Mexico, and Canada during the last quarter of the nineteenth century in an effort to better establish the ideal Christian community and promote economic self-sufficiency. In 1874, Brigham Young introduced the United Order system as a direct response to the forces that threatened LDS economic and political independence and as a final effort to build the ideal community envisioned by Joseph Smith. . . . While orders differed from each other, two main types persisted. In the St. George type, members contributed their economic property to the order and received dividends and labor income according to the relative amounts of capital and labor contributed. The second type of United Order was communal. Members contributed all their property to the order, shared more or less equally in the common product, and functioned, ate, and worked as a well-regulated family." From L. Dwight Israelsen, "An Economic Analysis of the United Order" *BYU Studies* 18 (Summer 1978), 536–562.

"The basic philosophy underlying the Welfare Services system of The Church of Jesus Christ of Latter-day Saints was succinctly stated by the Church's sixth President, Joseph F. Smith: 'It has always been a cardinal teaching with the Latter-day Saints, that a religion which has not the power to save the people temporally and make them prosperous and happy here cannot be depended upon to save them spiritually, and exalt them in the life to come.'

"The present-day system for helping the poor had its roots in the Great Depression of the 1930s, . . . [when church leaders] in urban areas contacted nearby farmers who faced prices so low that it was not profitable to harvest their crops. Arrangements were made so that idle urban members could harvest the crops in return for a share thereof. The produce thus obtained was stored in Church-controlled warehouse facilities and distributed according to need. Drawing upon that experience, Welfare farms were soon established under Church ownership in areas surrounding Mormon-populated cities. Other Church units undertook processing and manufacturing projects based on the rural produce. Bishop's storehouses were created for storage and distribution, and products were moved from location to location by a Church-sponsored transportation system. A sheltered workshop program, Deseret Industries, was introduced in 1938 to create jobs for the unemployed and the handicapped, refurbishing used clothing, furniture, and household goods for retail sale at low cost. With the return of prosperity in the United States following World War II, these facilities were expanded to offer short-term emergency work and commodities during recessions, strikes, and natural disasters, as well as employment assistance to the aged, the handicapped, and others with limited ability for self-support. As the complexities of urban life increased and other obstacles such as unemployment and the need for various types of counseling became more evident, a Social Services agency was added. When needs became apparent, other Welfare service functions were also added, growing into the system that currently operates, primarily in the

United States and Canada." From Garth Mangum, "Welfare Services," http://www.mormons.org.

3. Dalton Conley, *Honky* (Berkeley: University of California Press, 2000), 119.

4. Sitting in a doctor's office not long ago, I read an article about the raising of a middle child, my position in the birth order. The author talks about her own experience as one where she "swung between being one of the 'big three' (when there was work to be done) and one of the 'little three' (when a privilege was at hand). Mostly I just did my own thing." She goes on to summarize some of the findings of Kevin Leman on birth order: "Predictably, sandwiched middle-borns tend to be good at compromise and negotiation. . . . Used to waiting their turn, they're usually unspoiled and realistic. But feeling overlooked and upstaged leads to their being more secretive and insecure than firstborns or babies. Eager to carve a special identity, middle-borns tend to be sociable (finding their place in a network of friends) or independent (going their own way, even if it means being a rebel) or sometimes both." Levin Leman, *The New Birth Order Book,* quoted in Paul Spencer, "The Perils of Parenting a Middle Child," *Woman's Day* (June 26, 2001), 112.

5. The Young Women's Mutual Improvement Association and for younger children, "Primary."

6. An organization for young women ages twelve through eighteen, in which activities are designed to "strengthen relationships, develop skills, and build testimonies of Christ."

"The Primary is an organized program of religious instruction and activity in The Church of Jesus Christ of Latter-day Saints for children from eighteen months of age until their twelfth birthdays. Its purpose is to teach children the gospel of Jesus Christ and help them learn to live it." *Encyclopedia of Mormonism,* ed. Daniel H. Ludlow (Macmillan),

quoted on www.mormons.org/basic/organization.

7. She also left me with something else very important: "We judge others by their actions and ourselves by our intentions."

8. www.mormons.org/basic/organization, taken from *Encyclopedia of Mormonism.*

9. Woman, in the cult of true womanhood presented by the women's magazines, gift annuals, and religious literature of the nineteenth century, was the hostage in the home. In a society where values changed frequently, where fortunes rose and fell with frightening rapidity, where social and economic mobility provided instability as well as hope, one thing at least remained the same—a true woman was a true woman, wherever she was found. If anyone, male or female, dared to tamper with the complex of virtues that made up true womanhood, he was damned immediately as the enemy of God, civilization, and the Republic. It was the fearful obligation, a solemn responsibility, which the nineteenth-century American woman had—to uphold the pillars of the temple with her frail white hand.

"The attributes of True Womanhood, by which a woman judged herself and was judged by her husband, her neighbors, and her society, could be divided into four cardinal virtues—piety, purity, submissiveness, and domesticity. . . . Without them . . . all was ashes. With them she was promised happiness and power." From Barbara Welter, "The Cult of True Womanhood: 1820–1860," *American Quarterly* 18 (1966), 151–174.

10. Defining *power* as "the ability to both make and effect decisions."

11. David O. McKay, *Gospel Ideals* (Salt Lake City: Deseret Book Co., 1953), 452–454.

12. From the journal of Alice Johnson Read, quoted in Kimball Young, *Isn't One Wife Enough?: The Story of Mormon Polygamy* (New York: Henry Holt, 1954).

Philomena McCullough

The Curse

Credit cards, phone bills, doctor bills, lawyer bills, and insurance. Even though I refuse to work for the Man, I end up working for the Man. Sometimes I can't help crying. Crying, however, is not a traditional Ojibwe occupation. Children are taught at a young age not to cry. It makes a person vulnerable to enemies and disease. The gete-Anishinaabe (old-time Indians) understood this. My grandma, too, understands this. I don't recall ever seeing her cry. She is my antidote. I call her when I feel pitiful and she tells me a story. She reminds me that I have more than she ever dreamed of having.

My grandma, Bess Polivka, grew up in Odanah on the Bad River Reservation at the end of the lumber era. From the late nineteenth century to 1925 the Sterns Lumber Company removed the grand, elegant white pine trees from the reservation to make grand, elegant homes in southern Wisconsin and northern Illinois. During the peak of the period, Odanah was a bustling little city. It had its own newspaper, two movie theaters, and an opera house. Unfortunately the affluence was short-lived. For many parts of the United States the Great Depression began when the stock market crashed in 1929, but it struck Indian communities earlier and harder. By the time Grandma had turned sixteen (1925), the

Sterns Lumber Company left town. They had removed most of the salable trees, leaving the community without an industry and with land resembling a war zone. The deep, lush forests were now stumpy fields. The Indians were left with nothing.

"When I was growing up," Grandma tells me, "we didn't even have anything to hope for." For women in Odanah, life meant marrying young and having babies until you satisfied God.

I cannot feel sorry for myself after hearing her stories. She, too, lived according to her principles: personal freedom and education, balanced by a strong sense of familial responsibility. These led her far from the reservation boundaries—both spatially and philosophically.

She found a teaching job right after she graduated from college—at an Indian boarding school in South Dakota. She left right away because her father was sick, and he needed money to raise her young brothers and sisters. My grandma never lived in Odanah again. She eventually made her home in Chicago, Illinois. Made a beautiful life with love and humor and books and ideas. She is one of the most well-read people I have ever met.

Indian communities often disparage those who leave. Call them apples, red on the outside, white on the inside; brutalizing those who "succeed." Could she, a well-educated woman with aspirations, have survived if she had stayed?

Today she is one of the oldest members of our tribe (possibly the oldest). There's no doubt that her decision to emigrate enabled her to survive the economic, biological, and psychological war waged every day against Indian people. Most of her contemporaries have succumbed to various preventable conditions.

Today I go back to Bad River as often as I can. I participate in many of the traditional harvesting activities, visit with people, and then go back home to my niche in the city. I try not to be a tourist; but the idea of community responsibility nags at me. What is my part? How can I use my education to make a contribution? Living and working on the reservation, however, seem impossible. No jobs, no place to live. It's the twenty-first century and I am left with the same dilemma as my grandma faced when she was twenty-four.

If feminism is going to matter to real women and native women and low-income women, it needs to focus on what brings them together—really basic things. And for native women that is often food. Food for subsistence—for sharing—not ritual—food brings people back to the reservation. Food for economics. For example, among the tribes in Minnesota wild rice is a big commodity; that way people with no jobs have money for the winter. While the slaying of the deer in my experience described below was symbolic, it was much more than that. It was more about someone having food in the freezer for the winter.

We had been riding up and down Government Road all night, Amoose in the driver seat and me riding shotgun. We stopped at every green flicker in the night. Most of the time it was nothing. Sometimes it was a deer hidden deep in the brush.

We hadn't had any luck and were ready to head home when we saw her. A yearling doe flashed by just twenty feet from the side of the truck.

"Get out your gun and turn on the light." Amoose spoke in a low tone. "Don't shoot yet, wait until you can get a good shot." We were on the south end of Bad River close to the farmers' fields. He didn't want me shooting holes in any farmhouses.

I got the rifle and followed the deer in the scope as she ambled out in front of the truck. She stopped for a moment and looked at us.

"Can I shoot now?" I whispered over to Amoose. By this time my arm was shaking from the weight of the rifle. I could barely see her in my scope.

"YES SHOOT NOW!" I pulled the trigger, not believing that I could make the shot.

But the bullet was true. It pierced her back and broke the spine. She hobbled in front of the truck, gave up at the shoulder of the road.

Nothing had prepared me for the power of those next moments. After I put down tobacco, Amoose handed me a knife. I could not believe what I was about to do. My hand shook as I cut through the thin layers of skin. He grabbed the knife away and made a smooth slice down her abdomen. The skin and fat parted at the cut and revealed the most perfect set of organs.

"Well, get down there and pull that stuff out. . . . It's your deer." For the next half an hour Amoose coached me. It took all of my strength to remove the gut sack, but I wanted to do it right. I tugged and pulled and cut. Finally the gut sack fell out onto the gravel. Were we giving birth? Transforming this life into life for many others? Was she forgiving me and my family for leaving so many years ago?

Anne-Marie Basso
Kim L. Morrison

Imagining Cinematic Lesbian Identity

"The master's tools will never dismantle the master's house."

—Audre Lorde, *Sister Outsider,* 1984

The women's movement has historically been dominated by White middle- and upper-class heterosexual women. White feminists have more often than not viewed their oppression (as women inferior to White men) as the most important of all oppressions. The women's movement's struggle for women's rights has focused on equality particularly between middle-class White men and White women (at times consciously and at other times unconsciously). Defining oppression based on this self-centered viewpoint has resulted in a movement that declares it is for all women but in reality ignores women of color, women of the poor and working classes, and queer women. Audre Lorde addresses this dismissal, saying,

> Somewhere, on the edge of consciousness, there is what I call a *mythical norm,* which each one of us within our hearts knows "that is not true." In America, this norm is usually defined as white, thin, male, young, heterosexual, christian, and financially secure. It is within this mythical norm that the trappings of power reside within this society. Those of us who stand outside of that power often identify one way in which we are dif-

ferent, and we assume that to be the primary cause of all oppression, forgetting other distortions around difference, some of which we ourselves may be practicing. By and large within the women's movement today, white women focus on their oppression as women and ignore differences of race, sexual preference, class, and age. There is a pretense to a homogeneity of experience covered by the word *sisterhood* that does not in fact exist.[1]

Lorde points out that the dismissal of difference by those in power makes it difficult for women of all backgrounds to benefit from the women's movement.

The dismissal of difference is not only an attitude coming from white heterosexual women. Lesbian history and lesbian literature are imagined by those who have access to research, write, and produce, whether in a novel or on screen—lesbians who most often have access are White. The dismissal of racial issues in the personal lives of White writers and directors is reflected in the art they create. Society shapes women of color by a White discourse describing the Africanist presence as deviant, wild, and reckless and white as supreme, pure, and virtuous. By juxtaposing White and Black characters, a wholesome White identity is reinforced in lesbian films. This paper explores the strategic formation of distorted representations of women of color in order to secure a credible White identity in the lesbian film *If These Walls Could Talk II: 1972*.[2]

If These Walls Could Talk II: 1972 attempts to point out that the women's movement in its binary thinking has persistently failed to incorporate difference; however, by the power of inversion the film itself fails to incorporate difference by presenting a predominantly White lesbian experience. In the following scene the film focuses on the difference in sexual orientation:

Diane: The College told us we can't have our meetings on campus any more. They don't want to support us because they think we are a lesbian group.

Linda: But, they can't do that.

Diane: Yes, they can do that Linda. Look, we have to be really clear about what kind of group we are. We feel it's too risky to include your issues right now.

Linda: Are you kidding me?

Diane: First we have to fight for the real issues of feminism, equal rights between men and women. There isn't any room for you guys.

Diane dismisses the relevance of lesbian sexuality while honoring heterosexuality. Diane, a White woman, presumably uses the mythical norm to define the one way she does not fit in as the "real issue." When Diane chooses her oppression as the most important, she disregards the lesbian experience and ends up acting in a heterosexist manner.

Similar to the women's rights group declaring "equal rights between men and women" as the "real issues of feminism" in 1972, the White race sets itself up as natural and normal, self-evident and immediately apparent in this film of 2000. Linda is the main character of the film, and her housemates take supporting roles. Apart from Re Re who is African American, Linda and the other college housemates are White. From the start of the film, viewers identify with Linda and her friends. Because Linda and her friends react so strongly against Diane's statement that "the real issues of feminism are the issues between men and women," viewers receive a clear message that the women's movement in 1972 was heterosexist and left lesbians out and that this is unacceptable. But the film does not address race and class in the context of Diane's statement, or for that matter, anywhere in the film. Race and class are as much issues of feminism as heterosexuality or homosexuality. The history that is told in this film is a biased history coming from a White lesbian center.

If These Walls Could Talk II: 1972 presents racist notions of lesbians and the women's movement because the film itself falls short of a well-rounded critique of race within these histories. There are characters of color in the film but no main character of color. Interracial issues are ostensibly ignored in the film. According to Audre Lorde, "It is not our differences which separate women, but our reluctance to recognize those differences and to deal effectively with the distortions which have resulted from the ignoring and misnaming of those differences."[3] I believe it is because the writers and directors of this film had a "reluctance" to "recognize those differences and to deal effectively with the distortions" that the characters of color in this film are portrayed in a stereotypical way. In effect, the film warrants that White people are normal and people of color are "the other."

The film does not address the differences of Black characters from White, and it is obvious that the writers and directors lazily relied upon the signifiers they have been taught to attach to Black people when creating the roles of Black characters. Toni Morrison, in her book *Playing in the Dark,* addresses the implications of ritualistic representations of Black characters. Morrison (much in the way of Edward Said's study of Orientalism) describes her study of the ways Black characters are represented in American literature as "an investigation into the ways in which a nonwhite Africanlike or Africanist presence or persona was constructed in the United States, and the imaginative uses this fabricated presence served."[4] Morrison says she uses the word *Africanism* "as a term for the denotative and connotative blackness that African peoples have come to signify, as well as the entire range of views, assumptions, readings, and misreadings that accompany Eurocentric learning about these people."

This Africanist presence Morrison describes can clearly be seen in *If These Walls Could Talk II: 1972.* The character Re Re, a Black woman, assimilates to the larger White discourse on Black people. For example, the rest of the scene goes like this:

Linda: Diane, we started this group together.

Re Re: (yelling) Yeah, and I worked my butt off to get free birth control on this campus. What do you think, I was protecting my right to screw frat boys?!

White girl in room: (yelling) That's exactly the kind of attitude we don't need in here.

Re Re: We did it for you!

Re Re is the first character to yell and get angry when the women's rights group says that lesbian issues cannot be included. In this scene we see two other Black women. They are sitting in a room full of about twenty to thirty White women. But while the White women are attentive, both Black women look disengaged; their heads are tilted to the side and their eyes are looking down. The Black characters, when shown, are distorted in their representation by the ritualized myths society creates of the angry Black or the lazy Black. It may seem to the reader of this paper that this is an isolated incident and does not mean much. But if you look at this scene next to the other representations of Re Re in the film, there is indeed a pattern. Re Re swears several times in other scenes, while the White characters do not swear. Re Re rolls the joints in the scene when she and her three White friends smoke pot, and Re Re has a loud mouth that is very critical when the four friends go to a "dyke bar." She is continuously portrayed as the most deviant character.

White characters signify *pure, virtuous, responsible, calm, majority,* and they define the real issues. In contrast, the Black characters swear, signify *lazy, disengaged, angry, outspoken,* and are marginalized, left out of main character roles. These racial signifiers, fabricated by White people, are meta-narratives in American culture. "We are surrounded by homogenizing and normalizing images—images whose content is far from arbitrary" White identity is invested in surrounding images—advertisements, TV, news features, and so on. Images that secure White privilege, reinforce White as the supreme race, are predominantly presented. White people largely refuse to admit that the visual meta-narratives infused in daily life are truly "suffused with the dominance of gendered, racial, class, and other cultural iconography."[5] Bordo believes that our culture does not perceive interconnections between events, oppressions, and the images literature creates. Because American culture looks at stories as if they are isolated incidents, we prevent ourselves from moving beyond predated signifiers, delaying the creation of new signs.

Because of this refusal to look at stories as having their own place in an ecosystem, being influenced by and influencing other factors, all representations of African American women in the film are problematic. Because there are so few characters of color in the film, such little recognition of race, and because the Black–White binary relies on archaic codes, the result is tokenization. Although Elizabeth Higginbotham, in her essay "Designing an Inclusive Curriculum: Bringing All Women into the Core," is clearly referring to the education system, her stance applies here. She says, "This teaching strategy is often linked with the view that gender relations are the foundation for universal experiences. Within this framework, other sources of inequality, particularly race and class, might be acknowledged, but they are clearly less important then gender. As a result, scholarship on women of color in both women's studies and curriculum integration efforts is marginalized. Faculty tend to rely upon the experiences of white, middle class, heterosexual Americans as the norm and view all others are merely exceptions to the rule."[6]

The universal experience strategy is not lost in the queer subculture; it is only transferred, inverted regarding sexuality and repeated regarding skin color and class. The refusal to see and value differences of age, race, sex, and class perpetuates the separation of women. One reason the movie is not able to present all women in an equal way is because, in the words of Lorde, "We have no patterns for relating across

our human differences as equals."[7] There is no map for what constitutes equal behavior and how to go about doing something in a way that works for all women of varying races, classes, gender identities, and sexual orientations.

In 2003 White women continue to separate themselves from women of color, even after Jim Crow, because of continual lack of recognition of difference. The film *If These Walls Could Talk II: 1972* intends to deconstruct the rhetoric that the women's movement has been for all women. However, the film fails to incorporate difference because as a society we are programmed to ignore inequality. Refusal to recognize inequality prevents women from attaining the very equality we say we value.

N O T E S

1. Audre Lorde, "Age, Race, Class, and Sex: Women Redefining Difference." In *Literary Theory: An Anthology,* Julie Rivkin and Michael Ryan, eds. (Oxford: Blackwell, 1998), 631.

2. *If These Walls Could Talk II: 1972.* Director Martha Coolidge. With Vanessa Redgrave, Ellen DeGeneres, Sharon Stone. HBO, 2000.

3. Audre Lorde, "Age, Race, Class, and Sex," 631.

4. Toni Morrison, *Playing in the Dark: Whiteness and the Literary Imagination* (Cambridge: Harvard University Press, 1992), 6.

5. Susan Bordo, "Material Girl." In *Literary Theory: An Anthology,* Julie Rivkin and Michael Ryan, eds. (Oxford: Blackwell, 1998), 1001.

6. Elizabeth Higginbotham, "Designing an Inclusive Curriculum: Bringing All Women into the Core," in *Words of Fire: An Anthology of African American Feminist Thought.* Beverly Guy-Shelftall, ed. (New York: The New Press, 1995), 481.

7. Audre Lorde, "Age, Race, Class, and Sex," 633.

Cara Ann Thoreson

Developing a Feminism Identity: A Father's Role

In 1986, Gloria Steinem wrote a satire about what the world would be like if men menstruated. She argued that in such a world, men would brag about being a "three-pad man," tampons and sanitary napkins would be given out for free by the government, and women would carry the stigma of lacking this great gift of menstruation. She states, "In short, the characteristics of the powerful, whatever they may be, are thought to be better than the characteristics of the powerless—and logic has nothing to do with it." Upon my first reading of that article I shared in the anger, the irony, and the raging pleasure of it. At the end, Steinem argues that "In fact, if men could menstruate, the power justifications could probably go on forever. If we let them."[1] In that sentence, I heard the unmistakable call she was issuing to women. She was calling them to uncover their eyes to the misogynistic cultural artifacts that many women are brought up in society to accept. However, years later, when I set out to write this essay on how I became a feminist and the role men played in that identity, I began to look at Steinem's article in a different light. Beyond the anger and sarcasm was a call for equality . . . a call that I believe was directed at men.

Today, Gloria Steinem, through the Ms. Foundation for Women, continues to seek men's involvement in her crusade for gendered equality. In April 2003 the Ms. Foundation will transition their Take Your Daughters to Work Day program to Take Your Daughters and Sons to Work Day. Men's involvement, education, and healing are essential to the goals of feminism. In fact, feminist men have influenced the person and political activist I have grown to be. I was five years old the first time my dad took me to work with him. His office was a library of amphibians, both in books and jars. My dad was a professor of biology at an all-women's college. At that early age I began to appreciate the education of women. "I realized how important feminism is because you were born," my dad would say, a syringe in one hand, a salamander in the other. The women who filled the lecture halls amazed me with their knowledge, confidence, and beauty. Just as my dad's feminism started with me, my feminism began to bud in his classroom, listening to his lectures when I was five. As a feminist, my two greatest enemies are misogyny and ignorance, which I believe lead to inequality and oppression. As a feminist, these are the monsters I battle. Because feminists have often been demonized as man-hating, femininity-denying, tradition-rejecting, family-disoriented women, it is hard to conceptualize the idea of a feminist man, or even men's involvement in feminism. These stereotypes enforce confusion and antagonism between the sexes, and they miss the point of feminism all together: equality. The popular antagonistic portrayal of men and women through feminism, in essence, makes equality seem like a radical idea. First and foremost, feminism is about equality; it has stretched itself to envelop not only gender but also class, race, sexuality, and even animal rights.

Fighting Feminisms

I have been trying to find feminism for most of my life. Although my introduction to feminism was through my father—who sought to instill in me his interpretation of the feminist ideals of the 1970s—as I grew up and educated myself in the feminist lessons of my own era, I began to realize the dichotomy in which my father's feminism existed. While my father championed feminism for my sake, he did not do so for his own sake. While he could recognize the many disadvantages of women, he could not see his own privilege, a privilege that often caused those very disadvantages. Because of this, feminism in my life has often been marked by confusion and fraught with tension. The seeming oxymoron of a feminist man has continuously haunted me because the most notable champion of feminism in my life has been my father. In what follows, I will document my growth within feminism through my own experience.

Feminism is a unique form of Western political theory. While feminist theory and political theory are both about power, feminist theory is a way to discuss the world through a gendered lens. But feminism as a united, political concept does not seem to be working in the United States. Feminism has become a plural; a site of political difference, contestation, and diversity. Unfortunately, as Black feminists have noted, many White women are racist; as gay feminists have pointed out, not all female professionals support gay rights. Moreover, as more radical feminists have claimed, women may have gained access to previously all-male professions such as medicine, but this certainly does not mean that those who control medical training have adapted their curriculum to incorporate feminist theories or methodologies. Another concern is that the most vocal criticisms of feminism come from feminists themselves. Theorists argue that activists are not being thoughtful and responsible. Activists argue that theorists aren't doing enough. Feminists urge each other not to homogenize themselves by noting our intersecting identities—such as race, ethnicity, age, and so on—within the social body of feminism, while fretting that these very different identities will tear the movement apart. This tug-of-war within feminism is augmented by stereotypes and misunderstandings of and between men and women, and the tense relationships that grow out of them.

I believe that feminism, more than other forms of knowledge and theory, carries with it a sense of responsibility. While most forms of political theory are based on a "challenge and response" pattern, feminism does not have the same sort of united, singular response. As a modern image of revolution, the guidelines of feminism are often fluid and ambiguous. Rebecca Walker describes a certain kind of self-consciousness that comes with feminism today. She speaks to how, when editing the feminist anthology *To Be Real,* she often worried about what others would think of her. Did she learn enough from her mother? Was she doing it right? saying it right?[2] bell hooks argues that one *isn't* a feminist, but that one *does* feminism.[3] It seems to me that women are having a difficult time wading through the muck of differences between, definitions of, and action among feminists. My father taught me his version of what feminism was. Could learning feminism from a man, who still employs many "traditional ideologies," create a rupture in its very goals? I worry often, as Rebecca Walker does, if I'm doing feminism "right."

Creatively Feminist

I like the word *feminism*. I even like feminism as a category and a purpose. I also believe in a gender-just world. Feminism is not just about women's empowerment but is also a release of men from the masculinized stereotypes they bear. However, this inclusion is often met with a distrustful eye. Many of my feminist friends have told me that men's involvement in feminism is unwanted, unwarranted, and unfair. "What right do men have to crowd our movement? They already have all the power." Often feminism is viewed by feminists and nonfeminists as a man-versus-woman dichotomy. I believe this antagonism and distrust are built on conflicting and contradictory messages within society about the expected roles of women. Old systems of power often assumed specific gendered spaces: the public belonged to men, the private to women. These networks of power articulated to each gender that basic biological differences fit them to different tasks. Much feminist debate has uprooted these assumptions. Women have begun to choose different roles but must still operate within a patriarchal culture. Patriarchal

relations in Western society are structural and institutional. Often unintentional, they are integrated into our politics and language. The roles women are socialized to seek are now very complicated and diverse, ranging from those who opt out of the traditional role altogether, to the supermom who has and does it all, to the antifeminist who encourages all women to return to the home. Most women find themselves somewhere in between.

I am constantly waiting for the moment when feminism will make as much sense in my head as it does in my heart. As I wade through murky theoretical arguments by contemporary feminists about "ethical" feminism and the importance of sameness, difference, and equality, I wonder where my voice is heard. And when I float confused among metaphysical definitions of feminism, where the only weapon against the gender hierarchy is performance and parody, I grow apathetic and angry instead of inspired and liberated. And above all, where is *my* feminist voice, if that voice was coached by my father?

Feminist Fathers

Growing up, I was a feminist because my father was one. I can clearly remember my first feminist lesson, sitting with him at the kitchen table, a Barbie lying before me. "Don't let anyone tell you that this is beautiful," my father warned me. I wasn't allowed to play with Barbies. My father thought they were grotesque and oversexed-looking. I looked at the blonde bombshell and couldn't imagine anything/one more beautiful than Barbie. Her long flaxen hair made a mockery of my dark, unruly bob. Her long, thin legs reminded me of my ballet instructor's. She was tall, thin, and beautiful. She was everything I thought a woman should be. At that moment, I stood at the biggest crossroad of my seven-year-old life. My two idols were squaring off. Barbie would from then on become my secret plaything, my shameful hero. I was my dad's little girl and I would do anything, be anything for him . . . even a feminist.

From that day on my father and I began a journey, exploring feminism together. At night he would sit on my bed and read to me from *Little Women:* a story about a woman writer and the man who would complete her. My dad always told me that I should use my mind and think for myself, but he never questioned whether I would need a man in my life. "Someday, Cara, when you get married . . ." He began to tell me stories about his mother, his childhood, how things were and how they should be. "I was never really a feminist before you were born," my dad would tell me.

"I used to think that life was just easy for my parents, each in their own role. My mom quit her job as soon as she got married. But after you were born, I never wanted you to give up anything. My mom liked teaching, but she never thought twice about giving it up. I think I became a feminist because you were born."

My dad and I talked about Barbie, fish tanks, tree houses, and biology. He taught me that feminism meant speaking my mind and having self-respect and a positive body image. Those things seemed easy enough to me. However, as I grew, these three feminist life strategies became harder to achieve.

As my dad encouraged me to have a positive body image, I often ran brazenly around in my swimsuit on hot summer days. However, I never expected the shame I would feel when my dad poked my stomach and told me I was getting chunky, or when he suggested I try out a diet before I started high school. "It's hard for over-weight people to get jobs," he would tell me. Just as I never questioned my father's feminism, I didn't question the shame I felt in my too-big, too-much body. I was trying to digest the conflicting messages my father sent me over the years. He once told me, "Cara, you should be with someone who treats you like fine china." "Why china?" I should have asked. "Why something breakable?" But instead I nodded my head, soaking it all in. In my schooling of feminism with my father, I always had a guilty suspicion that women just might be better equipped at feminism than men, that they might know how to do it better. What was feminism really when wedged within these contradictions?

By comparing me to a dish, my father was unintentionally regurgitating many of the important life lessons American boys are taught. bell hooks states that "Like women, men have been socialized to passively accept sexist ideology."[4] Men, stereotypically, are the bearers of privilege and power. Women, as their complement, are commodified, oppressed, and suppressed. My father's feminism was only as old as I was; it still had to compete with a lifetime of socialization. By assuming both my heterosexuality and my submissive, breakable position in that relationship, my father's feminism became confused. Men, by their very shape as masculine-gendered beings, embody the same systems of oppression that feminists fight. So what happens when a man, who still bears the scars of socialized gender inequality, teaches a young woman feminism?

Growing Pains

In high school my father began to lose ground in his position as my idol and feminist teacher when I fell in love with the captain of the cross-country team. He slid a little more when I kissed a boy on the soccer team. And by the time I got to third base with the first baseman on the baseball team, my feminism had become perverted, distorted, and lost. As I frantically searched for a man who would treat me like a dish, I learned that men were not often gentle and usually wanted me to do the dishwashing. These men were nothing like my father. I was also finding it hard to navigate the mixed messages I was receiving from my dad. I should be independent, but I should also be on the search for a man who would complete my identity as a woman. I should be outspoken, but the guys I dated cared more about what I looked like and didn't want to know or didn't care what I stood for. Sex and sexuality are tied to socialized gender dichotomies in which roles are assumed and power is unevenly distributed. As a heterosexual woman, I could never seem to fulfill my sexual desires without slipping into the expected role. My feminism began to get squeezed out.

As I went from man to man, I didn't seem to notice that over those four years of high school my self-esteem had grown weedy and undernourished and my feminism was nearly forgotten. Not until my dad found me sprawled melodramatically on the kitchen floor, declaring desperately to him that I had been dumped, did I begin to question my identity as a woman and a feminist. "Why do you put up with these jerks?" he implored. "You are so much more than this, why do you want to be with this guy who doesn't even appreciate you?"

I felt betrayed and stumped. Growing up I had been my dad's biggest fan, his most promising prodigy. I had tried to live by his conflicting lessons. I was to be a self-confident, Barbie-hating woman, who watches what she eats so as to be desirable to men. I was acting self-assured and independent, but inside I felt needy and exposed. How could Dad's lessons have failed me now? I had found a man that treated me like fine china. He had beat up one of his competitors to prove how he loved me, to prove I needed protection. He had promised me that he would always be there for me. He had told me that I was the most beautiful thing he had ever seen. I practically felt that my shatterable self had been put on display. With him I felt more like a dish than ever in my life. This one was The One. And he dumped me. I hit the floor like broken glass. Who would protect me now? Who would beat up the bad guys? Who would reassure me that my body was good enough? Who would make me a woman? Who would support me now that even my father had betrayed me?

Me, that's who. But not for at least another four years.

During my four years at college, I discovered a type of feminism that my father had never taught me. I learned that men were oppressors and should not be dealt with. I learned how to be angry at men. I learned to hate the way men unfairly hold the majority of the political, economic, and social power. I learned to assume that all men hated women at heart and planned to fight back with that same hatred. I read and absorbed the *Restocking Manifesto,* which proclaimed: "We identify the agents of our oppression as men. Male supremacy is the oldest, most basic form of domination. All other forms of exploitation and oppression (racism, capitalism, imperialism, etc.) are extensions of male supremacy: men dominate women, a few dominate the rest. All power situations throughout history have been male-dominated and male-oriented. Men have controlled all political, economic, and cultural institutions and backed up this control with physical force. They have used their power to keep women in an inferior position."[5]

I discarded the ultra-macho men from my high school years and replaced them with "feminine" men, and later replaced men with women. When my anger collapsed with my desire to belong, I tried to adjust my life accordingly. I associated feminism with oppression; I thought the only way to do it right was to belong to an oppressed group, to make martyrs of women. I tried to behave as any man-hating feminist would. After all, how else would I avoid misogyny? I embraced a Foucaultian life: power is everywhere, oppression is unavoidable.[6] I chose lesbianism partly to avoid confusing heterosexual gender roles and also because I thought the only true feminist was a repressed one. The victimization explicit in my collegiate feminism was perfect for me. It seemed to collapse the lessons my father had taught me. I was outspoken; writing papers on feminism, marching through the streets with my colleagues, yelling, "Take back the night." I had self-respect, appreciating my own skills within an all-woman community. I had a positive body image, without the purportedly critical male gaze.

I lost track of the true feminist goal: equality. I chose a sexuality that was not my own. I chose victimization in order to ignore my privilege. I also made some huge assumptions about lesbianism being linked to feminism. Ultimately, I repressed my own sexuality because I believed it would oppress me, that men would oppress me. For heterosexual feminists, it is often a struggle to reconcile our feelings for men with whom we enter into intimate relationships and our rage against misogynistic male culture. Although I am part of the privileged majority (heterosexual), expected gender roles can still feel confining and limiting for both men and women.

bell hooks writes about how feminism became a bourgeois White phenomenon. What she describes is a fight over privilege, by the privileged. "They did not want to acknowledge that bourgeois white women, though often victimized by sexism, have more power and privilege, are less likely to be exploited or oppressed than poor, uneducated, nonwhite males."[7] By claiming my lesbianness for political reasons, I was trying to navigate this antagonism that hooks describes without recognizing an important slippage between my oppression and my privilege as a White, middle-class, heterosexual woman. Although this slip was my own, I believe its roots lie in my feminist training with my father.

I believe my father tried to be an active feminist before he could even react to feminism. He tried to be a feminist before he could begin to hear feminisms and understand their claims. My father nobly attempted to carry out feminist agendas before feminism had a chance to saturate his perspective. hooks argues that there is a special bond between men and women in oppressed groups that doesn't exist between the privileged. They bond over political solidarity and exploitation. They need each other to achieve their goals, while many White women create an antagonistic perspective of feminism and see men as the problem, not a necessary part of the solution. However, are men not also oppressed by gender stereotypes? Men are often expected to be emotionally and physically tough, successful breadwinners, and they rarely have the choices and flexibility that women do in regards to staying home with the children. Is it possible, then, that in feminism, women need men to achieve their feminist goals?

Feminist agency should belong to men and women, just as it belongs to women of all different races, classes, sexualities, religions, and political standpoints. I encourage debate, change, self-discovery, and constant questioning. I don't believe there is a utopian feminist destination, but we invariably find pieces of it on our journey. Barbara Kingsolver states it perfectly: "The most important thing in life is to find what you hope for and live inside that hope."[8] My hope is equality; my method is feminism; and only by including women *and* men in that journey can I expect my goal to be achieved.

The only way for me to be proactive, not reactive, about my feminism and femininity is to get to know myself and understand the source of the mixed messages my father gave me. This introspection continually leads me to further unpack feminism and how men can play an important part in it. I realize that as I change and grow up as a person, as my surroundings, friends, and perspective change, my feminism will change as well. I realized that even as my father was passing down some of the potentially harmful gendered lessons from his youth, he was also passing down some positive and inspirational notions about equality. Overall, I have found that I want men in my life and also in my feminism.

I realize that my father and I still have feminism in common. I discovered that the gap that separated his slightly chauvinistic, fatherly feminism from my feminine, activist feminism really wasn't that deep or wide. My father and I could share feminism based on privilege and change, recognizing our privilege and constant progress. Through my father's version of feminism I learned how important and hard it is to recognize your privilege while working for your cause. My father has had many advantages: he is a White, middle-aged, middle-income man. Growing up as his daughter meant that many of his advantages were also mine. My father, who was reared

on patriarchy, did his best to show me a world where I didn't have to sacrifice the things his mother did. My father tried to show me a world of opportunities. And when the taint of oppression and tradition threatened to bleed into his feminist lessons, I had to forgive and teach the teacher of the greatest lesson I'll ever learn. I also had to let go and allow my dad to have his own version of feminism, just as women have given allowances to each other in the feminist community for decades.

Feminism is in a continually transitional stage. Many of the principles that feminists have fought so hard for over the years are now part of the fabric of the nation. While progress is showing, equality has yet to be achieved. Feminists often tumble and scrape over the tactics to use to achieve their goals; however, this energy proves that the movement is alive. I'm not willing to give up the "responsible thoughtfulness" of feminist theory, while also not backing down from the hopeful polemic of my work. I will always fight for women's rights, while never again giving up on men or myself. Social scientists are often criticized and revered for complicating and problematizing situations that often seem clearcut in our society. Within these ruptures I have found the space to move, a place to claim my own imperfect feminist identity and agency, and have discovered that "complicated and problematized" is the creative space where I would rather be. Feminism is not only about women anymore. It is a lens with which to view the world and its inequalities and oppressions. Mindy Stombler states that "Feminism today is about figuring out ways to have equality or social justice without ignoring the differences among women and between women and men."[9]

I realize that this is a difficult approach to the subject, but within it, there is also a call for hope. My goal is to raise questions and awareness, not give out any answers—to inspire others to think about their own feminism and femininity, their influence and power. I have not achieved perfection in feminism but seek to make it an active, effective and thoughtful part of my life—as I hope you will do.

I called my dad to tell him that I had proposed to my boyfriend. "Just remember," he told me instead of congratulations, "I'm on your side." I told him I knew it. He always had been on my side as a father and a fellow feminist. Later in the conversation he asked me, "Cara, do you remember that T-shirt I used to have with the bicycling fish on it?" I remembered it. Under the picture was screened the phrase: A woman needs a man like a fish needs a bicycle. "Do you still think that's true?" he asked. My dad and I had talked through my growth and settling into feminism my whole life. These conversations had forced us to grow together, had made us better feminists. "Yeah," I answered him, "I think it's still true. Women don't *need* men, but I believe feminism does."

NOTES

1. Gloria Steinem, "If Men Could Menstruate." In *Outrageous Acts and Everyday Rebellions* (2nd ed.) (New York: Henry Holt, 1995), 366–369.
2. Rebecca Ealker, ed. *To Be Real: Telling the Truth and Changing the Face of Feminism* (New York: Anchor Books, 1995).
3. bell hooks, *Black Looks: Race and Representation* (Cambridge, MA: South End Press, 1992).
4. Ibid., 269.
5. Restocking, *Feminist Revolution* (New York: Random House, 1975).
6. Michel Foucault, *Discipline and Punish: The Birth of the Prison* (New York: Vintage Books, 1979).
7. bell hooks, *Black Looks,* 266.
8. Barbara Kingsolver, *Pigs in Heaven: A Novel* (New York: HarperCollins, 1993), 139.
9. Mindy Stombler, "Fraternities." In *Encyclopedia on Men and Masculinities,* ed. Michael S. Kimmel and Any Aranson (Santa Barbara, CA: ABC-Clio Press, 2002), 17.

Defining Ourselves, Being Defined by Others

- What has been central to the development of your identity? In what ways do these articles resonate with your experiences?

- If you are female, what role have men played in your development? If you are male, what role have women played in your development?

- How are terms like *dyke* and *queer* used to describe lesbians? Do you see these terms as positive or negative?

- Can men be feminists?

 f u r t h e r   r e a d i n g s

Bordo, Susan. *Unbearable Weight: Feminism, Western Culture, and the Body.* Berkeley: University of California Press, 1993.

Findlen, Barbara, ed. *Listen Up: Voices from the Next Feminist Generation.* Seattle, WA: Seal Press, 2001.

Morrison, Toni. *The Bluest Eye.* New York: Pocket Books, 1970.

Steinem, Gloria. 1986. *Outrageous Acts and Everyday Rebellions.* New York: NAL, 1986.

Walker, Rebecca, ed. *To Be Real: Telling the Truth and Changing the Face of Feminism.* New York: Anchor Books, 1995.

West, Traci, *Wounds of the Spirit: Black Women, Violence, and Resistance Ethics.* New York: New York University Press, 1999.

part THREE

Contradictions: Theory and Activism

The articles in this section mention only a few of the contradictions people face when trying to reconcile the assertions of feminist theory and the reality they live every day. We do not pretend to have covered, or even mentioned, all issues remaining to be seriously engaged by feminism and feminist theory. Nor is this an attempt to document where change has been advocated but not achieved. Many disciplines in the academy have been little affected by the experience of women, and there are many ways in which women are still subordinate to men in our society. Issues of social class and aging have not been sufficiently explored by feminists. As mentioned in the introduction to this book, much remains to be done in reconciling American feminism with the situation facing women in other parts of the world, particularly those in the Southern Hemisphere. We do hope this final section will further discussions of these and other issues.

Shari Popen, author of the first article, is a professor whose critique of mainstream academics covers much more than women's studies. Here she argues that women's studies, as a discipline, has been co-opted by what she calls "academic capitalism," the result of which is the loss of the "revolutionary potential" of this field. In assuming a "curatorial role," women's studies simply *preserves* the past and, in the process, loses its critical role. Cynthia Moulds shares this critique and responds with a personal account of her experience as a women's studies professor. Her essay demonstrates the difficulty of overcoming the market culture in academia when students are not used to challenges to their ideas of what is appropriate in the classroom and what is expected of them outside.

The third article, by Camellia Phillips, speaks to the complicity of feminists in the domination of Native Americans through their failure to actively support Native American struggles for sovereignty and self-determination. Here she picks up on a statement by Pam Colorado, which asserts that "Nothing . . . in feminist theory addresses the fact of our colonization, or the wrongness of white women's stake in it." Phillips argues that feminists must come to grips with the contradiction that allows them to *assert* that their struggle is for "the liberation of all people," while ignoring, for the most part, the struggles of Native Americans.

Margaret Chapman points to another area where feminists have missed "some critical aspects of social justice" through, for the most part, the exclusion of men from the movement. In exploring this issue Chapman interviewed a male social activist who had been instrumental in promoting women's issues on the campus where both were students. The interview is printed as part of the article.

The final piece in this section is drawn from a much longer conversation among four social activists, each of whom has had a strong relationship to feminism but also been involved in many other social and political issues. They cover a wide range of topics, not always in linear fashion, ranging from the kind of activist environment they have "inherited" to the importance of history, the importance of recognizing that gender is a social construction, and the relationship between academic learning and social activism.

Shari Popen

The Advancing Curatorial Role of Women's Studies

Academic Feminism Under Academic Capitalism

"What worries me most is that this will indeed happen: you will graduate, marry, grow fat around your nerves of social responsibility, and moss over your sense of outrage. You will become responsible only to a life of material privilege paid for by other people's deprivation and the demeaning of your own spirit."[1] That quote is taken from an address that Nadine Gordimer gave to students in South Africa in 1971. Today we can read it into our own academic lives as feminists. In trying to rethink what we have compromised away for an activist women's studies program, I turned to Gordimer, whose words are written and spoken out of a finely tuned and active political consciousness. The great battle, it seems to me, facing feminists in the academy is the monumental effort to hold the line against the encroachment of academic capitalism. Arrogant in the logic that its terms must be followed, it has conducted a stealth assault on the social promise of our work as feminists. It has significantly reterritorialized the academy and shifted relationships of need, power, and geography within our collegial spaces. Adding to the frustrations, the discipline of women's studies, and

with it the politics of feminism considered more broadly, have not responded well to such shifting scales. We have grown fat around our nerves, as Gordimer warns.

Indeed, is there not something disturbing about intellectual work in the academy today? So many people, on and around campuses, are dissatisfied and repressed by the highly administered capitalist organization of knowledge. For many of us, it feels as if the air has been sucked out of our colleges. Fields of study and disciplines are laying claim to what's left of their intellectual authority and professional significance by aligning themselves in various ways with academic capitalism. Or, weary of what seems increasingly quixotic, we more and more look to our personal lives outside the academy for meaning and richness. I do not want to find fault with this shift, but to indicate the fault lines that it creates for feminism in the academy.

To look at publisher's catalogs and browse bookshelves, women's studies appears to be a very active and dynamic field. Likewise, professional organizations and journals continue to support scholarly work. Despite these signs of well-being, there is a growing sense that women's studies is in crisis. By many accounts, institutionalized feminism, understood as a political and ethical project, has lost its moorings. It has emerged in the university as a discipline but, as I will argue in this chapter, without its history, and therefore its promise, of confronting real issues. There is some discomfort in critiquing a space that has nourished so many of us and that has generated and sustained a serious theoretical critique of the injustices women face worldwide. Despite the sense of disloyalty that taking these ideas seriously conjures up, academic feminism deserves a new appraisal.

It will be the ongoing argument of this chapter that academic feminism, or women's studies, has claimed for itself a minor curatorial role, a scholasticism amidst the capitalist–consumer culture that has invaded and occupied every space of the modern university. Our cares, as guardians, shift to what can come in, rather than what can be taken out. This has already begun to occur across the academy, as practices and systems are distorted to conform more directly to market thinking. For women's studies, this amounts to a corruption of academic feminism and a loss of belief in its revolutionary potential.

Our failed collective vision, dangerously myopic, blinds us to the larger reality—the ruthless forces of global capitalism manifested as patriarchy on steroids. Global capitalism and its institutionalized forms in the academy are hypermasculine, highly planned, highly controlled wars of great reach and scale. To think that we in the academy are left relatively untouched or are smart enough not to be seduced is to miss the point, and the advertising. Corporate culture institutionalizes the ambiguity and arbitrariness of intellectual authenticity in multiple and subtle ways as life becomes the fiction and TV the reality—from the TV shows *Survivor* and *Who Wants to Be a Millionaire?* to the manufacture and technologies of everyday fear and consumerist

desires. As Michael W. Apple says, common sense is produced that makes it difficult for actors to see the ideological and material structures that organize the daily realities of life.[2] In such a context, it becomes illegitimate to ask troubling questions about the social and political purposes of academic projects and grant proposals.

Global capitalism in its current triumphalist phase is total, and totalizing, because it represents a profound erasure of memory. Our collective memories in this culture play out as if they were designed to furnish a theme park. We seek professional refuge in a language that is insulated from the instrumentalities of political–economic power. Called by its real name—finance capitalism—this form of capitalism has seamlessly merged with a commodified culturalism, in which relations of production are increasingly dematerialized, or mediated through abstract symbols. As we engage in an unapologetic embrace of academic commodification, we reduce our study, and hence our field of effect, to objects of consumption. According to Waters, material and power exchanges in the economic and political arenas are progressively becoming displaced by symbolic ones, that is, by relationships based on values, preferences, and tastes, rather than by material inequality and constraint.[3] Intellectual capital and critical literacies mean less and less as our careers are redefined and commodified by this prevailing, indeed neo-imperialist, culturalism.

Who or what do we become once we adopt the symbols and begin to speak the language of the capitalist–consumer discourse? The cultural practices they at once reflect and make possible mark or form our minds by habituating them to certain forms of attention, certain ways of thinking and conceiving of ourselves and the world. Such cultural redescriptions are not neutral.

They can supplant civic discourse, reshaping our characters and conduct. The two discourses are incompatible—the older language of republican civic virtue, public service, duties, and obligations that framed the promise of women's studies cannot be reconciled with the newer economic language of the market. And in the capitalist–consumer culture that has penetrated the university, this newer discourse, because its idiom seems straightforward and unpretentious, appears to have special authority. To intellectuals struggling to reclaim lost authority, this has a certain appeal. However normal, natural, and unexceptionable the discourse of markets and competition seems, it carries with it cultural understandings and practices that seep into how we understand what we are about as a society. Precisely because of its pervasive scope, we should all make ourselves more acutely aware of what is lost between the two discourses for women's studies. As market thinking becomes more central to the academy and seeks to displace an earlier culture, it is central to feminist thinking to see what it misses, marginalizes, trivializes, or undermines and destroys. To redescribe education in the language of the market is not to speak in a normatively neutral or innocent idiom. There are very real and problematic implications for intellectual authority and social action grounded in fundamental senses of fairness and justice.

Practicing feminisms in the cultural territory that has become academic capitalism risks leaving women's studies without a politics based in social justice and with a thin pedagogical belief that changing individual consciousness is an end in itself. The politics of identity that has taken hold among us has powerful effects. Our intellectual survival in this dystopian vision is reduced to a narrowed and individualized ca-

reerism. Dissidence is expressed through a turning away from the collective center, through pursuing local or even self-autonomy rather than the politics of transforming society. Complicit with the logic of corporate culture, academic feminism no longer poses a serious threat of activist dissent to colleges intent on preserving the status quo and former entitlements. Those forms of dissent have been eroded largely from within by careerist impulses among us and the consensualist values of corporate culture. This is true of us as faculty and as students. My own undergraduate and graduate women show increasing signs of adopting "Stepford wife" conformities, intent less on what runs beneath than on the shiny surface of things. Indeed, diversity itself—the expression of different ideas, different views and ways of being—has not only been stylized but also commodified into a form of cultural tourism based on a notion of popular aesthetics and the arbitrariness of social forms. In its current state, dissent has become a mere annoyance to college administrators that can be controlled with the promise of professional capital—in the form of important committee or course assignments, conference support, promotion, and so on, or the threat of its reduction.

The problem for academic feminism, I suggest, is not only a methodological one. It is also a disciplinary one, driven perhaps by overspecialization or textualization on the one hand and a failure to confront, deal with, and broker the participation of the people studied. In a sense, events and circumstances have overtaken the need and the raison d'être of the discipline and its practices. While we may have been accused at an earlier time for naively aspiring to effect social transformation through raising consciousness, the contemporary movement is disquieting for the opposite reason. It reflects a resigned abandonment of social concern in the bid for professional status and individual recognition. Interdisciplinarity and public collaborations only mask this lack of ethical focus. And the larger shift from ethics to aesthetics only serves to ghettoize women's studies within broader social feminisms, narrowing our academic concepts to the formalistic and symbolic. This is essentially a subtle return to earlier scholasticisms, and our efforts at raising substantive inquiry have acquired as much worldly promise as questions about angels on the head of a pin.

To be fair, this is not entirely our fault. It must be granted that the history of women's studies has been animated by contradictions and divergent impulses. Likewise, universities are political and economic institutions, and as such they serve political and economic interests. Among other things, universities are traditional places and agents of social control. University scholarship has in many ways been an important source of the ideology that has not only produced but supported women's oppression. This newer form of academic capitalism is highly seductive in many ways. It engages a spirit of triumphalism that is generated by American expansion globally—economic, political, and cultural expansion. Indeed, buoyed by the smug ideology of social Darwinism, those who have triumphed need no longer listen. In their conceit, according to Joel Samoff, since they know what is right and since it is their power (rather than negotiation) that secures their interests, they can instruct rather than learn. As well, since the triumph, they believe, proves the correctness of their perspective, they need not feel reticent or guilty about telling others what to do.[4]

Corruptions, Complicities, and Contradictions

As intellectuals, we are not immune to, though perhaps we are more isolated than most from, cultural shifts. Perhaps in the long run this will be our lifeline, but it also contributes to our failure to see beyond the classroom or lab to the everyday practices of profit, and the current alignment of culture with global capitalism. Academic feminism must, if it is not to lose sight of its history, seek out the contradictions, complicities, and corruptions in its own academic project and in its conjunction with the corporate university. This requires that we reset the terms under which academic feminism is practiced and renegotiate the limits of our careers.

In the commodified academy feminism has experienced a series of fundamental and felt contradictions. Under-theorized and unresolved, they remain invisible and unchallenged. The historical orientation of academic feminism to social justice has been corrupted. It is increasingly difficult in our multiple isolations to look closely at how our own choices and decisions have cumulative consequences for university life as a whole. We have allowed ourselves to act largely in accordance with our own perceived self-interest, to grow fat around our nerves of social responsibility. Only when we let go of uncritical attachment to precepts that may have served women well in the past can we see that within the current framework, these precepts perpetuate profound social inequities.

Feminists in the academy are likewise not immune from the broader fundamental problems that concern the viability of intellectuals as a social group. The distinctions that we make in theory and in principle are not always very helpful in practice. Women's studies, too, is caught up in the changing function of intellectuals. This is not to make a simplistic populist argument but to claim that our field is increasingly characterized by excessive intellectualism and reliance on insider jargon. In our attempts to negotiate our intellectual spaces, we are having great difficulty in finding an appropriate critical framework. At the heart of women's studies is the founding idea that real social knowledge would weaken and erode prejudice. The crisis of confidence that is growing in our ranks has undermined our confidence that our social knowledge can chart, with any authority, the structures of material reality. As we scramble to regain our footing, it seems likely that the field is being reconstituted to preserve the interpretive and authoritative scope of a form of textual analysis. The textualism that is privileged in this move is a form of neo-scholasticism, an advancing curatorial role for women's studies in the modern university, which significantly reduces its politics. In saying this, I do not want to raise questions about particular schools of thought or theoretical models within women's studies, but rather to position the field more broadly against institutional changes.

And finally, I worry about the toll that these complicities and contradictions in the contested space between academic feminism and academic capitalism are taking on our bodies. Not merely the bodies of research and practices that are women's studies, but in this precarious self-exile, our embodied selves. Indeed, as we feel our more outspoken views become increasingly censored, we can recognize that the chilly climate for women on campus, no longer a matter of idiosyncratic intention, is now systematic. Despite administrative rhetoric to the contrary, and perhaps despite the increased numbers of women on campus, women's lives in the corporate university are lived largely in fear, silence, and isolation. And this after thirty-plus years of women's studies programs.

To live with these contradictions and a corresponding loss of collective vision is to live with the consciousness that we are betraying women and censoring ourselves. Speaking our minds is always embodied, and silencing those embodied minds attacks both mind and body. According to a recent article in the *New York Times,* autoimmune diseases, in which the immune system attacks the body's own tissues, strike women far more often than men, and minorities far more often than the dominant White and heterosexual culture.[5] The numbers are staggering and cannot be denied, nor are they attributed solely to genetics. If postfeminism fails to record these ratios as evidence of women and minorities silenced, reduced from the fullness of our humanity, it must content itself with those who marvel at the emperor's new clothes.

For our purposes here, the logic of this shift in the university can be analyzed by paying attention to three corruptions[6] that paralyze feminists as social actors and distract us from our historical purpose. Together they amount to a form of transcendence, or flight from our history and from material feminism. First, the spirit of triumphalism that propels this emerging form of capitalism more broadly brings with it the delegitimization of dissent. This puts at risk any form of women's studies that is itself dissenting. Second, the shift in global economics is increasingly total and totalizing, capturing our social institutions in its mandate. Under this form of unregulated capitalism, the private realm and private interests or individual differences are elevated over the public, and over public matters and different ideas. Feminism, historically responsible to public matters and the political representation of people, is itself privatized. And third, aligned with the first two, but probably the least noticed and most controversial shift, is the expanding valorization of epistemology among the disciplines. This has led to privileging the individual and dangerously relativizing knowledge and truth. Under the sign of an individualizing epistemology, feminism loses its essential public ethic. Posing among the increasingly clinical social sciences and humanities, themselves undergoing a behavioral revolution, academic feminism too is reduced to an abstraction by pure theory or technique.

The university has become a new kind of community, one of acquisition and consumption, of special interests and investment. This is more than a difference of scale. It is a new phase of capitalism in which market finance has invaded and reterritorialized every material and symbolic space. There is little left of the ideas of the community based on propinquity or the common good left in the commodified university. This is expressed in the changing nature of academic work, a turning inward toward private scholarships and the acquisition of, in Pierre Bourdieu's words, symbolic capital, of which tenure is the most prized. Publication, teaching, and program or course development have now been thoroughly commodified and subsumed within a political economy of production, even bio-production. Captured within this logic we can see the emergence of the commercialization of coursework, disputes over intellectual property rights and research patents, the discourses of outcomes, and cost and return analysis.

The consumerist model that currently is remapping the academy appeals to people who are affluent or who have achieved some means of affluence or capital in the academy. It also appeals to those who have substituted the narrower model of rights for a sense of responsibility for the common good. The model of consumerism elevates the discourse of individual choice—including the choice of research topics, areas of scholarship, and course construction—to an ultimate value, an entitlement, an individual right to be protected against erosion. In the pervasive climate of social Darwinism that has deeply penetrated not only social life, but social institutions, what is conveniently ignored is how individual gains from working the system inevitably come at the expense of others.

Against this model, people are systematically rendered invisible and disposable, excluded because they lack the resources to purchase goods and services. Sustaining this tension, this delicate balance of rights and responsibilities, and restoring people to social space, is not exclusively a feminist problem. But because feminism as a social movement has sought justice and equity, it is a problem for feminists. If we want feminism to move beyond individual self-interest and to restore its power—and danger—as a social movement, it may require accepting some degree of inconvenience or restriction on choice as academics.

Secondly, the triumph of consumer society is a triumph of all private matters over all public matters. American society and its public institutions seem caught in a form of insular individualism that avoids acrimonious and unpopular public discussion by relegating many ethical and political issues to the status of individual choice. Following Dolores Hayden's history of domestic feminism,[7] it is possible to analyze how universities have themselves adopted the isolating model of a suburban ideal, separating public from private spheres and rendering it difficult to combine collective interests. For many of us, these academic jobs have become our dream houses, increasingly isolating us and rendering us more susceptible to advertising and mass media trends. There is little solace in retreating to some form of purity, outside the economic arena. That is wrongheaded. It hinges on a view that we can decontaminate women's studies, but in fact it serves only to further enmesh us in the conservative restoration of a romanticized vision of purity and health. The university is being actively redesigned to sustain the technologies and relations of surveillance and domination. Accompanied by a renewed familial notion of domestic harmony in university affairs, these academic jobs that house our teaching and scholarship serve to buttress these patriarchal oppressions and to mediate or obscure the contradictions inherent in academic capitalism for feminism. Audre Lorde's warning has gone unheeded. We are using "the Master's tools" to design and rebuild our academic houses.

If the project of feminism, as a social movement, is in the end the production and sustainability of political public spheres, that project depends, I argue, on the cultivation of an intermediate ethical practice that must take into account this individualized status but also go beyond it. We must ask hard questions and accept responsibility for making hard decisions about who gets what and at whose expense. As David Trend cautions, this emphasis on individual rather than collective voice is part of a long history of intellectual conceit in which self-selected activist authorities presume to tell the masses what to think.[8] It reflects a lingering vanguardism, Trend believes, and contributes to

the commodification and sale of otherness to mass audiences.[9] That drains the public realm of political possibility and empties academic feminism of its powerful activist impulse.

And third, legitimating the technologies of the commodified university is the valorization of an individualizing epistemology. This shift is accompanied in part by privileging process, theories of learning or knowing, and the self as individual. Rather than defining the end of education in purposive terms, it is conceived instrumentally as the functional product of the process of learning, as the individual acquisition of information and skills. These epistemologies also function to validate the curatorial role by reinforcing inquiries dedicated to privileging questions of who knows and speaks, rather than inquiries that challenge systems and structures more directly, what is or exists. This discourse has become so dominant among us, and our scholarship and practices so embedded in it, that we have buried the memory of what it replaced—almost.

To our credit, the contemporary reflexive turn within women's studies has engendered a necessary self-critique, acknowledging that there is no single or overarching public interest to represent, but only diverse and contested interests that do not all have equal voice. This holds potential for ending past colonialisms and imperial practices as well as challenging more recent neo-imperialisms and neo-colonialisms. The positive side of this sensibility signals more humility and less dogmatism. But the darker side of this critique, the postmodern celebration of dissonance for its own sake, is paradoxically a form of consensualism. It has rendered ethics as well as visionary thinking problematic, thus discouraging political engagement. Coupled with the increased isolation that accompanies the epistemological model of possessive individualism and the faculty job as dream house, this becomes a retreat from a public politics that can turn into cynicism, and more dangerously, despair—a loss of faith in working collectively toward a better world.

One can without too much trouble catalog the weakened state of women's studies programs on campuses, the mounting suppression and censorship. It is no secret that gender discrimination against women in the academy is rising, as is discrimination against women beyond the university generally. This is evidenced by widening salary gaps, broadened inequities in ranks, and the slowed advancement rate for women. The workforce itself is being feminized, or domesticated, and parallels the new international divisions of labor.[10] The bottom ranks of faculty are increasingly being filled with women and minorities at lower salaries, at a time in which tenure itself is being threatened. Partnered with these shifts is the rapid casualization of the workforce, which includes the rise of adjunct or part-time faculty and graduate students working at poverty level, with no benefits or retirement plans, on a just-in-time basis.

There is also an expressed consciousness that feminism, having accomplished its task as a movement, is over. In the current era of conservative restoration, this can be a dangerous idea. It not only works to provide a justification for the enhanced careerist impulse among us but also to lend credibility to more socially conservative positions that run against the grain of feminist projects. We have, according to this view, entered a postfeminist era, one in which women are free to choose among greater life options. I do not want to deny the progress that has been made and the hard work that many of us did to move women forward in the world. But it is important to view that progress against the context of a conservative restoration that is boldly remapping the spaces of what is possible for many of us. The current rhetoric of back to basics and neotraditionalisms return women to a world in which we are increasingly experiencing emotional and material backlash, in which the rhetoric of choice camouflages the difficult ethical and political judgments that we daily face. In this "Alice in Wonderland" context, in which things are not as they seem, one can only conclude that the earlier promise of a liberatory, feminist women's studies has fallen dramatically short.

Likewise, many of us in the academy are struggling with our roles and responsibilities as intellectuals, teachers, and feminists. Driven by an anxiety that we are endlessly recycling theoretical debates, there is a growing disquiet that women's studies itself has been colonized from within. This raises a fundamental contradiction for feminism in the academy—one that is all too evident in our departments and classes and at professional gatherings. We claim a special empathy for, an understanding of, and an ethical relationship with the people whose life circumstances we study and for whom we claim some advocacy. Yet if we are so close to the people and communities struggling against systemic poverty and for freedoms of self-representation, these people should be flocking to us for knowledge, wisdom, insight. They—the women on the ground beyond the academy—should be coming to our meetings, enrolling in our courses, reading our books, and even joining our ranks. In the United States this is not happening. The participation of the studied is stunningly low and expresses no confidence in the activities and knowledge of university-based feminism.

Add to this the ways in which colleges and universities are increasingly being put out of reach for minorities by the combined forces of academic capitalism and the conservative restoration—the shutting down of affirmative action programs, raising of tuitions, emphasis on high-stakes testing that disproportionately disadvantages minority students. Indeed the moral currency of civil rights language itself is under broad attack. We may be developing a disconnection from many local and informed feminist activists and the bulk of the people who are dissatisfied with the status quo but disenfranchised from any political process and inactive. Some of us have developed our own supportive subcultures on campuses and find colleagues more frequently in the academic diaspora that is becoming our intellectual network, but in doing so we have lost touch with others who then become long-distance spectators. Increasingly feminists and allies on college campuses, as compared to women in the community, look entirely different, have different tastes and preferences, and talk differently about different things. Academic feminists often live in university neighborhoods or enclaves and are largely insulated from, rather than immersed in, the larger population and the everyday practices and concerns of women beyond the academy.

Even more crippling is that instead of responding to this situation and finding ways to bring new life and vitality through inclusion, our disciplines and scholars seem increasingly intent on defending diminishing careers, privileges, and academic turf. Many of us too are tired, worn down by the Sisyphean nature of the struggle. Amidst this disquiet, a sense that a scholarly community is being lost, we seem to have lost our subject matter, vitality, and wisdom—even

risking our historical claim to a revolutionary sense of justice and freedom. And tragically, because we find ourselves a fragmented community of researchers, we find it harder to see such communities in others. Since our own discipline, subject matter, or field has become de-essentialized, we de-essentialize much of the social world around us. From this diminished view, we fail to see that others are standing on their own political feet and engaging directly with societal injustices that we have lost connection to. Feminism, in terms of its social effect, is by many accounts stronger on the ground outside than we have let it be inside the university. Scholasticism has penetrated women's studies, preparing the ground for the curatorial role we have constructed for ourselves.

A Modest Proposal

Feminism is a politics, and like all politics has its roots in a political movement. The women's liberation movement, an active force for social change since the late 1960s, has been historically charged with changing existing power relations between men and women in society. We must now face the genuine possibility that feminism in the academy has failed to fulfill its inherited revolutionary social promise and is in serious disrepair. Moreover, it is also possible that, because of dramatic shifts in the academy itself, academic feminism as a collective movement is unlikely to survive beyond its current careerist and curatorial impulses. Although perhaps not widely held, these apprehensions are not unfounded. Women's studies programs have never fit easily within the academy. But this points to a more thorough unsettling of the political in our time. Indeed, the recent spate of books with titles such as *Is Academic Feminism Dead?*[11] and *Femi-*

nist Amnesia[12] testify to a more generalized concern.

For some time now, as part of this reflexive turn, we have privileged discursive analyses and epistemologies. This I admit has been intellectually fun and in many ways provides a welcome therapeutic escape from depressing daily events. But perhaps we have chased this wild goose long enough, as Bonnie Zimmerman has warned.[13] It may be time to return our work to its essential tensions, those that continue to haunt our collective memories. In the end this may even provide a tonic that engages us politically and takes us beyond the current therapeutic and highly commodified practices. Significantly, I look to that stronger tonic to restore wisdom to our bodies of scholarship and our embodied selves to health.

Women's studies programs (as part of social movements) find themselves in turmoil. The dilemma is not just one of scale or communication, although they contribute substantially to what is put at stake. It is also one of authority—partly and honestly, a problem of our own making. The human sciences and humanities as disciplines have gone a long way to undercut their own legitimacy and worth in everyday social lives within and beyond the academy. Under the guise of rethinking modernism and the master narratives, we have conspicuously ceased to talk about structure at all, instead openly embracing a stylistic rhetoric and a hegemonic semiological approach to criticism. We are having a wonderful time rearranging the deck chairs on the *Titanic.*

Michael Apple, in his analysis of the politics of official knowledge, has lamented that we have been too concerned with our elegant abstractions and have forgotten about the connections we have to make with real life. For too many of us,

Apple says, our only political work is writing for other theorists.[14] Cultural scholars and women's studies scholars in particular have rightly, I believe, displaced an objectivist, scientific, or positivist ethnography. But too often the findings are celebrated for telling more about the author (and her own society) than about the people we might seek solidarity with beyond the academy. We have become a bit too narcissistic. This is an unintended consequence of a critique that rightly examined the questions of what constituted knowledge, and who had the authority to speak. That critique seemed a healthy corrective to more imperial, ethnocentric approaches, but the result has gone astray.

In our rush to see everything in discursive terms, Apple cautions, we are forgetting to focus on *material* conditions. Although, he says, "discourse *does* have its own materiality, I think there are very real dangers, as well as benefits, of seeing the world as only a text. I am not being a class essentialist or economic reductionist here. However, *living under capitalism means something, and I believe this should not be forgotten"*[15] (italics mine). That academic feminism has been territorialized and remapped by academic capitalism must not be forgotten.

Apple's words speak to the dilemma for feminism and betray its alienation from practice. I agree with Lynda Stone that we need to pay attention to a form of discrimination in higher education that contributes to the failure of academic feminism to connect with real life: "the devaluing that feminists in professional schools feel from their academic sisters. . . . Moreover, almost no (or very few) education feminists and academic feminists work together."[16] This division, I believe, not only further estranges us but also helps sever practice from theory. And it makes it harder for us to see more generally how education as a field has developed historically and philosophically. Education feminists, as Stone claims, are devalued as applied scholars in a university that valorizes pure research, significantly silencing a critical analysis of education, pedagogy, and power. What could be brought forward from educational feminists, and educational theorists generally, is effectively dismissed. By addressing this academic estrangement, we may also find reasons and ways to breach the estrangement between academic feminism and women beyond the academy.

Edward Said has observed that this progressive withdrawal from asking questions and assuming responsibility in a world in which knowledge is increasingly specialized and fragmented disallows any radical or effective engagement with general issues. Gordimer's concern about lives lived out in pursuit of material privilege is realized. Increasingly in this academic culture, we are working under no illusions that what we do theoretically is truthful or has meaning that reaches to a larger world. We have to ask to what extent theory itself is a mask for personal ambitions and thus an accomplice to academic capitalism.

On what terrain might contestation and feminist alternatives emerge? The nature of that site and that struggle is by no means clear. What is clear is the impossibility of traditional forms of struggle. The new imperial power not only is resistant to the old weapons, but it actually thrives on them. They have become immanent in its disciplinary forms. We have to ask, then, what does it mean to take an oppositional position today? New types of resistance or forms of political action will have to be found to challenge

the new dimensions of sovereignty. We need a much stronger, collective form of scholarship if our findings are to stand up under the scrutiny of audiences who can seriously think about and use our work.

There is nothing inevitable or inexorable about the triumph of the neoliberal academy. We have to stop being so frightened or seduced by its mechanisms that we are complicit, in retreat, or do nothing. Nor must we allow ourselves to be seduced by a negative politics—of fear, rejection, and withdrawal. Our feminist priority, I suggest, is to critique those disciplinary forms of power and conflict that have emerged in the neoliberal academy and begin to construct new forms of resistance. It is also incumbent upon us to challenge our own domestication or complacency in the midst of those forms and our complicity with them. And we also have to recognize and analyze the failure of feminism as an identity politics and the ways it furthers neoliberal powers and incapacitates our political efforts.

It is only possible from here to point to openings. It will be important for us to integrate research more thoroughly with education, public service, and planning. That means becoming and sustaining more worldly scholars who can understand their own work—from lectures to ethnographies to publications—as itself a form of cultural presentation. We have to help expand the ability of people—regular people, common people, people at the grassroots—to create, debate, and manipulate their own sociocultural circumstances. Knowledge of any kind should be used in the real world, where it can be tested in the crucible of action and where one's own actions can themselves become the objects of theoretical reflection. According to David Trend, it will mean redefining the very territory and terms of activism. It will involve changes in the definition of political intervention and where it can occur.[17]

Samuel Delany has developed a distinction between contact and networking that is helpful here.[18] Networking situations, he says, start by gathering a population with the same or relatively similar needs. A publicly engaged feminism must seek out contact, which is random, the gift of human variety. Contemporary society fears contact, and mass media help construct those fears and panics. Indeed, the gated community that the commodified university has become mitigates against contact and paves the way for academic forms of communitarianisms that cushion the university and make it impervious to stronger feminist challenges. The practices of the university and its systems of rewards or symbolic capital are designed for networking, not contact. It is incumbent upon us to make alliances with those who point to the weaknesses and failures of the administered academy, and especially for academic feminists, the highly administered academy.

For Jane Jacobs, responding to the politics of colonialism and postcolonialism meant that one's speaking must be measured by a responsibility to anticolonial politics.[19] We cannot be a preserve of the elite nor succumb to the seductions and competitions of the capitalist–corporatist shift in the academy. To do so leaves us with impoverished and taut spaces within which to study and teach. It gives us a narrow curatorial role over women's studies—attention to what can be brought IN, not what can be taken OUT. Careers as curators can be erected in the corporatized academy, but at the expense of the more principled and emancipatory responsibility that women's studies has historically charged itself

with. We have to teach *as if* we have nothing to lose except our fear. For in that is not only resistance, but freedom.

NOTES

1. Nadine Gordimer, *The Essential Gesture: Writing, Politics, and Places* (New York: Penguin Books, 1989), 96–97.
2. Michael W. Apple, *Official Knowledge: Democratic Education in a Conservative Age,* 2nd ed. (New York: Routledge, 2000), xxi.
3. Malcolm Waters, *Globalization* (New York: Routledge, 1995), 124.
4. Joel Samoff, "Institutionalizing International Influence." In *Comparative Education: The Dialectic of the Global and the Local,* ed. Robert F. Arnove and Carlos Alberto Torres (Lanham, MD: Rowman and Littlefield, 1999), 57.
5. Natalie Angier, "Researchers Piecing Together Autoimmune Disease Puzzle," *The New York Times* (June 19, 2001), sec. F, p. 1, col. 3.
6. I take the use of the term *corruptions* from Michael Hardt and Antonio Negri's book *Empire* (Harvard University Press, 2000). For Hardt and Negri, *corruption* is the pure exercise of command, without any proportionate or adequate reference to the world of life (p. 391).
7. Dolores Hayden, *The Grand Domestic Revolution* (Cambridge, MA: MIT Press, 1981).
8. David Trend, *The Crisis of Meaning in Culture and Education* (St. Paul: University of Minnesota Press, 1995), 126.
9. Ibid., 127.
10. For an excellent analysis of the feminization of labor, see Mechthild U. Hart, *Working and Educating for Life: Feminist and International Perspectives on Adult Education* (New York: Routledge, 1992).
11. *Is Academic Feminism Dead? Theory in Practice,* ed. by the Social Justice Group at the Center for Advanced Feminist Studies, University of Minnesota (New York: New York University Press, 2000).

12. Jean Curthoys, *Feminist Amnesia: The Wake of Women's Liberation* (New York: Routledge, 1997).

13. Bonnie Zimmerman's comment was made during a plenary session at the conference *The Future of Women's Studies: Foundations, Interrogations, Politics,* held at the University of Arizona, October 2–21, 2000. A much shorter version of this chapter was presented at that conference.

14. Michael W. Apple, *Official Knowledge,* 167.

15. Ibid., 171.

16. Lynda Stone, ed., *The Education Feminism Reader* (New York: Routledge, 1994), 2.

17. David Trend, *The Crisis of Meaning,* 128.

18. Samuel R. Delany, "A . . . Three, Two, One, Contact: Times Square Red, 1998." In *Giving Ground: The Politics of Propinquity,* ed. Joan Copjec and Michael Sorkin (London: Verso, 1999).

19. Jane M. Jacobs, *Edge of Empire: Postcolonialism and the City* (New York: Routledge, 1996), 8.

Cynthia M. Moulds

Feminist Approaches to Social Justice: Activism and Resistance in the Women's Studies Classroom

"Learning about feminist theory's assumption of activism requires a social and public act [in the curriculum]."

—Cynthia K. Drenovsky, 1999[1]

"To learn ideas that run counter to values and beliefs learned at home is to place oneself at risk, to enter the danger zone."

—bell hooks, 1994[2]

"Knowing and not doing are equal to not knowing at all."

—Fortune cookie[3]

Entering the Danger Zone

Okay, so I'm naive. On the first day of class on my first day of teaching Introduction to Women's Studies, I handed out a survey in an attempt to "break the ice" and pair students up to interview each other. In my rather blatant attempt at ascertaining what type of class this was going to be, I included the question "Do you consider yourself a feminist?" Out of a class of twenty-nine students, three said yes, three were unsure, and the other twenty-three said no. I went home depressed.

When I went looking for a feminist student group on campus, I didn't find one. When I went looking for a meeting of feminist faculty, there wasn't one. When I checked the campus calendar for discussion groups or brown bags on feminist pedagogy, there weren't any. I went home depressed.

When I introduced the Community Action Project, in which students would have a chance to see the reality of our communities dealing with some of the issues we were going to talk about in class, they looked at me with blank stares. A student asked, "Do you mean we have to do volunteer work?" Groan. "Forced activism?" More groans. "What? Do work outside the classroom?" Gee, I thought they would get excited about the idea. Okay, I was naive. I went home depressed.

My Own Story

When I graduated in 1983 with a bachelor's degree in business management, I swore never to set foot on a campus again! I was in culture shock about the state of the real world and how little my college career had prepared me for it. I had nightmares that I had never received my diploma after all, and the bills coming in from the federal government, asking me to pay back my student loans, were a cruel joke. I later realized that the crux of my disillusionment was the belief that academia had no connection to the real world.

Here I am, almost twenty years later, a teacher with a master's degree and my foot in the door to obtaining a Ph.D.! What gives? As Gloria Steinem and Jane Roland Martin state, "I [now] believe that it is critical to bridge the great gulf between those who search for knowledge and those who wish to improve society."[4] My activism with regard to access to educational and financial resources for women, breast cancer education, and international politics and development led me right back to academia. Where else could I combine my community activism with the continual need for intellectual stimulation and gained knowledge but women's studies? I mistakenly thought I could "have my cake and eat it too." Yes, I teach women's studies at a midsize liberal arts college. Yes, I love it. Yes, I attempt to bridge the gap between academia and the community. And yes, I bring awareness to students who do not understand feminism. But

I find myself in a place where many other women in academia reside: part-time, adjunct, unheard, and underpaid. As one of the other professors labeled me, I am "an ad-hoc, adjunct instructor with no clout!" I am also very good at my job, have twenty years of feminist activity under my belt, and have consistently received outstanding student evaluations. The quandary lies in attempting to work within a political institution where patriarchy, hierarchy, elitist language, and the "right" credentials are thought to be essential. But alas, I persevere! I believe in the potential of women's studies to transgress boundaries and transform institutions even though, as Sheri Popen says in the previous essay, "women's studies has never fit easily within the academy." Neither do I!

At one point in my illustrious career as a women's studies instructor, I was also the program assistant to the director of women's studies. During this period I collaborated with faculty, staff, and students in developing curricular activities; supervised senior projects, internships, and independent studies; maintained records and budget files; arranged and conducted women's studies faculty, advisory, and curriculum committee meetings; planned the women's studies student colloquium; arranged for and promoted guest speakers; and established a feminist collective on campus. When the position of director of women's studies opened, I attempted to apply. I was locked out. I could fulfill all the requirements except "must be tenure or tenure-track Ph.D. faculty." By the way, our women's studies program does not have any faculty positions, tenured or not. Even if I had my Ph.D. at the time, I could not have been hired! Most of our women's studies faculty reside in other disciplines. The one place in our institution of higher education where I thought the rules could be bent, the one group of colleagues I thought would look beyond the hierarchical structure, the one place where I thought I would be evaluated by my experience because it was relevant and appropriate for the position ignored me, rendering me invisible. It seemed so antifeminist!

My own resistance and concerns as to the position of feminism and women's studies in academia, along with the essay by Shari Popen, pose some of the challenges faced by feminist academics. How do we work toward feminist social change, given who we are, who our students are, and the academic and community institutions within which we work?

The Link Between Women's Studies and Activism

When women's studies first hit campuses in the 1970s the link between academia and activism, due to the women's liberation movement, was strong and obvious. It now seems women's studies has been absorbed into the institutional box of academia and has lost much of its vigor, reflecting a general shift from the political to the sociopsychological and academic. Have we gotten off track? Women's studies seems to have marginalized activism in the classroom. Whereas the initial classes of women's studies were politically charged, radical, and controversial, today's classes often ignore the individual voice and lived experiences of their students. "In turning female and male members alike from the lived experiences of real people in the real world, and especially from society's desperately urgent problems, the academy creates a brain drain within the culture at large," states Jane Roland Martin, Ph.D., author of *Coming of Age in Aca-*

deme.[5] Most students seem "blinded by women's token advances," thinking equality has been reached and they can do "whatever they want" without barriers based on their gender.[6] However, in all the women's studies courses I have taught, some students end up talking about their lived experiences (which I encourage) and realize they have suffered sexual harassment, dealt with body image problems, known victims of domestic violence, seen their brothers earn more money in summer jobs than themselves, experienced the chilly classroom, been date-raped, and have indeed been discriminated against because they are women. I believe in order to examine the political and transformative nature of feminism, students in women's studies, and in academia at large, must turn questions of inequity into activist practice by applying feminist knowledge to social change in the community. Feminist pedagogy promotes diversity, voice, collaboration, and community-based learning— components suggested in the improvement of education, yet its potential contribution goes unacknowledged. As prominent mainstream magazines ask, "Is feminism dead?" and affirmative action is falling to the wayside, young women are afraid of the "f" word, reproductive rights are coming under attack (again), and fundamentalism and conservatism are on the rise, it is imperative that women's studies maintain its hold (although precarious) on the critical role of bridging the gap between theory and practice. What does it all mean?

One of the many challenges inherent in women's studies is defining the terms *feminism, feminist,* and *feminist activism.* One student, on the first day of Introduction to Women's Studies, lamented, "I didn't know this was going to be about feminism!" Another challenged, "Are you a man-hating lesbian?" Another, "I thought we were going to celebrate women artists." There are diverse definitions and misconceptions. For purposes of this chapter, I choose to use the definitions posed in the introduction of this book: "Feminism is the belief that the female perspective and experience are both legitimate and illuminating of human experience and that to marginalize this part of the human experience is to construct a false picture of the world as a whole. . . . A *feminist* believes that women's experience, historically and cross-culturally, is illuminating of all human experience; believes and acts on the idea that women's experience has been violated, undervalued, negated, and often trivialized and laughed at; and whose philosophy of life includes the idea of emancipation for all people whose lives have been so defined."

I turn to the *Dictionary of Feminist Theory* for a definition of *activism:* "*Feminist activism* is action for social change that encourages political or symbolic activities which can directly challenge women's oppression and the social constructions of gender. Generally, feminist activism precedes the creation of feminist theory but is subsequently strengthened and renewed by theory."[7]

One of our first exercises in the Introduction to Women's Studies course is to ascertain what stereotypes, misconceptions, and definitions the students themselves have for the terms *feminism* and *feminist*. It is indeed a scary place to go! The opponents of feminism have done an excellent job of ambushing the term, and the often-hostile responses include "femi-nazi, man-hater, bra-burner, anti-family, lesbian, and a hater of children," to name a few. Usually this prompts me to introduce the article by Lisa Maria Hogeland, "Fear of Feminism: Why Young Women Get

the Willies," which says, "Feminism asks questions—difficult and complicated questions, often with contradictory and confusing answers—about how gender consciousness can be used both for and against women. . . . fear of feminism, then, is not a fear of gender but a fear of politics. . . . the fear of political reprisals is very realistic. . . . there are powerful interests opposed to feminism. Women have real reasons to fear feminism and we do young women no service if we suggest . . . that feminism itself is safe. It is not."[8]

How then do we incorporate activism into women's studies courses, considering the challenges, resistance, and fear?

The Community Action Project: Students as Social Activists

Regardless of students' individual relationships to the words *feminism* and *activism,* women's studies aims to empower them to see themselves as agents capable of acting together with others to build coalitions, foster public awareness, and create social change. A primary objective in feminist education is enabling women and men to see and understand the important connections between what is studied in the classroom and the lives of women outside the educational setting. What are the manifestations of the oppression of women in our communities? What are the ramifications of our society's designating women and things associated with women as inferior, of lesser value? Feminist theory developed out of the need for changes, and women's studies is largely about activism and advocacy. Unlike other theories, social activity and advocacy are basic assumptions of feminist theory. Feminist theory is a body of writing that attempts to describe, explain, and analyze the conditions of women's lives . . . and also proposes strategies for action to improve the conditions in which women work and live.

I believe women's studies cannot be adequately taught without a community action component, without an attempt at self-examination and political commitment. Numerous departments offer opportunities for internships, service learning projects, or community action projects, so what is the difference in women's studies? Although some internships may have a political emphasis, the difference between an internship outside of women's studies and a community action project within women's studies is the politically gendered aspect. We look at activities that are specifically geared toward eliminating oppression against women, those that question the existing social constructions of gender, class, race, and sexual orientation and attempt to change the structure of society—all through women's lived experiences. Service learning projects, quite prevalent at our university, do involve interacting with community, reflecting on the experience, and putting theory into practice. However, most service learning projects do not look at the underlying socially constructed stratifications perpetuated according to gender, class, race, and sexuality. The term *service* itself carries the connotation of providing service to those less fortunate, a missionary expedition if you will, while visions of servile women dance through one's head! Service learning does not ask the question How and why are most of these people less fortunate than I? Nor does it look at power relations and social location as factors. When asked to do a community action project from a feminist perspective, the class first discusses "situated knowledge," re-

flecting on their place in the world. We discuss gender, class, race, sexuality, and other areas of difference. What preconceived notions do students have? How have their lived experiences influenced their ideologies? How does their privilege color their views of the world? Where do they sit on the hierarchy of gender, class, race, and sexuality? What prisms do they see through? We talk about how feminist theory and feminist methodology recognize that the position of the researcher or activist *does* shape the research or action. A discussion on feminist methodology is included to emphasize that feminist research is research *for,* not *on,* women and is meant to challenge the masculinist perspective inherent in most organizations, polities, and issues they will approach.

The logistics of doing an activism project in a ten-week course are daunting. However, I believe so strongly in my responsibility as a feminist teacher to expose students to social action from a feminist standpoint that the benefits outweigh the challenges. Often in the course of learning about women's oppression, students find themselves feeling depressed and hopeless, wondering "now that my eyes have been opened, what can I do about all this?" The course ends on a positive note, using successful examples of feminist activism that have made a difference. Students also channel what they are learning into some type of activism throughout the term, hopefully reducing those feelings of frustration. Students find that the classroom can be a place where one can build community, re-envision power, and act as a catalyst for social change.

"My community action project was *the* most important thing to me during the term because I actually felt like what I was doing made a difference." —Maria

"A light bulb went on in my head when I started to understand the dynamics of why women stay in abusive relationships. I had never thought about the cycle of abuse or why she may have been petrified to leave. I saw my aunt in a whole new light. I hope to volunteer at the shelter this summer."
—Bina

"By bringing the two guest speakers from The XXX Gender Group to class, I felt I was able to bring awareness to an otherwise taboo subject, that of transgendered people. It worked really well with the discussion on the social construction of gender!"
—Yvonne

Most students who have done a Community Action Project in our Introduction to Women's Studies course leave with a sense of empowerment, which is exactly what a women's studies classroom is all about. Students break the silence around women's issues, take charge of their education, and actively engage in learning. They see outside the classroom!

However, not everyone chooses to see . . .

Resistance

"I don't want to be empowered, just give me a reading pack!"[9]

When I introduce the Community Action Project in class, I am met with stares of confusion, furrowed brows, and actual groans; once someone walked out, never to be seen in a women's studies class again! The challenge with a ten-week course is to start the project early enough to provide adequate time to complete it, yet at the same time introduce the relationship between feminist theory and social activity and advocacy, without which the meaning of the project is lost. The Introduction to Women's Studies at our university is considered a "general university requirement" (GUR), and thus the composition of the class runs the gamut from the occasional diehard feminist to the "this will be an easy *A*" student to the antagonistic male. It makes for an interesting dynamic and precludes my lamenting that I'm preaching to the choir. It also makes for a largely apathetic group who is used to a rote, assembly-line approach to learning and uncomfortable with a classroom that differs in any way from the norm. They are used to a male model of teaching wherein the teacher is the expert and they are the mute, unknowing subjects. Many women are used to being passive in class, especially as undergraduates. Several students claim its volunteerism to be forced and believe "other" has no bearing on their life. The deconstruction of the system they are familiar and comfortable with is frightening, especially when it may reveal their own privilege. Another complaint I hear is that classrooms are not meant to be political; "colleges exist neither to indoctrinate activists nor to create saints."[10] Yet I remind them that feminism is meant to challenge the status quo, to ask troubling questions about the social and political forces behind women's oppression.

Resistance does not lie with the students alone. Several faculty feel these projects are not "academically rigorous enough," and if they do not include a fifteen-page paper or a test on the content, where's the merit? One professor went so far as to tell me not to give too many *A*'s or the course assignment may come into question (as if that would be the first time women's studies has been challenged!). Other external influences are also at work on today's campuses that are counterproductive to examining social and political issues. For a discussion on "academic commodification" see the preceding article by Shari Popen, who asserts, "The older language of republican civic virtue, public service, duties, and obligations that framed the promise of women's studies cannot be reconciled with the newer economic language of the market." On Western's campus we have seen the antifeminist Independent Women's Forum standing in Red Square next to the Pro-Lifers. Yes, believe it or not, *feminism* is still a dirty word, and activism conjures up visions of burning bras and hairy armpits.

The following examples of the Community Action Project experience contain quotations directly from the students involved; however, the names of people and organizations have been changed.

The Continuum Called Gender

Bridget came up to me after class and rather tentatively asked if she could change the topic of her Community Action Project. "I've been thinking about the part of the assignment where you mention we should "push our boundaries," "venture outside our comfort zones." I'd like to interview members of the Transgender Support Group. She blushed. "This would really push my levels of comfort, and although I am afraid, I want to take on this challenge. I think it will be good for me." To this day the individuals Bridget interviewed about transgender issues are guest speakers in the Introduction to Women's Studies course.

Bridget decided to look at how the transgender lifestyle appears to "fight societal condition-

ing of proper gender behavior." She decided she wanted to bring the transgender issue to our classroom. Three members of the group discussed with her classmates the social construction of gender and how gender is a continuum and not a binary concept. Donna spoke of her transition from a male to a female and how she was treated with less respect as a female than she had been as a male. Her partner Lee, a female transitioning to a male, was amazed at how much more attention his opinions received as a male. All the talking in the world on the social construction of gender could not have made the impact on the students that Donna and Lee made. Out of twenty-six evaluations at the end of the term, nineteen students mentioned the presentation given by the gender group as "really opening my eyes."

Radical Menstruation

When you visit our local co-op to buy tampons, don't be surprised to see a skull and crossbones on the boxes of those products that contain dioxin and are not made from organic cotton. Although I refuse to give up the names, I know who "defaced" those packages! Students decided to do something about an article I had brought into class about the dangers of dioxin to a women's body and how most mainstream tampon companies were using this chemical in their products. Tampons are made from cotton and rayon, which is commonly bleached with chlorine. This chlorine-bleaching process results in a toxic byproduct called dioxin, which has been called one of the most toxic substances ever created by humans. The students asked, "Why is it acceptable to have toxic substances in our feminine hygiene products?"

The first step for this project was research on the facts, after which one of the students designed a pamphlet called "Radical Menstruation," which she distributed in class, on campus, and in the community. She set up a table in the student center and the community co-op with information on dioxin in tampons, alternative products, and even a pattern for homemade non-bleached cotton pads.

Poetry for Peace

Using the spoken word as her weapon, Carrie performed for the class a selection of her poems dedicated to women who resisted war and advocated peace. She joined the local Peace Vigil on each Friday of the term to share her poetry with the community and talked in class of the "maleness" of war and the accepted idea of "collateral damage" and violence as a solution to conflict.

Dialing for Doulas

Brad, a large, robust man, was in front of the class, squatting to demonstrate one of the most natural positions for delivering a baby while being supported by his sister, who was a doula. When he handed in his community action project proposal, the last line read, "I also plan on compiling a journal of my thoughts as I take this journey, as it is one I am slightly scared to go on."

Brad decided to research natural birthing options in our community and compile a resource guide with names and information on doulas and midwives. I pointed out the need to look at the mainstream birthing process in our local hospital and to do some research on how far the process was removed from "natural" childbirth. He ended up talking about how women's positions in the delivery room are adjusted to accommodate the doctor and that if the

birthing is taking too long, the doctor will often call for a cesarean. He was able to make the connection between women's oppression and the birthing process. "I had no idea that something as natural as childbirth could be affected originally by male doctors' need for convenience. The statistics on cesareans in our local hospital was appalling up until just a few years ago."

Coming Out

Ruth wanted to help her friend. She decided to focus her energy "on the lesbian experience within the framework of our society." Her friend had "expressed her 'coming out' story with undertones of anger and uneasiness because of the animosity directed toward her by her parents, friends, and other classmates." Ruth interviewed members of the campus LGBTA (Lesbian Gay Bisexual Transgender Alliance), asking for their feelings on feminism, support in the community for LGBTA individuals, and the social construction of gender roles. "Because I was totally accepting of my friend's sexual preference, I was surprised that she received such negative responses to 'coming out.' There are so many feminist issues surrounding sexuality, and I had no idea that many lesbians originally felt left out of the feminist movement."

The Second Shift

"That phrase should strike fear into the hearts of women everywhere," said Robyn. Robyn had read *The Second Shift,* written by sociologist Arlie Russel Hochschild in the 1980s. The feminist movement liberated many women, especially white, middle-class women, to leave their homes and work. However, the workload inside the home did not then become a 50/50 split; thus the term "second shift." Robyn decided to sign up for a local parenting class to see if she could ascertain if in the year 2000 anything had changed. "By analyzing the information and guidance provided to parents and observing the general atmosphere of the class and instructor, I am curious to understand the expectations for both parents and how they differ."

The Day-Care Dilemma

As a single parent of two young children and a full-time student, Janet "was painfully aware of the lack of resources for adequate and affordable child care in the community." She proposed compiling a resource guide for mothers and fathers with the fees, scholarships, availability of care and resources available within each option. I pointed out that the lack of day care services nationwide is an implication of deep-rooted societal ideologies about working mothers and the business world's reluctance to accept the importance of child rearing and women's entrance into the workforce.

But I Want to Keep My Name

One of the international students in my class, a Korean feminist, proposed to two feminist organizations in the community and one student feminist organization on campus "to start a movement to keep the woman's last name after marriage or to use surnames of both parents." Soon Lee interviewed 123 people from campus and the community and asked, "Should women change their last name to the man's when she marries?" Of her random sample (admittedly subjects mostly in their twenties) 70 percent did not agree with the custom of changing a woman's last name after marriage. She then sent her findings to the feminist organizations she

had identified and proposed they start a movement!

Additional Comments from Student Evaluations

"This was the most challenging class I have taken at Western. I was very intimidated at first, but now I feel like 'one of the girls.'" —Rebecca, 2000

"I think it would be great if the class as a whole went out on campus and invited males to come to come to the class or if we simply tried to educate in Red Square [the center of campus, outdoors]." —Basu, 2001

"This class should be required for males to graduate!" Erin, 1999

"This project has changed my perspective on so many issues that I notice people's behavior more and how it affects others. I am also more confident in myself as a woman." —Angie, 2000

"It really is valuable to go out there and see what these issues entail. Textbooks and lectures only do so much. One thing I discovered is that I AM a feminist! I have this fire inside me that really wants to go out and make a difference." —Carrie, 2001

"We talked about the frustrations of the university and the system and about working 'in the field.' Well, the more I thought about it, I came to realize that this is the 'field' because this is your culture and what you are doing does do good and we might not see it right now, but we may do things differently in the future." —Jeff, 2000

Transformation Is Possible: The Ongoing Value of Student Activism

Each student submits a reflective piece at the end of the term, examining his or her assumptions and ethnocentricities around gender, race, class, and sexual orientation and attempts to deconstruct the Community Action Project to expose socially constructed systemic biases. We discuss the notion of forced volunteerism, voyeurism, observation versus activism, burdening the organizations or individuals, time constraints, feelings of misplaced pity on the part of some students, assumptions on both our parts, and so on. The Community Action Project offers students a self-conscious way to connect feminist theory to social problems, to expose social ills or issues, and to raise a little consciousness. A feminist perspective can inform all of society's urgent problems, especially those related to issues of gender equity, racism, homophobia, war, and globalization. One needs only to pick up a mainstream newspaper or a popular magazine, turn on the television, or peruse the Internet to find evidence of the urgency of these social ills. Here are some examples:

A report issued by the Research Organization Catalyst predicts that, if the small annual increase in the number of women sitting on Fortune 500 boards does not grow beyond its current rate, women will not achieve gender equity there until the year 2064.[11]

The United States is a "C" student when it comes to gender equity in education, according to the National Coalition of Women and Girls in Education.[12]

The House Constitution subcommittee held a hearing yesterday on the "Partial-Birth Abortion Ban Act of 2002" (HR 4965) that aims to outlaw or significantly chip away at a woman's right to choose a safe and legal medical procedure.[13]

U.S. House rejects Anti-Racism bill, 3/24/1999.

Gay and lesbian youth are two to three times more likely to commit suicide than other youths, and 30 percent of all completed youth suicides are related to the issue of sexual identity.[14]

Collectively, women lose over $100 billion annually in wages due to pay inequity. According to a recent study by the Institute for Women's Policy Research, a 25-year-old woman who works full time year-round for the next 40 years will earn $523,000 less than the average 25-year-old man, if current wage patterns continue.[15]

I feel a sense of urgency almost daily as I research issues surrounding women and ask, "Why can't the classroom be a place of activism?" What a perfect place to infuse concern, acts of defiance, and stronger bonds between students and their social and political environments. This is the essence of feminism.

Feminism challenges the notion that existing structures are the fixed reality of life and suggests that these structures and values are alterable, open to reconstruction and redefinition using a feminist lens.

Feminist scholars long have imagined alternatives to traditional bureaucratic government consonant with the insights gleaned from feminist research and women's organizational experiences. Unfortunately, reinventing government from a feminist perspective has not captured either policymakers' or citizens' attention. Even within the discipline of public administration, women's scholarship and experiences have remained largely on the periphery, with discussion limited to a narrow range of topics such as equal opportunity, affirmative action, comparable worth, and numerical representation in public bureaucracies. As Camilla Stivers notes, "feminist theory offer[s] new theories of power, virtue, of the nature of organization, and of leadership and professionalism. . . . Yet few if any of these ideas have made their way into conversations in public administration. . . . As it stands, feminist insights and women's experiences are no more a part of the "new governance" (entrepreneurial government) than they were a part of the old (bureaucratic government).[16]

"After all one could easily graduate, get a 'good job,' make some money, get a busy life, and live in a cloud of denial that there are social issues we as citizens need to do anything about. Besides, who has time?"[17]

Academia may be the only place where some students get a glimpse of activism. And, despite the initial reservations about these activist projects, it has been reaffirmed time and time again that, at least on the part of the students, they have been transformative.

"I am so glad I took this class, it has forever changed me."

"I listen, and I forget. I see, and I remember. I do, and I understand." —Akan saying.

Excerpt from Introduction to Women's Studies Syllabus

Your Community Action Project (CAP) Guidelines

A primary objective in feminist education is enabling women and men to see and understand the important connections between what is studied in the classroom and the lives of women outside the educational setting.

Feminist theory is a perspective that developed out of the need for changes, and women's studies is largely about activism and advocacy. Unlike most other theories, social activity and advocacy are basic assumptions of feminist theory.

The assignment (see examples below and your syllabus): Choose a topic relating to women's lives, and decide on an action project which makes the connection between the issue theoretically and the issue in the "real world." This project can involve a community agency, a campus group, or an action that you design yourself. *Change* is a keyword in this project; look at an agency, a person, or a project that has or is attempting to initiate social change. Or initiate the change yourself. The assignment also includes weekly progress reports and a reflective paper due with final presentation of your project. The goals of this assignment are as follows:

- To see the connection between the issues we have discussed in class and how these issues transition from classroom to community (connected learning).
- To see yourself as an agent of change.
- To understand the feminist notion that "the personal is the political."
- To help alleviate the frustration that may arise when discussing the issues behind

women's oppression in the classroom. In other words, this assignment aims to combat the oft-asked question, "What can we do about any of this?"

Please follow these guidelines:

- Please be respectful: mindful of others' privacy, ensure confidentiality, respect busy schedules, be on time, and be professional.
- You may work alone or in a group.
- Discuss expectations and set reasonable goals.
- Apply general course themes: look at issues of power, privilege, difference and sameness, hierarchy, subordination, oppression, and socialization (gender, race, class, and sexuality processes). How do these play into your project?
- Examine your assumptions and ethnocentricities as you go.
- Watch your biases about your subject.
- Step outside your comfort zone.

Include a 3–5-page self-reflection paper on your experience that answers these questions:

- How did this project enhance your understanding of the course's theories, research, topics, and overall learning objectives?
- Did you see active confrontation of oppression; whether yes or no, how did this make you feel?
- Did any ethical issues come up for you?
- How do you "position yourself" within this project?
- Has this changed any of your previous notions, assumptions, and/or ideas?
- What confused you? surprised you? excited you? frustrated you?
- Did you learn any new skills?

- How did you see "feminism" in this project?
- What do you make of this assignment?

Present your Community Action Project in a suitable finished format, such as a portfolio, a performance piece, a journal, a three-dimensional display, and so on. Have something to show for your efforts. Here are some ideas and examples:

- Produce a student feminist newsletter.
- Develop an informative webpage on community resources that deal with women's issues.
- Produce a 'zine.
- Observe or interview community participants at an agency, discover its mission, its resources, its published materials, the clientele served, and so on. Present the information in a creative way, and do an analysis from a feminist perspective.
- Do an ethnography (literally, *ethnography* means "write about people") on a particular woman; document her life as a woman (maybe even as a feminist!) in a creative manner.
- Check out a local agency that supports and benefits women, and provide an informational compilation of their resources in a portfolio or other creative means of sharing the information.
- Educate the campus about a women's issue.
- Do a workshop for students (college, high school, grade school) or the community.
- Volunteer in a community agency.
- Work to increase the participation of women in politics, or work on a specific political policy affecting women.
- Interview an individual actively working to improve women's lives.

- Volunteer to provide shopping, gardening, or housework for an elderly woman, and interview her about the changing role of women in her lifetime.
- If you know someone who has been sexually assaulted or abused in some way, perhaps you could do the research for this person to provide some resources and to learn how to better handle the situation.
- If you're interested in education, you could visit a classroom and see if you notice differences in gender behavior and socialization.
- Observe/participate in YWCA programs or programs related to transgender issues, sexuality, sexual orientation, and so on.

Here are some issues to consider (this is not an exhaustive list):

Day care	Sexual harassment
Violence	Safety
Body image	Motherhood
Religion	Women and war
Media image	Title IX
Reproductive rights	Breast cancer
Gender construction	Women immigrants
Women and race	Sexual orientation
Welfare reform	Politics
Health issues	Eating disorders
Date rape	Women and work
AIDS	International issues
Domestic violence	Same-sex marriage
Self-esteem	Feminist organizing

NOTES

1. Cynthia K. Drenovsky, "The Advocacy Project on Women's Issues: A Method for Teaching and Practicing Feminist Theory in an Introductory Women's Studies Course," *Women Studies Quarterly,* 27, 3–4 (fall/winter 1999).

2. bell hooks, *Teaching to Transgress* (New York: Routledge, 1994).

3. Ellen Messer–Davidow, *Disciplining Feminism: From Social Activism to Academic Discourse* (Durham, NC: Duke University Press, 2002). Messer-Davidow used as an introductory quote a fortune cookie from Vina's café.

4. Gloria Steinem, In *Coming of Age in Academe: Rekindling Women's Hopes and Reforming the Academy,* ed. Jane Roland Martin (New York: Routledge, 2000), x.

5. Ibid.

6. Ibid.

7. Maggie Humm, *The Dictionary of Feminist Theory* (Columbus, OH: Ohio State University Press, 1995), 3.

8. Lisa Maria Hogeland, "Fear of Feminism: Why Young Women get the Willies," *Ms.* (Nov./Dec. 1994): 18–21.

9. Gayle Letherby and Jen Marchbank, Voices in Gender and Education Conference, University of Warwick, March 1999.

10. Frank H. T. Rhodes, "A Battle Plan for Professors to Recapture the Curriculum," *The Chronicle of Higher Education* (Sept. 14, 2001): B7.

11. http://www.catalystwomen.org/research/overview.htm, accessed on 6/30/02.

12. http://www.ncwge.org, accessed on 6/30/97.

13. http://www.feminist.org/news/newsbyte/uswirestory.asp?id=4105, accessed on 6/20/97.

14. www.ama-assn.org/sci-pubs/msjama/articles/vol_282/no_13/jms90031.htm11k, accessed on 2/11/2003.

15. www.aflcio.org/yourjobeconomy/women/equalpay/about.cfm

16. DeLysa Burnier, "Reinventing Government from a Feminist Perspective: Feminist Theory, Women's Experiences, and Administrative Reality," presented at the Fourth Women's Policy Research Conference, Washington, D.C., June 3–4, 1994.

Margaret Vaughn Chapman
with Robin Elwood

Expanding Feminism and Experimenting with Labels: Where Do Men Fit Within the Movement?

I came to feminism as a young woman who had personally encountered sexism and violence from men in my life and, as a result, became increasingly critical of the masculinist culture surrounding me. Like many girls growing up, I was hypersensitive to the fact that many of the boys and men in my social circles were stronger than I was, and if they felt compelled, would use their power to put me "in my place." These men maintained their control through cutting words about our bodies or our choice of clothing and, at worst, violated us physically.

Feminism offered answers to my disillusionment with humanity, created an outlet for the outrage I felt as a woman in a world plagued by inequality of all kinds, and provided a framework that would take me into the realm of the political. Through my early studies in feminist theory, I devoured the mainstream classics, from Mary Wollstonecraft and Sojourner Truth to Mary Daly and Angela Davis. I became an activist and proudly identified as pro-woman. I worked vigorously within an alliance of young feminists whose initial chief concern was how to spell *women*. Should it be *wimmin, womyn,* or left alone? We wanted the power to define ourselves apart from men—from those who had co-opted and usurped our power for so long. And while this reclamation of identity is important, it wasn't until later that I realized that we were missing some critical aspects of social justice and effectively alienating significant numbers of women and men.

We organized events in the classical second-wave sense. By offering educational and consciousness-raising opportunities, we were sure that we could activate women. If they only knew how oppressed they were! We discovered, however, that the women in our small town did not, on the whole, feel oppressed. What had we experienced that they hadn't? Were they completely oblivious? Was I making mountains out of mole hills? What was going on?

Then I found bell hooks. As I read *Feminist Theory: From Margin to Center,*[1] hooks opened up an entirely new definition of *feminism* that enabled me to fit together multiple levels of oppression, and I realized that the White feminist ideology that I had embraced was classist and narrow, and that even though I worked actively to rid the world of racism and heterosexism, I was doing it *all wrong*. Doing it all wrong because up until that point I didn't understand the discreet ways in which injustices overlapped and perpetuated each other . . . that to eradicate suffering, to work for justice meant to build alliances. This, I found, was no easy task. It meant truly accepting my privilege as a middle-class White woman and opening my ears and my mind to the struggles identified by my sisters and my brothers whose experiences were different.

My brothers. *My brothers.* What place has that concept in the feminist movement? After all, I had begun my feminist adventures determined to identify myself completely outside of men and was virtually convinced that to work with men risked sacrificing our core goals of working as strong and focused feminists. But as I progressed as an activist, I came to work with more men involved in struggles for justice. Some of them even claimed to be feminists themselves! This was simultaneously heartening and, honestly, insulting. Who did these guys think they were? They were reaping the benefits of male privilege and then professing to despise it. How hypocritical!

But perhaps not. I decided, through my relationships with good men who were true allies to the feminist and social justice struggles with which I was involved, that maybe there was space for men. Just how that space is defined, and exactly what we should call those men, is another question. Through discussions with friends, I've found that the jury is still out on this matter. I think most of us would agree that if the feminist movement is first and foremost a women's movement, then it must be said that men have a responsibility to listen to women in the movement, to acknowledge their privilege and to avoid co-opting the agenda at all costs.

But can men be feminists themselves? When you get down to the essence of feminist struggle, can a man who hasn't walked in my shoes really understand masculinist oppression? But if he's fighting sexism alongside his sisters, does he really need to walk in my shoes? After all, for a movement whose goal is progressivism, we seem infuriatingly obsessive about hair splitting and labeling. But as feminists, we are keenly aware of the power of language and the power to define. . . . So what's a woman to do? I decided to explore the issue directly by talking with a friend and an ally, Robin Elwood, who identifies as a male feminist. What follows is our conversation. Does he make the cut? Can men be feminists? You decide.

How It All Began

M: What does feminism mean to you, personally? How did you get involved?

R: That's a big one. I got involved sometime in high school, in a small eastern Washington town. I mean a small town—I lived in a rural area, and the town with the nearest school has about five hundred people, total. In small-town middle and high school, gender policing is really obvious and brutal—boys harass girls, girls harass other girls, and it's very obviously connected to control. You can see people internalizing it, and it's heartbreaking and enraging, but it's part of community identity, and I don't know where even to start changing it.

I think partly because of who my parents were and the way we lived—we didn't have electricity when I was young, or television ever. I was never very successful in forming social connections. I was very much an outsider to TV culture, to the music, to interaction skills with folks my own age. That lack of cultural capital contributed to failure in my attempts to be an accepted part of the dominant culture.

My parents are relatively liberal, and while I've never heard them call themselves feminists, I've always seen them as people who were aware of gender issues and sexism. In particular, I've always seen my mother as an immensely capable woman who works incredibly hard both physically and intellectually. As a result of these things, the policing of gender roles always seemed like a mindless cruel game to me; it never seemed natural or positive.

M: When did you first hear the word *feminism*?

R: I heard it early in high school. The local library had a few feminist books by White women—*The Beauty Myth* and *Backlash,* as well as Suzanne Pharr's book *Homophobia.* I identified as feminist at that point, but I didn't have access to an activist movement and I didn't know how to move in that direction in that setting—I put up political posters in the halls, wrote poetry and diatribes, and put in time until I could leave. A school that size lacks the resources that some urban and suburban schools have; there's not any critical mass of "alternative" students, there are no examples or mentors. Of course there is diversity—but no one is really "out" in public, whether they're queer or politically different or from a different culture, or whatever. And because I felt rejected by the mainstream, I assumed that I was not part of it—that it was something unrelated to my thoughts and behavior.

And then I came to the university—ready to make social justice the center of what I was doing. I wasn't really clear about what kind of social justice I would focus on, but I knew that I wanted to be active. Fighting homophobia, sex-

ism, and racism were my main interests. Then, during my second day of walking around campus and looking for a work-study position, I saw this sign that the Women's Center was hiring. So I went to speak with the two women who coordinated the program that year. I asked them, "Can men do work-study positions here? Do you have men in the program?" It had been a totally moot question up until that time, so they had no answer for that. But they told me to come back later while they thought about it. They decided to give it a try. And so that certainly impacted me—I spent the next five years there. It was a feminist-supportive environment . . . and it made feminism a central part of my activist identity and social life.

On Being an Exception

R: That's one of the odd things about the women's center—I made my feminist identity by being an exception. It only worked because I was the only guy there, and I was twenty, and painfully shy and short on social skills. So I could be very supportive of the decisions women in the space made. It didn't erase any kind of privilege or the fact that my presence affected the dynamics of the office, but at a day-to-day level, I believe it made a big difference in my interactions. It's a point you and I have talked about before, Margaret; it's that gap between theory and practice—without minimizing male privilege, it seems that my age and temperament did have a practical effect that wouldn't show up on paper. Theoretically, I should have been a horrible interruption and source of tension. And that possibility was there. But it actually worked pretty well for years. At the end of five years, there was a difference—I was the oldest person in the office, I'd been there longer than anyone, I had really strong feelings about strategy and course for feminism, and I expressed them. And it was quickly becoming inappropriate for me to work there.

M: You couldn't be the mouthpiece for the Women's Center.

R: No . . . my voice was made strong by my history of organizing events, working in coalitions, discussing issues with friends, having a strong personal stake in a successful feminist movement, and by a lot of time spent thinking and working on the issues. But it was also made strong, or at least loud, by male privilege and a long tradition of men assuming we have the right to define anything, be experts about anything, and have access to every space. And there was nothing I could do to "relinquish" that or really do enough to mitigate its effects.

M: It makes me think about the civil rights movement, and how, when White people started getting into the movement . . . a lot of people came to feel that White people really needed to work on other White people and to educate them. For me, that seems like a critical part, for men, too.

R: And that's where I have not been as effective. I have not started formal men's discussion groups, but, then, most of my friends are women, so . . .

M: Do men freak you out too?

R: Hell, yeah! Most men scare the shit out of me! Although I do work one-on-one with men who are my friends. But that's not in a formal "now we're working on sexism" setting—I've tried to put my whole life into one piece—social life, love life, work life, friendships, spare time— I have never sought very clear separations. Most of my close friends have been women, all of my

partners have been women—there aren't that many men in my life to work with.

M: Do you think your presence in the Women's Center was positive for other men?

R: This could sound self-centered, but there aren't many current examples in this county of men working in feminist situations for feminist politics—and I think there does need to be that! I think the sight of men working with other men is important too. I think we can't rely on a single model—there are different possibilities, and too many challenges to use just one strategy.

Why Not Start a Men's Group?

M: A real activist group of men working on feminist issues—I think it would be awesome! Imagine!

R: Absolutely! It's something I need to work on; I have not done enough of it!

M: That brings me to a discussion of human nature and power, though. Say you do have a bunch of guys; is it going to be a funky relationship? Where did I get so cynical? I have to wonder if they wouldn't come out trying to tell the women's movement what to do? So maybe we should keep guys apart, have one or two scattered in organizations?

R: In practical terms, it's one method—maybe we should try every method we can think of, see what works, and change accordingly. The men's groups I have seen here . . . they are useful to participants, but they are not turning out vocal advocates who can talk compellingly about gender or create effective actions or events. This is not to downplay the importance of discussion or dialogue—but I have always been more effective at organizing events, rallies, publications, and the like. And discussion groups around here are not doing counseling, not publishing women's poetry, not advertising protests, not crashing meetings to demand better lighting, not distributing safety whistles, not raising funds for free women's self-defense classes. And those things are important to me. But I realize that starting a men's group, and convincing other men that sexism is even a problem, is crucial.

M: Oh, and that is no fun.

R: It's no fun, but it needs to be done. It does need to be done.

M: Should you have done that instead?

R: I'm not coming to this interview with answers to that. I feel it was useful to me to work in the Women's Center, and at the time my coworkers valued my help—but whether it was ultimately useful to the women there, to the center, to the movement . . . I don't have that answer.

M: I've struggled with similar issues regarding my tenure at the Native American Mentoring Program.

R: You worked there for a good while.

M: It was two years. It was the same kind of issue. When I applied for the job, I was one of two or three people applying. There were no native people applying for the job—the recruitment and advertising efforts could have probably been better, and it was a relatively new program at a very White academic place. And so I took it, but I still question whether I should have done that. This year, though, I'm so psyched about this year—the program is so much better now!

R: Even the quotes on their T-shirts this year demonstrate how progressive and vibrant it is—it's obvious the program is better.

M: They have three native people on staff, and the program is going to function so much more fluidly and proactively. But looking back—in practice, we were able to do some awesome work with me as a White person working there. And my commitment to social justice, White though I am, still served to open up a space that enabled them to be where they are now.

R: It's that slippage between theory and the local real world. Both of us have worked in spaces that were questionable, and where our long-term presence might not be desirable. And certainly, in the Women's Center, issues of privilege were never absent or irrelevant. But work got done that would not have happened otherwise. Women got help at hours when the office would otherwise have been closed. We created a photo display of misogynist, racist, homophobic, and classist graffiti from men's bathrooms that we would not have done without me there.

M: That was so kick-ass!

R: That was a good project. I was really happy about that one.

M: Okay . . . but are there some areas of feminism that you agree should be off limits to men?

R: Yes.

M: Like what?

The Ally Thing

M: The word *ally* gets thrown around so much these days.

R: There is so much mainstream university funding behind that word right now!

M: Yeah . . . to me, I always thought the term *ally* was really tied to political struggle. But now . . .

R: Now it's something you can do without interrupting your dominant-culture college experience.

M: Yeah . . .

R: Here at least, there's a men's anti-rape group—but their underlying message is that you can end sexism without . . .

M: ending patriarchy.

R: Yeah! It's such a rapidly co-opted term!

M: So Men Against Rape is a great start. I'm glad they're there. I was very excited to read that they were starting, because not many men do much of anything. But they're not really enough. So, as feminists, is it our job to try to make them political? Or should we just be glad that they are doing their thing, they're doing something?

R: It would be great if enough feminist men converged on our fair city to revolutionize Men Against Rape . . . but that's unlikely. And I would like for that change to happen!

When I came into college I started from a politicized wanting-to-end-patriarchy place, so I've never felt that close to liberal groups who are trying to sway folks who are in the center. And I'm never sure—are they a first step for men becoming political, or are they a safety valve that lets men feel okay about the normalized violence in our society without having to take hard steps to challenge it? A funny thing that it reminds me of: at the last Take Back the Night march, which is women-only here, the men against violence group was going to set up luminaria around the march's endpoint, and they brought hundreds of bags and candles . . . and no lighters! And I said to myself—this is not a movement I want to join!

M: No one brought a lighter?

R: Well, there were three or so, but not nearly enough! I mean, that's just ineffective planning.

I don't care how great the discussion is—we still have to be effective on the street!!!

Labels: Third Wave?

M: What do you say to those folks who say that men can't be feminists?

R: I don't fight about that . . . I don't really get that stuck on labels. If it makes people more comfortable, I'll label myself a feminist ally or someone who works on gender issues, or who works with feminist activists. Around the friends I've worked with for a long time, I call myself a feminist, because there's a history there of shared work; they know who I am. But I would not try to impose that term on people that aren't comfortable with that. I don't really know myself: can men be feminists? It depends on how you define it and upon what issues you are working. And it's a diverse movement, so I think the answer varies depending where you are. I've visited cities where there are pro-feminist anarchist men's groups, and *feminist* is noncontroversial as a label. I've worked with women who felt that only women really could use that word. To me, the important thing is that the work is getting done, not what it's called, and my experience is that men can do some work that contributes to feminist causes.

M: So as labels go, would you consider yourself a third-wave feminist?

R: No. I'm not entirely sure what's third wave and what's not. But the third-wave anthologies that I've read have not really convinced me that it's really so different. A lot of it seems to be sort of urban/postmodern/academic, which is very useful for people coming from or to that background, but it isn't really where I have an informed voice. And the focus on reclaiming lipstick or appearance, which you mentioned earlier—and Rebecca Walker's anthology spends a lot of time on that issue—again, it's not my puddle to jump into. Obviously, for many of the women I know, those are hard, hard questions. And, as a man, those are hard questions for me to deal with myself. But it's not me who has the right to answer for women, or even really be involved unless I'm asked. When women I know, as individuals, answer for themselves, I try to support their decisions.

I do think that the strong emphasis on inclusiveness and connecting supposedly "different" struggles, on truth-telling about scary topics, about bringing out the limits of solidarity, are very important to the third wave. Certainly, the emphasis on personal voice drives my writing! And since I'm of a certain age with a certain college background, I suspect it affects me more than I realize. Lots of third-wave writers are great, and I'm blown away by what they have to say. But that goes for lots of second- and first-wave writers too, and I often see the similarities between facets of past movements and younger writers, rather than the "new movement" separation.

I'm worried that if we call young radical voices third wave as if the issues are really new, we'll erase our knowledge of the radical folks or the working-class voices, or the women and men of color who have been raising these same issues in the past. And if we distance ourselves from the fact that the mainstream ignored those voices as much as possible, then we might fail to see parallels between then and now.

Final Question

M: So, did your cat really pee on your leg?

R: Um . . . yes. It's embarrassing.

NOTES

1. bell hooks, *Feminist Theory from Margin to Center* (Cambridge, MA: South End Press, 1981).

Camellia Phillips

Taking a Stand on Stolen Ground: The Need for Feminist Movements to Support American Indian Sovereignty

It seems to me that the feminist agenda is basically one of rearranging social relations within the society which is occupying our land and utilizing our resources for its own benefit. Nothing I've encountered in feminist theory addresses the fact of our colonization, or the wrongness of white women's stake in it. . . . feminists appear to share a presumption in common with the patriarchs they oppose, that they have some sort of inalienable right to simply go on occupying our land and exploiting our resources for as long as they like.

> —Pam Colorado, Oneida, 1985 letter to Ward Churchill, Keetoowah Cherokee[1]

Evidence of the colonialist content of much of Euroamerican feminist practice has been advanced, not just at the material level, but in terms of cultural imperialism. Andrea Smith, . . . writing in Indigenous Woman, recently denounced the feminism of the "New Age" persuasion for "ripping off" native ceremonies for their own purposes, putting them on notice that "as long as they take part in Indian spiritual abuse, either by being consumers of it, or by refusing to take a stand on [the matter], Indian women will consider white 'feminists' to be nothing more than agents in the genocide of [native] people."

> —M. Annette Jaimes, Juaneño/Yaqui, and Theresa Halsey, Standing Rock Sioux[2]

In 1992, M. Annette Jaimes, Juaneño/Yaqui, along with Theresa Halsey, Standing Rock Sioux, published the groundbreaking essay "American Indian Women: At the Center of Indigenous Resistance in Contemporary North America." Focusing on the accomplishments and experiences of American Indian women in struggles for sovereignty and decolonization, the essay outlined a crucial critique of feminism and its relationship to American Indian women.

Based on the writings of Native American and First Nations women scholars and activists, their fundamental argument can be summarized in Pam Colorado's reflection that "Nothing I've encountered in feminist theory addresses the fact of our colonization, or the wrongness of white women's stake in it."[3] Colorado's critique is crucial. If the feminist movement is in fact fighting for the liberation of all people, then it must also fight for sovereignty and self-determination of American Indian nations. Any movement that does not believe in, make space for, and support American Indian sovereignty is inherently colonial and can never fully challenge colonialism and its related forms of oppression, such as racism and patriarchy. If feminism is truly devoted to achieving justice and equality, it must develop new frameworks, or learn to utilize existing frameworks, such as human rights, that can actively support American Indian nations' struggles for self-determination.

While since the publication of Jaimes's essay some White women have been increasingly looking at their own stake in White supremacy and joining growing antiracist movements, on a practical level White feminists have yet to integrate a decolonization/indigenous sovereignty agenda into their work. As a middle-class White woman, the experience of being raised and educated in a corner of the Pacific Northwest where the primary racial divisions were between Indians and non-Indians has continued to shape my perspective and awareness of American Indian nations and issues. Now involved in social justice work, I feel it is essential to further a discussion on why non-Indian, particularly White, feminists must begin to understand their work in relation to struggles for indigenous sovereignty within the geographic border of the United States. What most White women fail to recognize is that they are both beneficiaries of the spoils of colonialism and participants in colonization. This lack of recognition can translate into frameworks, strategies, movements, and programs that reinforce, rather than challenge, colonial practices. As Janet McCloud, Tulalip, one of the leaders in the struggles for American Indian fishing rights, challenged in a 1984 lecture:

> You join us in liberating our land and lives. Lose the privilege you acquire at our expense by occupying our land. Make that your first priority for as long as it takes to make it happen. Then we'll join you in fixing up whatever's left of the class and gender problems in your society, and our own, if need be. But, if you're not willing to do that, then don't presume to tell us how we should go about our liberation, what priorities and values we should have. Since you're standing on our land, we've got to view you as just another oppressor trying to hang on to what's ours.[4]

Continuums of Colonial Violence

Violence against American Indian nations and people has been a crucial and ongoing element of Euro-American colonization, land theft, and genocide in North America. While feminist movements have prioritized antiviolence work, most have yet to take into account the multiple dimensions of colonization and violence. Yet historical and contemporary manifestations of colonial violence continue to shape the conditions faced by American Indian nations today. As asserted by Luana Ross, Salish, "Colonialism was and is an act of violence."[5] Andrea Smith,

Cherokee, further reveals that colonial violence—perpetrated and tolerated as a method or outcome of colonization—imparts the message that American Indian people are "not entitled to bodily integrity."[6] In practice, this violence against American Indian people is not considered a crime in either a legal or a social sense. She explains that "the history of mutilation of Indian bodies, both living and dead, makes it clear to Indian people that they are not entitled to bodily integrity. . . . In the history of massacres against Indian people, colonizers attempt not only to defeat Indian people but to eradicate their very identity and humanity. They attempt to transform Indian people from human beings into tobacco pouches, bridle reins or souvenirs—an object for the consumption of white people."[7]

When Smith writes that colonizers "attempt to transform Indian people from human beings into tobacco pouches, bridle reins or souvenirs—an object for the consumption of white people," she is speaking literally. The mutilation of Indian people, including women and children, is well documented, even in Euro-American histories. At the same time, her statement resonates with many contemporary manifestations of colonization, such as the practice of stealing Indian bones and artifacts for White-owned museums or "researchers," or the theft of Indian spiritual practices by White shamans.

Through the centuries, colonial violence has taken many forms. The initial colonization of the Americas through land theft and genocide were an act of violence that relied upon and consisted of acts of violence. Widespread rape of American Indian women was one of the most insidious and complex of these violations and poses the most contradictions in feminist discourse. According to Andrea Smith, rape against American Indian women is not only a tool of patriarchy as it has been constructed by White feminists, but more directly "serves as a tool of racism and colonialism."[8] Inés Hernández-Ávila (NATION) has similarly noted that the conquest of the Americas has physically and metaphorically involved the sexual conquest of indigenous peoples.[9] In the Euro-American justice system, rape of Native American women continues to be devalued in a similar way.[10] With the end of initial conquest, colonial violence has adapted new manifestations. North America continues to be occupied by a Euro-American-controlled state, which uses threats and acts of violence to enforce its laws and existence. Furthermore, the treatment of American Indians within the United States, both in government and in mainstream society, is inherently dehumanizing—including everything from the use of caricatures of American Indians as sports mascots to the mass incarceration of American Indian people to blatantly racist anti-Indian organizing and policies.

The land, however, remains linked to nearly *all* these forms of colonization and continues to ground American Indian resistance. The legal, historical, and cultural relationships between Native North Americans and the land distinguish the struggles of indigenous peoples from other struggles for justice. Within this relationship, already complex issues of racism and patriarchy take on additional meanings, as evidenced in what Luana Ross, Salish, has referred to as neocolonial racism[11]—racism specifically directed against American Indians that is informed by the ideologies that have been used to justify and facilitate violence against American Indian peoples. In her poem "Gate #9," Chrystos, Menominee, reveals how neocolonial, or what could also be called anti-Indian, racism intimately links attacks on American Indian people and land. She writes that

> Whites "hate us" because they've treated us inhumanely—savagely   Any of us who have survived are ugly reminders of their past and present viciousness   *We are witnesses to the fact that these lands, all of them, town and reservation alike, are our home. No white person (or indeed, no non-Native person) has a "right" to be here*   When we survive (especially if we're sober and activists, as I am), we are "unpleasant" reminders of everyone else's invasion and/or genocide.[12] (italics mine)

As Chrystos explains, at the root of much racism against American Indians is the land, and the fact that American Indian people and nations "are witnesses to the fact that these lands, all of them, town and reservation alike, are our home." Gail Small, Northern Cheyenne, of Native Action explains that as an American Indian woman "you're born into a struggle. . . . I knew I was going to be fighting for our land."[13] Even the ground upon which non-Indians live, build homes, raise children was stolen through genocide and violence—and the genocide of Native North America is a reality that is, for Whites, both unpleasant and ultimately exploitable.

Cultural and Spiritual Appropriation: Making a Profit

Anti-Indian racism is not only deeply integrated into Euro-American cultural practices and social structures but is used by non-Natives for financial and personal gain. Currently, stereotyped images of Native Americans are used by non-Natives to sell bottled iced teas, butter/marga-rine, corn flour, corn tortillas, cigarettes, and pancake/waffle mix, among other things. Even more blatantly, Native Americans are the only racial/ethnic group still used by corporations, universities, public schools, students, and fans as sports mascots. One group of Native American activists has spent nearly a decade fighting the Washington Redskins[14]—who now, for only $1 a month, offer fans the opportunity to purchase email addresses ending in "@redskins.com." Suzan Shown Harjo, Cheyenne and Hodulgee Muscogee, reveals that the term *Redskins* "arose in the 1600s and 1700s, with the colonists' practice of paying bounties for dead Native adults and children. When wagonloads and gunnysacks of corpses became a transportation problem for bounty-hunters and a disposal problem for traders, scalplocks instead of heads and red skins in lieu of whole bodies were accepted as evidence of Indian kill."[15] The marketing of caricatures of Native Americans can be directly traced to what Andrea Smith describes as the "mutilation of Indian bodies" and the "transform[ation] of Indian people from human beings into . . . object[s] for the consumption of white people."[16] The Redskins represent the glorification of violence against Native Americans. Like other degrading images of American Indians marketed to the mainstream by non-Indians, the Redskins reinforce the dehumanization of Native Americans and create an atmosphere in which American Indian nations that struggle to assert their human rights as indigenous peoples and sovereign nations are already discredited.

The appropriation of spiritual traditions by Whites—known as White shamanism—also follows established patterns of colonization and poses significant barriers to meaningful relationships between non-Indian feminists and American Indian activists. While American Indians have been massacred and persecuted for practicing their traditional religions,[17] Euro-Americans are increasingly appropriating elements of American Indian belief systems and often *selling them for a profit.* Like the use of the term *Redskins,* this crass appropriation is a violent denial of the past and ongoing struggles of American Indian peoples to preserve their cultures and communities. Chrystos addresses this directly when she opens her poetry collection *Not Vanishing* by assuring her readers that "while I am deeply spiritual, to share this with strangers would be a violation. Our rituals, stories & religious practices have been stolen and abused, as has our land."[18] Spiritual appropriation fits neatly into the established patterns of colonization of American Indian lands and peoples, occurring at the intersections of the legal and social denial of American Indian peoples' rights to practice cultural and spiritual traditions, and White people's perceived rights to access and possess Native American cultures and spiritual traditions. Like American Indian land and American Indian bodies, American Indian culture and spirituality are perceived by Whites as open and willing to be taken and violated.

While White shamanism taps into a real spiritual need felt by many Whites, the practice cannot be separated from its colonial and genocidal implications. In their 1992 piece, quoted in the beginning of this article, M. Annette Jaimes, Juaneño/Yaqui, and Theresa Halsey, Standing Rock Sioux, explore the relationship—or rather lack of respectful interaction between—"Native American Women and Feminism," charting the intersection of colonialism and spiritual appropriation within some elements of the mainstream White feminist movement. As stated by Andrea Smith, "as long as [feminists] take part in Indian spiritual abuse, either by being con-

sumers of it or by refusing to take a stand on [the matter], Indian women will consider white 'feminists' to be nothing more than agents in the genocide of [native] people."[19]

While a decade has passed since Jaimes's, Halsey's, and Smith's assertions, abuse of Native American spiritual practices by White people, many of whom consider themselves progressive feminists, continues to grow. At the same time, White feminists have failed to take a unified stand against spiritual appropriation. This can perhaps be partially explained by what Wendy Rose, Hopi/Miwok, identifies as the "spiritual barrenness"[20] of Euro-American society. Rose admits that "white shamanism has touched upon something very real. An entire population is crying out for help, for alternatives to the spiritual barrenness they experience, for a way out of the painful trap in which their own worldview and way of life have ensnared them."[21] Regardless of their spiritual need, however, on a very basic level White people need to learn to listen to and respect Native peoples' requests that they not appropriate American Indian spiritual practices. The ongoing refusal of Whites to acknowledge the very real impact of White shamanism continues to occur in a number of forums, including spaces created directly for the purpose of facilitating communication between American Indian people and non-Indians. In 2000, for example, I attended a screening of *White Shamans and Plastic Medicine Men,* facilitated by filmmaker Daniel Hart and Luana Ross. Following the film White people in the audience forcefully argued that they *deserved to and needed to* learn from Native American people and spirituality—despite direct requests from numerous American Indian people in the audience that White people stop stealing Native American spiritual and cultural practices. When White people are able to sit in the same room with American Indian people and refuse to even listen to what they are saying, it demonstrates how White shamanism silences and discredits the voices of American Indian people and nations—and how White shamanism can have a very real and negative impact on American Indian nations' struggles for self-determination.

On the Ground: White People Organizing Against American Indian Sovereignty

Washington State (where I was born and raised) provides a clear example of just how widespread and publicly "tolerated" anti-Indian sentiment and the corresponding anti-Indian movement[22] really is—and reveals its concrete implications. One recent and notable instance of this is the "controversy" surrounding the Makah whale hunt. In the late 1990s, the Makah Nation sought and won the right to hunt gray whales—a practice from which they had abstained since the 1920s when the gray whale became endangered as a species but which was guaranteed under the 1855 Treaty of Neah Bay, in which "the Makah Nation ceded much of the Olympic Peninsula to the federal government in exchange for the right to fish, hunt and go whaling."[23] With their treaty rights upheld, the Makah elected to publicly pursue their first whale hunt in eighty years. Almost immediately, a number of animal rights and environmental groups, including Sea Shepherd (headed by Paul Watson), Project Sea Wolf, Ocean Defense International (ODI), World Whale Police (WWP), and the website www.stopwhalekill.org, emerged to "challenge" the Makah's right to hunt whales. While these groups and their members came out with some shockingly racist arguments and perspectives

(such as signs and bumperstickers availing people to "Save a whale, harpoon a Makah"),[24] what is most revealing is the response of "average" White people to both the whale hunt and the racist arguments set forth by anti-whaling groups, who soon began to ally themselves with established anti-Indian politicians, such as then-senator Slade Gorton and then-representative Jack Metcalf.[25] As the hunt neared and in the months following, letters to the editor poured in to local newspapers and, though some expressed support for the Makah and American Indian sovereignty, even more viciously attacked the hunt, the Makah, and American Indian nations and people in general. *Seattle Times* reporter Alex Tizon revealed that "by one count [of incoming letters and phone calls to the paper], protestors outnumbered Makah supporters 10–1."[26] The true magnitude of the violent racism leveled at the Makah can best be understood through the letters and statements themselves. Some examples from the May 23, 1999, issue of the *Seattle Times*:

> We should tell the Makahs (and all other "Native Americans") that, in the words of Star Trek's Borg: "Resistance is futile! Prepare to be assimilated!"

> These aren't whale warriors, they are welfare warriors.

> Just saw some pictures of a bunch of testosterone-laden, high-fiving, party animals dancing on a dead whale. Whoops! I guess they were Makah tribal members spiritually reconnecting with their deeply respected tribal past.

> There are people on this planet whose ancestors engaged in human sacrifice, slavery, cannibalism and head-hunting. While these

may not be on the same levels as killing the largest mammals on earth, they illustrate the points of progress and change. . . . O great Makahs, there is no glory or honor here. You have fallen much lower in the eyes of the world than you can possibly imagine.

My daughter has never had a prejudiced bone in her body. Now she hates Indians.

If a people can pick and choose which old tradition to resume, does that mean descendants of white slave-holders should go out and capture themselves some slaves because they used to do that?[27]

What is surprising about these letters and their violent racism is not that people wrote them, but that papers published them, often either without comment or at most under the shallow pretext of "letting readers decide" if the letters were racist or not.

During the months surrounding the actual hunt, it became clear that anti-Indian sentiment in the Pacific Northwest and elsewhere (many of the letters were from people outside the region) was not only widespread and vocal but also generally tolerated—and thus supported—by the "mainstream," including liberal Whites, conservative Whites, and the media. During local newscasts, for example, excerpts from letters such as those quoted above were displayed on the screen—all for the sake of journalistic integrity or portraying both sides of the story. In reality, however, it seems that the Makah controversy was also a great way to sell papers or attract viewers and listeners. At the same time, the response of progressive non-Native groups, including feminists, while present, failed to gain equal air time, leaving the overall impression

that most non-Native people in the Northwest would prefer to see American Indian sovereignty dismantled. Throughout the Northwest these types of controversies are repeated over and over again. In my own town, letters to the editor asserting the need for laws to protect the rights of White people living on reservations, bemoaning the "special rights" of American Indian nations and people, or attacking the water or fishing rights of neighboring American Indian nations, are commonplace. One year after the first Makah whale hunt, for example, the Washington State Republican Party, in a move led by John Fleming, a non-Indian with property on the Swinomish reservation, "passed a resolution in their June, 2000 convention calling for an end to tribal government."[28] Though later rescinded, the resolution reflects the political agendas of many anti-Indian politicians in Washington State and elsewhere, and their close relationship with grassroots anti-Indian and anti-sovereignty movements. Tracing the growth and arguments of the anti-Indian movement, Zoltan Grossman reminds us, however, that "it can never be emphasized enough that the main threat to Indian peoples and their rights does not come from the anti-Indian movement, but from the government and corporations that the anti-Indian groups often front for."[29] When politicians and other policymakers are "in bed" with anti-Indian groups, however, public support for anti-Indian policies and rhetoric can and does translate into policy.

Sovereignty, Human Rights, and Feminism's Roles

Despite ongoing attacks on American Indian sovereignty within the public debate and the U.S. legal system, the struggles of American

Indian nations for self-determination and sovereignty continue to grow, in the process redefining the role and meaning of sovereignty itself. Just as the cultures and experiences of American Indian nations are infinitely varied and adaptive, so the concept of sovereignty is shaped by individual nations, cultures, histories, situations, and needs. The assertion of sovereignty, in whatever form, is an act of empowerment. Luana Ross explains that "sovereignty is a fragile concept whose meaning is shaped and reshaped by legislation and court decisions. At the same time, sovereignty is inherent; it comes from within a people and their culture. Some would argue sovereignty cannot be given to one group by another because ultimately it comes from spiritual sources. Whatever the case, sovereignty cannot be separated from a people or their culture."[30]

Sovereignty is of necessity a malleable goal. Inherent within the struggle to achieve sovereignty is the process of decolonization.[31] Issues that fall under the jurisdiction of sovereignty, in a general sense, include self-determination for indigenous peoples in regards to land, language, culture/spirituality, citizenship, and law. Sovereignty is in turn defined by the land, language, culture, spirituality, and law of each indigenous nation. Since "sovereignty cannot be separated from a people or their culture," it also empowers American Indian nations to assert the value and importance of their own cultures, laws, spiritual practices, and languages.

Sovereignty is also clearly a legal concept—guaranteed to American Indian nations by the hundreds of treaties signed with the United States as well as the Universal Declaration of Human Rights and other international documents—and can be enforced on legal grounds. According to Rebecca L. Robbins, Standing Rock Sioux, "North American indigenous peoples continue to hold a clear legal entitlement—even under U.S. law—to conduct themselves as completely sovereign nations unless they themselves freely determine that things should be otherwise."[32] American Indian nations have sought to exercise their "legal entitlement," utilizing both national and international forums. American Indian nations throughout the United States continue to bring cases before U.S. courts in which they attempt to exercise rights guaranteed to them through the many legally binding treaties they have signed. And in many cases, such as the Makah, American Indian nations are winning. At the same time, nations and activists have learned to utilize international forums to address conditions facing indigenous nations within the United States. Haunani-Kay Trask, Native Hawaiian, proposes that the rights of indigenous peoples in the United States must be addressed within the context of human rights rather than civil rights, since "injustices done against Native people, such as land dispossession, language banning, family disintegration, and cultural exploitation, are not part of this intrasettler [or colonizer] discussion and are therefore not within the parameters of civil rights."[33] Though Native Hawaiians are in a different legal situation than American Indian nations, the issues remain much the same: land, language, culture, religion, citizenship. There are many contemporary examples of indigenous peoples utilizing a human rights framework to fight for sovereignty and self-determination, both through direct appeal to the United Nations and through the application of human rights standards within the United States.

As a movement, feminism must learn to actively support sovereignty. Feminists and others working for social justice need to create a broader framework/movement with significant space for struggles for American Indian sovereignty; a human rights framework can, in part, provide this space. The challenge is to develop an anticolonial, antiracist feminism that takes into account the positions, needs, goals, and strategies of American Indian nations and people. Non-Indian feminists and others working for social justice must speak out against anti-Indian racism and anti-Indian policies—and must take a vocal stance opposing violence against American Indian people and nations, including caricatures of Native Americans used as sports mascots, White shamanism, anti-Indian rhetoric and groups, and other attacks on American Indian land and peoples. At the 2000 Color of Violence Conference, Luana Ross reminded those in attendance that supporting American Indian activism and sovereignty is not only crucial to struggles for social justice but in fact is a responsibility of all non-Indians living in the Americas, when she asserted that "I want you all to remember that you are on Indian land."[34]

Feminism's role in supporting American Indian and other indigenous peoples' struggles for sovereignty and decolonization is complicated. As a movement, feminism must learn to actively support sovereignty. Feminists and others working for social justice need to create a broader framework/movement within which there is significant space for struggles for American Indian sovereignty; a human rights framework can, in part, provide this space. The challenge is to develop an anticolonial, antiracist feminism that takes into account the positions, needs, goals, and strategies of American Indian nations and people. Non-Indian feminists and others working for social justice must speak out against anti-Indian racism and anti-Indian policies—and must take a vocal stance opposing violence against American Indian people and

nations, including caricatures of Native Americans used as sports mascots, White shamanism, anti-Indian rhetoric and groups, and other attacks on American land and peoples.

At the same time, non-Indian feminists must learn to create an anticolonial feminism without expecting American Indian women to "join up" or "direct the movement," but instead focusing on listening to American Indian women and supporting the work they are doing. Non-Indian women must learn to listen, because Native American women are speaking, though their words and ideas may be difficult for non-Indian feminists to hear. Of the many Native American women activists, there are some who reject and some who accept the feminist label, though nearly all are doing woman-empowering work. In recognizing the role of sovereignty in feminism, there is a need for feminists to acknowledge both of these perspectives. Perhaps what is most clear is what non-Indian feminists should not do: appropriate, objectify, label, dismiss, consider themselves the "experts" on indigenous peoples and American Indian nations.

At the 2000 Color of Violence Conference, Luana Ross reminded those in attendance that supporting American Indian activism and sovereignty is not only crucial to struggles for social justice, but in fact is a responsibility of all non-Indians living in the Americas, when she asserted that: "I want you all to remember that you are on Indian land."[35] It is far overdue for White feminists and feminist movements overall to respond to American Indian sovereignty and our ongoing apathy in relation to it in a concrete and visible way. White feminists must educate themselves about issues surrounding colonialism and sovereignty, while at the same time building meaningful alliances with women of color who have been organizing around the intersections of racial and social justice for decades. Perhaps most difficult of all, White women need to learn to listen to and learn from American Indian women and other women of color, without dismissing, co-opting, or appropriating their work. Fundamentally, White women must take a stand on American Indian sovereignty, because no matter what the struggle for justice may be, it continues to be fought on stolen ground.

NOTES

1. M. Annette Jaimes with Theresa Halsey, "American Indian Women: At the Center of the Indigenous Resistance in North America." In *The State of Native America,* ed. M. Annette Jaimes (Cambridge, MA: South End Press, 1992), 332.

2. Ibid., 333.

3. Pam Colorado, quoted in M. Annette Jaimes, *The State of Native America,* 332.

4. Janet McCloud, Tulalip, a talk delivered for International Women's Day at the University of Colorado, Boulder, April 1984, quoted in M. Annette Jaimes, *The State of Native America,* 314.

5. Luana Ross, speech at the Color of Violence Conference, Second Plenary Session. April 29, 2000. Transcript summary available from Incite! Women of Color Against Violence.

6. Andrea Smith, "Sexual Violence and American Indian Genocide," *The Journal of Religion and Abuse: Remembering Conquest: Feminist/Womanist Perspectives on Religion, Colonization, and Sexual Violence* 1.2 (1999): 31–52).

7. Ibid., 35.

8. Ibid., 32.

9. Inés Hernández-Ávila, "An Open Letter to Chicanas: On the Power and Politics of Origin." In *Reinventing the Enemy's Language: Contemporary Native Women's Writings of North America,* ed. Joy Harjo and Gloria Bird (New York: W. W. Norton, 1997), 235–246.

10. See Kimberlé Crenshaw, "Mapping the Margins: Intersectionality, Identity Politics, and Violence Against Women of Color," *Critical Race Theory: The Key Writings that Formed the Movement* (New York: The New Press, 1995), 367–368.

11. Luana Ross, *Inventing the Savage: The Social Construction of Native American Criminality* (Austin: Texas University Press, 1998), 3.

12. Chrystos, "Gate #9." In *Dream On* (Vancouver: Press Gang, 1991), 80–81.

13. Gail Small, speech at the Color of Violence Conference, April 28, 2000. Response to keynote address by Angela Davis.

14. Suzan Shown Harjo, "Fighting the R-Word," *ColorLines Magazine* 3.1 (2000): 18–19.

15. Ibid., 18.

16. Andrea Smith, "Sexual Violence and American Indian Genocide," *The Journal of Religion and Abuse:* "Remembering Conquest: Feminist/Womanist Perspectives on Religion, Colonization, and Sexual Violence." 1.2 (1999): 31–52) 35.

17. Luana Ross, *Inventing the Savage,* 137–138.

18. Chrystos, *Not Vanishing* (Vancouver: Press Gang, 1988).

19. Andrea Smith, quoted in "American Indian Women: At the Center of the Indigenous Resistance in North America," by M. Annette Jaimes with Theresa Halsey. In *The State of Native America,* ed. M. Annette Jaimes, 333.

20. Wendy Rose, "The Great Pretenders: Further Reflections on Whiteshamanism." In *The State of Native America,* ed. M. Annette Jaimes, 418.

21. Ibid.

22. While anti-Indian groups and campaigns do fall into a category of anti-Indian movements, with the overall goal of eroding American Indian sovereignty, the majority are extremely grassroots organizations. For example, many anti-Indian groups are made up of White people living on Indian reservations who agitate for "equal rights" for all people or, in other words, that White people on reservations

should not be subject to the laws and policies of American Indian nations on whose land they live. Other participants in anti-Indian movements include anti-Indian politicians, non-Indians fighting the rights of Indian nations to treaty-guaranteed fishing, hunting, water, or land rights, and more traditional White supremacist groups.

23. Camille Monzon, "Treaties Protect Indians' Right to Go Whale Hunting," *The Seattle Times,* editorial pages (Friday, Oct. 30, 1998).

24. Michael Elm, with Jason Spaulding and Mike Two Horses, "Some Examples of Racism in the Anti-Whaling Movement," CERTAIN: Coalition to End Racial Targeting of American Indian Nations. Article available at www.certain-natl.org/racism_in_the_ar_movement.html, October 2001.

25. Ibid.

26. Alex Tizon, "E-mails, Phone Messages Full of Threats, Invective," *The Seattle Times,* local news pages (Sunday, May 23, 1999).

27. "Readers Write About the Cultural Value of a Whale Kill" and "More Letters About the Makah Whale Hunt," *The Seattle Times,* editorial pages (Sunday, May 23, 1999).

28. CERTAIN: Coalition to End Racial Targeting of American Indian Nations, "Public Information Packet." Available at www.certain-natl.org, October 2001.

29. Zoltan Grossman, "Treaty Rights and Responding to Anti-Indian Activity," Center for World Indigenous Studies, the Fourth World Documentation Project. Available at www.alphacdc.com/treaty/anti-indian.html, October 2001.

30. Luana Ross, *Inventing the Savage: The Social Construction of Native American Criminality, op. cit.*

31. Ibid., 3.

32. American Indian nations face barriers to self-determination of *citizenship* through the imposition of "blood quantum" standards enacted by the United States Congress through the General Allotment Act of 1887. "Blood quantum" standards generally identify people with one quarter or more "Indian blood" to be American Indians and those with less to be non-Indians, completely disregarding the right of American Indian nations to determine their own citizenship based upon factors beyond the "degree of Indian blood" someone may possess. M. Annette Jaimes discusses the impact of blood quantum on American Indian sovereignty in-depth in her article "Federal Indian Policy: A Usurpation of Indigenous Sovereignty in North America" in *The State of Native America* (Cambridge, MA: South End Press, 1992), 123–138.

33. Rebecca L. Robbins, "Self-Determination and Subordination: The Past, Present, and Future of American Indian Governance," *The State of Native America,* ed. M. Annette Jaimes, 90.

34. Haunani-Kay Trask, *From a Native Daughter: Colonialism and Sovereignty in Hawai'i,* rev. ed. (Honolulu: Hawai'i University Press, 1999), 90.

35. Luana Ross, speech at the Color of Violence Conference, Second Plenary Session. April 29, 2000. Transcript summary available from Incite! Women of Color Against Violence.

Sherry Jubilo, Robin Elwood,
Anne-Marie Basso, and Kim L. Morrison

Taking It to the Streets: A Group of Activists in Dialogue

Sherry: My name is Sherry, and the tape recorder makes me nervous. So who knows what I'll remember to say, but I'm fifty-seven, and I'm White, working class, bisexual, identify as a feminist. I started out being an activist with low-income people in Iowa around welfare rights and housing issues and housing discrimination, and then went into Vietnam War stuff and feminist activism. I really met everybody here fairly recently, probably a year ago, oh, year and a half, probably when the hate crimes started in a small town near here.

Robin: I'm twenty-four. I'm a straight White male, and I've been doing various forms of activism for a good number of years. My parents do some kinds of activism, and I have tried to expand on that legacy. Most recently I spent five years working in a women's center at the university while I was doing a degree in feminist theory and political activism there. For the last year and a bit I've been working for a local shoestring-budget human rights group as the staff/organizer/gofer. I am the staff. It's very small and unorganized.

Kim: I'm thirty-four years old; I'm one of ten kids. And one of ten to graduate with a bachelor's degree. Oh, and I'm a lover of men and

women, but I'm in an interracial relationship with a women and have been in relationships with women for the past ten years. Culturally I'd identify myself the way culture identifies me: as a Black woman, I guess. But I identify as a Black Indian woman. When I have to identify.

Anne-Marie: I'm twenty-four and I am a White woman. I grew up in an upper-middle-class, non-activist family. I graduated in American cultural studies. I identify as a queer woman. I'm also in an interracial relationship.

■ ■ ■

Kim: I think we should ask ourselves, "What kind of activism movement have we inherited or think that we've inherited?"

Sherry: I think that's where young people find themselves. For me, it's more, "What are we left with? What are we stuck with or left with?" And it's more discouraging for me because being older and socially active since 1968 I can see that we haven't accomplished much and that the same patterns are repeated over and over. But for young people it's more "What have we inherited?" I didn't inherit much of anything.

Kim: I can say the same thing about being stuck with versus inherited. I was stuck with unresolved racism, homophobia in the women's movement, and the consequences of White privilege. However, I have inherited the tenacity to struggle for justice.

Sherry: I know, but I feel more responsible, especially for my part in not getting farther in a better, more inclusive way, not seeing what directions we were going, not risking more. We all have inherited stuff, it's just that we may not know it. When I was young, I didn't know about activism, even feminist activism in England in the early days.

Anne-Marie: We may not be aware. I am only just becoming aware.

Sherry: If we don't know about history, as I didn't when I was young, then we don't know we've inherited a bunch of shit—both good and bad.

Kim: It is important for everyone to know that you come from people that have been activists and have been on the front lines, that we all come from that.

Anne-Marie: Yet it is important to remember that we have not necessarily inherited front-line-type of activism in all aspects of our lives. For example, as a queer person I have inherited a rich history of front-line resistance. Take Stonewall, for instance. Yet when it comes to my White skin or class background, I do not feel I have inherited activism. I have inherited a history of oppressing others by way of privilege. As a White woman trying to resist a racist and sexist society, I have inherited a history of White women who have struggled for *White* women's liberation under the guise of "women's liberation," hence still practicing racism. I have to try to change the pattern in my own life, but the blueprint has not been written yet.

Kim: Historical context is lots of times lacking. We think that because we're here that things from the past have been dealt with, and that's my whole issue with the feminist movement. There's not a historical context coming from White feminists or White activists and even, I can say that of people of color activists too, that there's no historical context being brought into the forefront, and I think that needs to happen in order to not perpetuate . . . the things that we've been trying to work toward ending or eradicating.

Robin: I can't second that enough. If you know the some of the history of the Fourteenth Amendment, and how the abolition movement split, and how people like Elizabeth Cady Stanton joined up with vicious racists like George Francis Train, and went on these speaking tours using race as a way to get the vote for White women, saying, "Are you going to let these brute beast animal-like men get the vote before white womanhood?" If you know that history and how that didn't work, it perpetuated racism, it gave feminism a bad name, but it seemed like an intelligent choice to them at that time because of racism they already had. If that knowledge had been broadly understood in 1970s feminism, some of the same choices might not have been made. The results might have been [a less racist movement]. And now, looking at our movements, people are still willing to sacrifice one movement for another. And there's just case after case. That's what we're inheriting, movements that have done that, that have been willing to do that.

Anne-Marie: That's led to such things as the mainstream feminist group on campus putting up these signs in all the women's bathrooms about rape.

Kim: The statistic was something like "one out of three" women will be raped, and the one out of the three pictured was the Black woman. We have to realize, we're all interconnected, and once we realize that and digest it, maybe we can work together.

Robin: I think that takes long-term strategizing and a "do the movements no harm" test, or more education within our activist groups or whatever. We need that long-term understanding.

■ ■ ■

Robin: The community we all work in right now includes some ex-feminist collectives that do domestic violence (DV) work; there's a human rights group that I work for, there's some stuff on the university campus, which is where I feel most at home. But definitely as far as the larger community, we've inherited an activist movement. . . . Well, actually, I haven't inherited yet. It hasn't been handed over by the people who "own" it at the moment.

Anne-Marie: Does it ever get handed over? And if it does, what are you getting?

Robin: Maybe not, but definitely I can say that most of the movements don't effectively form progressive alliances that don't keep some form of oppression going. Like a lot of the local non-profits that do domestic violence issues don't do class issues so well, or have problems working with, say, people from the Indian reservation. I actually heard a story the other day about a search committee down at the DV shelter. Within the last year they interviewed an older Native American woman and someone on the search committee actually said, "well, we hired a Native American woman before, and it didn't work," implying, of course, that they shouldn't do it again.

Sherry: And the Food Co-op has done some similar stuff too.

Robin: Yes, and the task force either has or will at some point. But the inertia in the organizations, the power of those organizations, has meant that the issues are not integrated and it's still perpetuating domination.

Kim: This is true, even on campus. Students of color are marginalized even in the gay lesbian transgendered alliance. When I was pretty active on campus and read some of the student newspaper articles from the 1960s and 1970s, groups were working on diversity issues and trying to integrate cultural studies into the curriculum. It seemed like there was this wave of revolution and students of color and their allies were coming together and trying to push that to the forefront. You'd have this dynamic of things moving forward and being active and then it would stop. And it seemed like when it was picked up again several years later, it was still at the same place, or had even gone backwards, even to before it began. Some battles are won and then later lost. For example, there's no longer an ethnic studies department on campus. I'm sure some of the same issues will come up again. We organized around I-200[1] but that's not around anymore even though some of the issues we were fighting for are still there, and some of the issues are still here. They didn't get resolved. On campus, of course, you're there a limited amount of time, and people leave and new ones come who don't know the history—like what we were talking about earlier. They don't know the history of what people have done and how far they've progressed, what they did that worked and didn't work, and I find that that's a big problem. Anyway, as far as inheriting something, it's lost because people don't know about it.

I do think I inherited the uncomfortableness of being on campus as a student of color, which propelled me to be an activist. Becoming an activist, I began to create the type of community that I longed for. This lessened my uncomfortability, finding a group of people who were struggling to manifest the same values as I was and together creating community around campus and community issues.

Anne-Marie: Kim, you have inherited an uncomfortability, while as a White woman I inherited a privilege to be comfortable or uncomfortable, if I choose. I think part of the reason campus atmosphere hasn't changed is because a majority of students come from this White middle-class background, and they have the privilege to be ignorant of what is going on. That's what I had when I came in, and then I started to open myself to really learn about experiences different then my own. When White people do take a stand against human injustice, then they have to face being seen as deviant, and this is another reason people fall back on their privilege, acting as non-activist, in apathy.

Kim: And they have the privilege to do that, but I don't because as a Black woman I'm seen as deviant anyway.

■ ■ ■

Anne-Marie: I just think if there's one thing that I wish didn't have to be learned over and over again, it's that gender is a social construction, and that there is nothing natural or innate about being female or male. This is still controversial, but this whole idea, for example, that a female can't be the prom king, or what it means to be male, a mature male, or other things associated with gender are things that human beings made up but aren't born with.

Robin: Coming out of college, we feel that we know this, but when we get off campus and out of the theory book, and work with the human rights or other progressive groups, we simply assume that gender is a social construction, but we're working in or with organizations that don't get it.

Kim: Their ideas are totally, totally ingrained and almost impossible to change.

Robin: And in fact they use this [mis]understanding to their benefit. The task force has done this less than some groups, but they'll use the whole idea of "we're a good community of families, we need a better world for all children," which assumes exclusive constructions of heterosexuality and gender in order to win battles about race and diversity.

Anne-Marie: Even within the gay community, people don't think about that.

Robin: It seems like a lot is because people have tried to separate out issues of race, class, and gender, to make sacrifices for short-term gains for their particular group or issue. So you have the public rhetoric of groups like PFLAG [Parents, Families, and Friends of Lesbians and Gays] saying "It's not a choice, we're born this way" because that's easier to get people to accept. Groups have not taken on the whole idea of "it's all constructed" but rather agreed with the idea that homosexuality is natural in order to defeat very real vicious homophobia. And what are the results of that for other struggles and other times?

Kim: I experience that when I come into contact with people who say that they're transgendered, but then take on roles that are either male or female, or even putting the role onto me as being transgendered because I don't look male or female. I say I'm not transgendered, I'm just Kim. I don't want to be put into the transgendered box where I feel more manly or womanly because people might mistake me for being a man because my breasts aren't big enough or my voice is deep or I have broad shoulders. Well hell no, I'm just Kim, I don't have to take on that.

Robin: By not challenging in any serious way the institution of marriage or the concept of gender roles, people have been able to separate them out and say, "we're just protecting good, working families," while they are really celebrating an oppressive institution, and they do this in order to work for tolerance and acceptance of racial diversity or some other forms of diversity. As soon as people separate these issues out and then make a tactical strategy of "we won't fight that battle right now," they're reinforcing domination in other areas.

Anne-Marie: Going on with that, part of the reason that's so frustrating to me is I was on a panel up on campus for future teachers, and it was a queer panel, transgender-lesbian-gay-bisexual-and-family/community, and one of the PFLAG board members was saying that gender is not constructed, and that's why transgendered is OK. And someone in the crowd said, "Oh, I heard gender is culturally constructed," and the board member said, "No! I don't believe that at all. It's not a cultural construction." I had to speak up on the panel and say, "I completely disagree; I think gender is a cultural construction. There's nothing natural about men working on cars better than women, or women, not men, being prom queens or homemakers." So the activists with power don't always understand these issues and can perpetuate an oppressive belief system. People need to understand the difference between sex and gender.

■ ■ ■

Robin: In practical terms, there's lots of people doing important work. But where are the people making pamphlets, where are the people who are making posters?

Kim: There are 'zines.

Robin: But 'zines that go out into our own communities. Where are the people going door to door? reaching out to others? There's all this third-wave theory, or call it what you will, that's really taking some of these things to task, deconstructing some stuff, but the professors aren't out spreading it in their own neighborhoods off campus, the students are not by and large doing it. And those of us who try, as all of us have at different times, aren't always successful because certain groups are invested in preserving the status quo. Even in the human rights movement.

Anne-Marie: It's a huge job, though, like with this youth group I work with. I wondered, "How can I get that message to young people?" I never did because I didn't know how.

Robin: But at the same time, where is the mass of us who are working in our own communities to do this? One local professor has written and presented a critique of the nongeographical nature of academia. Academia does not encourage us to put down roots in a community and have theory that guides activism rooted in our family and friends. We all took classes on campus, reading theory written in New York that is supposedly applicable anywhere. Many of us have no grasp of the history of this town or this state, or who you talk to make stuff change.

I really think we can't change public perceptions through academic texts. That might be part of it, but it's getting out and doing talks in the community, it's making pamphlets, it's working with specific groups and pushing them in our communities to do that. And that's not something I was effectively taught to do, learning feminist theory on campus. The terminology I used on campus is not based in something I would stick up on the wall where I'm doing my laundry where people write racist shit, as happened the other day, yet again.

Anne-Marie: But how do we counter that effectively? Even 'zines and pamphlets, it seems, kind of get to the same people all the time.

Kim: I think in some ways it's happening. Some of the 'zines are effective, but it's slow and it's arduous work, and it's a struggle.

Robin: The tools I was offered on campus in classes have not always been useful. Some of them were, there were some really good classes, but they did not teach me how to phrase stuff in such a way as to write a pamphlet for the family down the street from me where I've been living for four or five years.

Anne-Marie: That would have been a great assignment too.

Kim: Experiential learning.

Robin: But that's not where most teachers' priorities are, it's not where most college students are. Mostly, people are writing papers for academia and for other students, for professors, for books that go to other universities. They're learning to communicate with other academics.

Kim: Which perpetuates that whole divide.

Robin: Yes, and that's a class divide, a racial divide, a divide between students and their home communities. Many of my friends, come, like me, from small rural communities. And we talk about this, that college has not prepared us to go back to those communities; we become either/or people. I have an identity that prepares me to be

an urban human rights activist, and I have an underlying identity of being a rural person, and I have often been unable to connect the two. And what does that tell us: that to be an activist you have to desert your family and move to an urban area? The books and classes . . . they prepared me to understand the constructed nature of gender and the nature of gender oppression, to some degree. What those classes did not teach me was how to go out and work for, let's be optimistic, for thirty years, in a human rights movement that has not got its shit together, where I'd be fighting those stupid stupid battles with mainstream groups over and over again that have no understanding of the history of what it means to be on the streets, on the front line. They even bargain away your right to be on the streets. In the past two months, all of us here fought those same battles twice, with the same people. Classes are not where I learned to be fighting stupid battles over and over. I learned that from being an activist.

Kim: Like you, Robin, I did not learn to be an activist in the classroom. I learned it from living my day-to-day life, and part of that learning has been the conversations I had with all in this room. We can also learn by putting ourselves on the front lines. By becoming a full participant in the movement, one can learn how to dismantle the injustices in their own community and in their own life. You learn as you go along.

Robin: And where is the third-wave theory that's going to help us do that? Where is the feminist theory, or womanist theory, or gender-inclusive theory? Where is the radical theory that will help us, that's going to tell college students how to be part of an activist community wherever they are and fight those same battles wherever they may be? Sure, they understand, you know, Foucault and his history of gender and surveillance and everything and can argue his points. But when it comes down to what kind of march you are going to organize, how do you argue for that? How do you argue for it over and over—over years with the same people who still don't agree with you?

Kim: I think that universities and classes and high schools really need to integrate community experiential learning, service learning.

Anne-Marie: A lot of schools are actually doing service learning, but I don't know about protest learning, or activist learning . . . kind of a difference of community service versus putting yourself on the margins and speaking up.

■ ■ ■

Robin: Overwhelmingly, the examples college students get on campus for activism are people who are working on the inside. It's almost overwhelmingly middle-class aims—cars, lifestyle, et cetera—because the people who become the leaders in the academic community, especially on campus, are often the people who were able and willing to step up classwise, to not rock the boat too much. And college activists are led toward those paths. It's just assumed you'll become "professional," with the limitations that accompany that. Because the radical community grassroots organizers are out in communities doing grassroots organizing, and they're probably not being paid, they're doing stuff like you're doing, Sherry, so the people who're held up as examples to follow to jobs or whatever are not representative of the real possibilities.

Sherry: Well, say when I was young, if I had a choice to be a college professor and affect thousands of students versus what I've done with my life, I would have been stupid not to try to teach

people. But I believe that some people on the inside had way more power, and at the time I didn't get to choose from a lot of options.

Anne-Marie: I wouldn't want to invalidate what teachers do because they do change and shape students; they did for me.

Robin: But at the same time, I see only a few professors doing the work in this town off campus, and if you look at what student activists go on to do, it's got to be connected. Most I know of follow the path of entering middle-class management type activist jobs, where they can't really do the work; they have to be careful and present a "professional" image.

Anne-Marie: I don't think I could be a professor and do activism; I think I would get so burned out.

Kim: I'd have to do activism on campus.

Sherry: But I know a professor who used to; there have been some.

Kim: I know that there have been students, or professors, who have come to rallies we have organized off campus; they have come and spoken and done other stuff.

Sherry: The difference I saw with the person we're talking about is that she actually was a feminist activist at the grassroots level in this town when I came here. She helped start Womencare shelter, she helped do pro-choice activism, so she's different than being just a teacher. But just being a teacher is a great thing. And she and I were part of those mistakes here in the 1970s. We were feminists here in the 1970s, doing this grassroots work.

Kim: So you were part of those mistakes, but look, you're here with me, you're dialoguing, you've been active with me, and so have a few professors.

Robin: We've talked about this a bit, the way that oppression actually plays out one on one. It gets masked as personality, and I've certainly seen that happen a few times in the last few years.

Kim: I've felt it.

Robin: I've seen people do that to you, Kim, where they react to you as being angry, too emotional, unreasonable, all these words, but they really hotly deny the source and legitimacy of that anger. I've had this conversation with people and suggest that maybe it's because you're a Black woman. They say, "No, Kim's just angry." They make it a personal thing, not a social one. I've seen this done to you often, like a stereotype or textbook example, but because it's one person they can put a name on it and say it's an individual difference, it's a personal thing, and act like it's not in play.

Kim: People acting out stereotypes. I am looked upon as being the angry Black woman rather than a passionate Black woman. Sometimes as a cool, dreadlocked Rastafarian, because I have dreadlocks. In reality my dreadlocks are a political statement whether I want them to be or not. I wear my hair natural versus trying to make it more like the accepted "White" hair. Yet once again this political statement is appropriated by the dominant majority. I find myself asking, "What can I appropriate from White America so they might see how their dreadlocks are derogatory to the risk I am taking by having natural hair." I am being branded yet again as the defiant other because I choose not to put unnatural chemicals in my hair. This stigma of having dreads result from an action that brings me closer to my true self. Some activists here in town, mainly White activists that have dread-

locks, have a false image of a Black woman with dreadlocks, and they interact with me via stereotypes.

Anne-Marie: Kim and I spend a lot of time together, and people in the liberal activist community sometimes reify her.

Kim: It's like I'm Sojourner Truth.

Robin: And they did it to Sojourner Truth too.

Kim: I think where I've felt people interacting with me via stereotypes the most is when people will engage with me on a philosophical level and debate textbook theory, but when it comes to the grassroots action, they are not present—or they're relating as if I'm not present. Or even when I cross the border into Canada—when I went across and was driving the car, and there were two or three white women with me, the border agent actually asked the other women, "Are you OK?" But when a White woman was driving, they didn't ask me if I was OK.

Anne-Marie: Or how about when you brought me to the emergency room at the hospital—they took me into a room by myself and asked, "Are you OK?" But when I brought you to the emergency room, they let me come in with you, and they never asked if you were okay.

Kim: In fact, they made me stay out when they took you back, like they thought I was going to harm you.

■ ■ ■

Kim: I would hope that my experience, and my talking about my experience, is going to separate me from any other Black person. To know where you came from and how you've evolved, instead of being put in some box. I think that would be really good, but that's not the way things go. We're put into this monolithic box. I just think we need to say where we come from, and that's part of my culture, you know, to say I'm the son or the daughter of Olla Morrison. That's much more meaningful than boxing me in with all other Black women.

Robin: I think it's important for us to remember that this is happening in the larger context of class supremacy, White supremacy, where we who enjoy that privilege can step out of it any time. It makes me think of bell hooks's essay in *Teaching to Transgress,* in which she talks about a colleague of hers who has this great fear that if she lets students speak from their experience, and speak on the authority of their experience, especially students of color, that they will dominate the class: "I'm a student of color and I know all these things," and they'll deny any voice to White students. bell hooks writes that, sure, maybe something happens that looks like that, but it's in context of White people just being able to assume that their claims carry weight and will be heard. hooks questions why this student of color feels she needs to do that in this situation, unless this classroom is making her feel voiceless and as if she has to assert her knowledge to be believed at all.

Kim: Some of the newer knowledge that she may have been coming into was about her own self, so she was gaining more information about where she's come from and how she fits in it. Maybe she was dealing with her own internalized racism, then dealing with racism and classism. When you have a little taste of this, when you have part of the story, but you maybe haven't taken that story a little further on, you're kind of stuck, and looking for ways to move on. I know that's happened with me before, that it's hard for me to hear people, or it's hard for me to articulate where I'm at.

Robin: I have been in classrooms where people do use things like class or gender to throw out someone's words. Sometimes I agree, sometimes I don't. I do think it's important to recognize that there's this underlying power struggle over who has the right to define things, and so it's not in a vacuum, it's in reaction to an established power dynamic that's unspoken, this unspoken assumption that White men like me hold that our experience goes for everybody.

Kim: That's why it's important, I think, that we say "This is my experience . . ."

Anne-Marie: I think it's really important to identify myself and where I come from, but that doesn't mean I have the same experience as every upper-middle-class person, and in fact, I have a really different experience than a lot of them. I had an older White professor at the university, and a lot of my classmates judge him and don't like him. It's like important for him to identify, you know, as a middle-class White male, but at the same time, we can't fall back on "because he is that he doesn't have new and progressive ideas." And we need to recognize that other pain that he's experienced in his life may have taught him things that make sense to us.

■ ■ ■

Kim: I have issues with the term *ally.*

Robin: I think this is a really good example of the way concepts get re-institutionalized and become meaningless really fast . . . a radical idea comes out that, for example, men don't have the right to define the experience of women in society, and men don't have the right to decide what women's problems are and how to fix them. That men need to center women's experience and to educate themselves and figure out what to do and how to work with other men. So there's potential there, but very quickly mainstream groups, like the lifestyle advisers, pick that up and make it into a class. It quickly becomes a thing to talk about, something students are told they can do in their daily lives without changing their behavior. There's this underlying message that "you don't have to be all political, you can be a happy White college student and go to lots of parties and still be an ally" . . . it gets mainstreamed out of existence so quickly, institutionalized so you have an ally-building network, you have an ally-building program that's doing very little, at least as far as producing activists who are willing to really risk privilege or be uncomfortable.

Kim: That ain't doing no fucking allying at all.

Robin: The other thing is, and for this example I'll use White people, or even just non-Native people, being an ally is a total mess in practice. Sherry and I have been dealing with that this last year, regarding a regional multiracial mainstream organization purging a Native American woman from the group, and in my opinion using sexism, pretty clearly using sexism, to kick her out of the organization. Depending on whom you talk to, it's either because she is power hungry or because she wants a fair wage for her work. And then you have some of the leadership of this multiracial organization, which has both White people and people of color in leadership positions, saying that White allies need to stay out of the issue because it's a fight among people of color. And the Native American woman who was kicked out of the organization is saying, "I need allies to support me to make sure my voice is heard, to rectify the wrong that's been done to me by this organization." And what you come down to in cases like this is that White people,

and I've seen this several times, use *ally* as an excuse to not think, to not figure out this shit. So many of the White people involved choose to side with whichever side they work with, or are friends with. And in some ways it's a fight over who is the "real person of color" and deserves allies. And obviously, however much of an ally you want to be, it comes back to your judgment in the end. You can't remove yourself as a privileged person from the decision-making process. I do believe that. In the organization I'm talking about, you want to be an ally, but you have to pick whom you want to be an ally to, because there a lot of people who need allies and they are in conflict. So being an ally can't be giving yourself a lobotomy and saying "Tell me what to do" . . . it still comes back to your judgment, and you still have to educate yourself about that. You still have to make decisions.

Sherry: Being an ally is complicated and often involves risks because the issues aren't clear-cut. I once went to a conference where tribal sovereignty workshops were canceled because of a conflict with the presenting organization, the Coalition for Human Dignity, which has a multiracial board. Some folks, including tribal leaders, were asking that the conference stop to deal with this problem. They said that group was treating them disrespectfully and not listening. These folks ended up walking out of the conference. Later, representatives of fifty-four Northwest tribes issued a press release, asking people to disassociate themselves from the coalition. When we got home, the conflict had extended to local politics with a Native woman, where people on both sides felt they were being allies. It became a Native versus non-Native issue, with sexism thrown in. So whose ally should I, as a

White woman, be? Or should I just stay out of it?

Robin: There are other ways it gets complicated for White people acting as allies. In complex real-world situations, it's not this easy obvious path. White people get a little bit of that treatment, of being called "immature" or "too emotional," "childish"—*childish* is a big word in this community. I've known several people who have jumped on board for something, and as soon as they see a little bit of that, feel any kind of criticism, it stops them dead, no matter what they know in their college brains, or how well they can talk the talk or what they know to be "right."

Anne-Marie: They can't hack the pain.

Kim: And I can?

Anne-Marie: You don't have a choice.

Sherry: That's privilege—having the choice of what should we do.

■■■

Sherry: It seems like whenever there's a problem, the response to it is a grassroots response. When there's something wrong, usually, a group of people get together, and say, "We have to do something about this, go into somebody's office and say it's wrong or picket the local museum because they're having something racist or sexist." Then at some point people say, "Oh, we're going to form a committee" or "We're gonna hire more people of color" or "We're gonna run a shelter," and then that grassroots energy gets lost. Some people get hired to deal with the problem or they get appointed to the committee, and that's more likely to be White people and middle-class people that get the job or appointed to the committee, and then the shelter or what-

ever ends up being run by White middle-class people out of what started as a grassroots organization. The food co-op started out with the food-conspiracy people buying food in bulk, meeting at somebody's house, and dividing it up; well, the purpose was cheap food for low-income people who wanted to eat more healthy. But it started at the grassroots, and so did the domestic violence shelter, and a lot of these things you're talking about on campus. I'm sure that the alternative college at the university started as "We have a problem here."

Robin: As a young activist, that's one of the things that I want to know more about. How does it happen that groups like Womencare, the co-op, the college, start out with radical energy and so quickly become institutionalized. They turn into just another bureaucracy that's maybe doing better stuff, but that has all those problems, that has racism in hiring, expensive food you can't afford, and so on. How do we stop that from happening again? Is this what it means to "work from the inside"?

Kim: But when people start taking these jobs in order to work from the inside, and they're in with other people who don't have the same ideas about social change, it's a nearly impossible situation.

Robin: So they buy into it.

Sherry: And then you're considered immature if you don't want to work from the inside. You're one of those immature women or people of color. I really think jobs and money are the heart of why people tell us we have to work on the inside because on the outside there's no jobs and money. For a short period of time people are willing to do grassroots stuff for nothing, but if people want to live a better way than they're living when they're young and poor, they're going to work from the inside.

•••

Robin: So how do we decide whom to work with? That's where I'm really split. On one hand I think that as a White man I want to find a way to work for what I believe in, for the societal transformation I want to see. At the same time, I feel pretty strongly that White people need to take on White liberal organizations and challenge them. We need to join those groups and refuse to be "professional" and break the solidarity of Whiteness. But it would be nice to work with a group that is totally there on the issues.

Kim: I don't know of any organization that is.

Robin: There isn't one locally. That's the issue. I think there should be one, at least!

Sherry: And that's where I know we made a lot of mistakes, but I think some things got taken over that were once on the right track. It doesn't mean that they weren't screwed up, but the co-op starting from low-income people who wanted to get cheap food. It might have still been run by men who do all the talking, but we could have dealt with that maybe easier than we can deal with an institution that's set up now with men and middle-class people in control.

Robin: The aspect that seems most direct to me, working in a multiracial organization as a White guy, is pushing them to do more on gender because they don't do much. I've tried to push them but haven't been very successful. This organization has a multiracial board, but radical people of color flee this organization. They fight like hell, then they move to Georgia or somewhere else. They fight like hell until they can't deal with this organization and place anymore. And there's a point at which it would be totally

inappropriate for me to be working there because the only reason I can deal with the shit is that I'm a White person who can afford to let some kinds of oppression go by me. But at the same time, I'm not selling out and I am rocking the boat, but it means I'm spending a hell of a lot of time and energy working with White liberals who may not go anywhere, as opposed to finding a group that . . .

Anne-Marie: . . . that sustains you. You need to be able to sustain yourself in order to give.

Kim: I've worked with various groups, you know . . . animal rights groups and different human rights groups and stuff like that, and they've worked with me on some of my activist issues. I think one of the reasons why I've been able to go to these different groups and work beside them is because a lot of those issues affect me too. And also people from different groups came to my side as activists on some of my core issues that I'm pretty outspoken about and that affect me in a way that, on a day-to-day basis, other issues such as animal rights don't. It's hard to say I'm affected because I'm a Black person every day, or a woman or a lesbian or whatever, every day. It's hard to put that together, but most of the people that I've come in contact with or have become associated with in my activist community are willing to hear me; there's a reciprocal experience going on. I can hear what they're passionate about too, and both of us show that interconnectivity. I think that that's important, and I think that without that it's harder to cross lines. That answer your question?

Robin: I guess one way I was thinking of framing it was when you move across country, as you're about to do, how will you decide what groups to work with? What will you need, what's your goal?

Anne-Marie: Harder for me is that I have major anxiety about going into the world and getting this "real job" or whatever. It's so competitive, and I feel like part of that is the patriarchy, so it does sort of apply. But it's so competitive you have to constantly prove yourself and say you're better. I even felt that in the volunteer work with PFLAG. It's like these eyes are down on you, watching and scrutinizing, sometimes I don't feel that way, but . . . If you look at it, it really is that way, they scrutinize what you do with your life. It makes me feel really bluueaghh . . . I don't want to feel that way in what I do. I don't know if that's my personal issue of confidence or a mix, or I don't know. But I definitely don't want to work in an environment that's really . . . I worked in a bookstore and it was just really racist and homophobic and sexist. I feel like I experienced sexual harassment there, and a mix of gay, whatever . . . I had to hear racist comments all the time. I don't want to work in that kind of environment even if I might change some things there. I want to do some kind of human rights work, but I haven't thought about it to the extent of what you're thinking.

Robin: How long would you work in a human rights movement where you're struggling with people who are in the mainstream and saying things about us being "outside agitators"? Will you feel that that's your battle? To work in that movement?

Anne-Marie: I don't have an easy answer to that because it was so hard and so draining. And I've started doing more with developmentally disabled adults, and I feel like that's just as important. But then the more I worked in that field, the more I learned about theories of working with developmentally disabled adults, and I started thinking, "Maybe I will keep having these issues with mainstream thinking . . . I don't know that yet because I still feel like I'm learning how to deal with people like that. And one of those people, I'm still supposed to go to coffee with her and have a conversation about it." And part of my ideal self says, "Well, if I can keep being in dialogue, they'll learn to change and I'll learn to communicate" and maybe that would be possible, but I don't know. There's not an easy answer.

Kim: You can only bleed so much to do it.

Sherry: I think the reason I stay working from the outside is that's just who I am. I'm not sure I ever really decided that, but I think some people are just outsiders. When I was young, things were getting changed. I saw that the civil rights movement and the antiwar movement happened in the streets, and people were changing from being in the streets, and I didn't see anything being changed from inside, but then, I just can't be the person on the inside. So I think there will always be people who are on the outside. I guess I don't have enough faith that it's going to happen so quickly that there won't be an outside. But the reason I do it is because it's what changed me. Seeing people risk their lives was what made me realize that I had to do something different with my life. If I hadn't then I wouldn't be who I am.

NOTES

1. Initiative 200, which prohibits Washington state government entities from discriminating or granting preferential treatment based on race, sex, color, ethnicity, or national origin, was passed by Washington voters on November 3, 1998.

Theory and Practice: Academia and Activism

 d i s c u s s i o n   q u e s t i o n s

- Have you taken courses in women's studies or in other disciplines where the experience of women has been a primary consideration? What was your reaction to the approach and subject matter of these courses? Was the reaction of other students obvious? If so, what was it?

- What biases do you bring to your studies of gender, class, race, and sexuality? What privileges do you enjoy in this society, and how have they influenced those biases (or lack of biases)?

- What is your reaction to the two articles in this volume written by Camelia Phillips, a White woman writing about the position and struggles of women of color? Is she trying to speak *for* these women? If not, what do you think she is trying to do? Whatever your answer to those questions, do you consider that she has been successful?

- What do you understand as "academic capitalism"? How is it, or might it be, manifest in disciplines other than women's studies? Do you agree with Popen that this movement in colleges and universities is a threat to the integrity of the various disciplines? Explain. Are there some disciplines in which this would not be a problem?

- What do you consider to be the role of projects such as those required by Moulds in her women's studies course? Do you think these projects are an unwarranted imposition on students? Why or why not? What are some other projects that might be relevant to women's studies classes?

- What other issues can you think of that might, in your opinion, require grassroots social action in order for significant changes to be realized?

 f u r t h e r   r e a d i n g s

Arneil, Barbara. *Politics and Feminism.* Oxford: Blackwells, 1999.

Bell, Diane, and Renate Klein. *Radically Speaking: Feminism Reclaimed.* North Melbourne, Australia: Spinifex Press, 1996.

Findlen, Barbara. *Listen Up: Voices from the Next Feminist Generation.* Seattle, WA: Seal Press, 2001.

hooks, bell. *Teaching to Transgress.* New York: Routledge, 1994.

Humm, Maggie. *The Dictionary of Feminist Theory.* Columbus, OH: Ohio State University Press, 1995.

Martin, Jane Roland. *Coming of Age in Academe: Rekindling Women's Hopes and Reforming the Academy.* New York: Routledge, 2000.

Messer-Davidow, Ellen. *Disciplining Feminism: From Social Activism to Academic Discourse.* Durham, NC: Duke University Press, 2002.

Walker, Rebecca. *To Be Real.* New York: Anchor Books, 1995.

c o n t r i b u t o r s

B R E N D A   A N Í B A R R O works as a researcher for the Economic Justice Program at the Data Center in Oakland, California. She recently completed her master's at the London School of Economics in anthropology and development and is interested in working with communities of color to weave together sustainable economic models with healing, music, and art.

A N N E - M A R I E   B A S S O is a cultural studies graduate from Fairhaven College, Western Washington University, and is now a graduate student in the Department of Library and Information Studies, University of Buffalo.

M A R G A R E T   V A U G H N   C H A P M A N, a homegrown West Virginian, embarked on her journey as a feminist activist while studying sociology in a small mountain town in Colorado. She went on to study political theory and public policy at Western Washington University, where she earned a master's in political science. She is a social activist and past director of the Native American mentoring program at Western Washington University.

D E N I S E   C O O P E R is a graduate of the University of Washington, with a degree in American ethnic studies and a math minor. She is a Southern girl, born in Savannah, Georgia, and raised in Anchorage, Alaska. She works as youth community organizer in Seattle's Central District and firmly believes in the power of Hip Hop and art to transform the world and help people get free.

R O B I N   E L W O O D is a straight white guy, active in feminist and community organizing. He is presently office manager with the Whatcom Human Rights Task Force, a grassroots group based in Bellingham, Washington.

C O N S T A N C E   F A U L K N E R, Professor Emeritus, Fairhaven College, Western Washington University, taught political economy, social theory, women's studies, and cultural studies.

C A R O L Y N   F I N N E Y is an African American feminist pursuing a Ph.D. in geography at Clark University. Her past research focused on the impacts of globalization on Nepalese women, emphasizing the relationship between capital, power, and identity and how women articulate and negotiate their needs across scales. Her present research explores cultural and environmental encounters in the United States, highlighting how they are gendered and racialized. All of her work is informed by a need to interrogate the production, representation, and dissemination of knowledge about people, places, and ideas.

SHELLY FRAZIER received an M.A. in political science from Western Washington University, with a concentration in political theory and American politics. Living in San Diego, she is applying for a Ph.D. program in political science that will allow her to further her studies in political theory and feminist issues.

SHERRY JUBILO is a white working-class bisexual feminist social activist who began her political activism working with low-income people in Iowa on welfare rights, housing issues, and housing discrimination.

SARAH MCCARRY has been published in *Clamor Magazine, Off Our Backs,* and *Listen Up: Voices from the Next Feminist Generation* (Seal Press, 2002). She also puts out the 'zine *glossolalia.*

MONICA MCCALLUM grew up on the Olympic Peninsula in Washington State. She ventured away from the area for a few years of traveling but then returned to nearby Bellingham, where she completed a degree from Fairhaven College in critical social theory. She currently works with a literacy program in Seattle and lives with her son, best friend, and a menagerie of pets (both real and imagined).

PHILOMENA MCCULLOUGH is an activist and graduate of the University of Minnesota Native American Studies Program.

KIM L. MORRISON is an information literacy/cultural pluralism librarian. Her interests lie in cultural studies, how people access information on marginalized groups from libraries, and whether their particular disciplines' discourse language, bias in subject headings, and cultural illiteracy of librarians working in academic and public libraries impact their access to marginalized information.

CYNTHIA M. MOULDS received an M.S. in gender and international development and is currently working on her Ph.D. in women's studies and international relations at the University of British Columbia Centre for Research in Women's Studies and Gender Relations, specifically examining transnational feminist activism and the potential for revolution. She teaches women's studies and serves as interim director of the Women's Studies Program at Western Washington University in Bellingham, Washington.

CAMELLIA PHILLIPS currently lives and works in Brooklyn, New York, where she is a grant writer with the community organization ACORN, the Association of Community Organizations for Reform Now. A middle-class White woman, Camellia was born and raised in Washington State, where she later earned a degree in writing social justice from Fairhaven College.

SHARI POPEN is a faculty member in the Department of Language, Reading, and Culture, University of Arizona.

WENDY SOMERSON earned her Ph.D. in English from the University of Washington. She lives in Seattle with her cat and enjoys snowboarding, eating chocolate, crafting, and working on the Northwest publication *Push: Queer Feminist Subversions*.

BECKY STATZEL is an activist currently living in Seattle. She started organizing around environmental issues in 1994 and has since spent time organizing electoral campaigns, unions, and activism around social justice issues. She is currently working with other White folks on helping to create a local antiracist White movement.

CARA ANN THORESEN is an anthropologist, a feminist, and a perpetual student. She recently graduated from the New School University with an M.A. in anthropology. She generally writes about feminism, body image, and media studies. She currently lives in New York with her husband.

SARA WEIR is associate professor and chair of the Department of Political Science, Western Washington University. She teaches courses in the fields of public policy and women and politics. Her latest project is a book about childhood cancer and identity.